Behold the

Lilies

DAILY MEDITATIONS FOR
CHRISTIAN WOMEN

Verna Mast & Susan Schwartz

ISBN: 978-1-941213-23-0
Cover design and layout: Teresa Sommers
Cover graphics: shutterstock, canstockphoto
Interior graphics: graphicstock

Upon the request of the original copyright holder, TGS decided to publish *Behold the Lilies,* a revised version of *Behold the Lilies of the Field.* Printed in the USA

Published by:
TGS International
P.O. Box 355
Berlin, Ohio 44610 USA
Phone: 330-893-4828
Fax: 330-893-2305
www.tgsinternational.com

TGS000874

Preface

Verna Mast had a dream to write a women's devotional book. We both were interested in writing, so we often discussed this topic. When she could no longer write due to her illness, I became concerned. Did someone know her plans for the manuscript? She had invested a lot of work in this project, and I didn't want it to go to waste. But no one felt able to broach the subject because Verna thought she would get better again. By the time she finally realized that death was inevitable, she wasn't able to talk about the book.

After her death, I was asked to finish the work. I accepted and began where Verna had stopped. However, something was missing. Then one day I received a packet on the mail that contained all the correspondence between her and the editor. Eagerly I read the pages of writing that answered my questions. It was second best to having Verna here as I finished the book.

I have placed one of Verna's last writings on November 7, the day of her death. The Lord called her away before He returned, just as she had written.

Verna is gone. Her voice is silent in death. Her gravestone in our church cemetery does not tell her life story nor express her dedication to her Lord. It tells nothing of all the hours she invested in this book. But though Verna is no longer with us, she left a lasting legacy for us who read these pages.

—*Susan Schwartz*

We gratefully acknowledge:

* Paul Yoder and Ira Huber for their encouragement in the writing and compiling of this book, and also for reviewing the manuscript.
* Martha Schwartz, Donna Miller, and Barbara Schwartz for proofreading the manuscript.
* Our ministers and brethren in the church, from whose topics we gleaned many inspirations.
* Our families for helping us with our other work and for being patient with us in our busy schedule to complete the book.

—*Moses & Susan Schwartz*

January 1

Come, my beloved, let us go forth into the field.
—Song of Solomon 7:11

A new year is dawning. As you stand at the threshold of this new year, you may wonder what the future holds. View this year as a vast field. Visualize a summertime meadow with hills that prevent your seeing the other side. Flowers bloom, birds chirp, and a refreshing brook ripples by.

Our Creator has placed you in this "field," and He will lead you along. He is the One in control of your surroundings. He is the One who created the roses with thorns, rainbows following showers, joy after sorrow, peace in the midst of pain.

As you stroll through this field, are you going to collect a lovely bouquet of flowers, or will you get tangled in the thorns and thistles and fail to see the beauties all around you? The flowers in your field should so enthrall you that the prickly nettles and thistles do not hinder you from collecting a fragrant bouquet.

Just as the daylily has fresh blossoms opening each day, these devotionals are intended to give you fresh courage each day. May these truths from God's Word sweeten your day and fill it with a warm glow of hope and cheer. When you gather a bouquet of lilies, you will likely be dusted with some of the bright yellow pollen, evidence that you have been collecting lilies. Allow the inspiration from these devotionals to cling to you like lily pollen, and you will bless others whom your life touches.

Your path may not always take you by the cool, refreshing stream. You may have to bear the heat of the day, which will cause you to feel faint. Rest awhile, and behold the lilies. God's promises are always fresh. He can make something good from difficult situations if you allow Him to do so. He will lead you to your desired haven as you place your hand in His and follow all the way.

And these things write we unto you, that your joy may be full.

—1 John 1:4

God created people because He wanted someone to commune with Him, someone to worship and serve Him. When we do what He has created us for, we can experience fullness of joy. When our relationship with God is severed, joy ceases.

There is some joy in earthly things, but it is as fleeting as the thing or the event from which it springs. If you find fulfillment in Jesus, things and events will pass but your joy will remain, and you can look forward to eternal joy. Martyrs went singing to their deaths because of this.

Many people believe possessions will bring fulfillment. Solomon said, "And whatsoever mine eyes desired I kept not from them" (Ecclesiastes 2:10). But in the next verse he mourns, "Then I looked on all the works that my hands had wrought, and on the labour that I had laboured to do: and, behold, all was vanity and vexation of spirit." Possessing few of this world's goods is no reason to be joyless. On the contrary, having few possessions can make us more joyful because there is less to distract us from the real purpose of life.

Many people believe marriage offers fulfillment, but Paul said of one who is unmarried, "She is happier if she so abide" (1 Corinthians 7:40).

Many believe they will find happiness in position. Haman had a prestigious position, but he was jealous and unhappy. There is joy and blessing in any position if the Lord places us there. Following his statement of joy in John 3:29, John the Baptist said, "He must increase, but I must decrease" (John 3:30). A demoted position did not dampen his joy.

God wants us to experience fullness of joy, and He knows how to maintain a relationship with us. It is up to us to listen to His promptings and abide in His presence.

January 3

Ye are the light of the world. A city that is set on an hill cannot be hid.
—Matthew 5:14

"I always watch for your light," my neighbor told me. Perhaps she finds comfort in seeing my light and in knowing that I am at home and she is not alone in the darkness.

My light tells her much about me. It tells her whether I am an early or a late riser or retiree. It tells her whether I am at home a lot or gone much. If my windows show darkness instead of light for a long time, she can guess that I have gone on a trip or that something has befallen me. I am the person responsible for switching on the light, and she notices if I fail to do it.

Someone is watching for your light too. It may be a young person seeking stability. It may be someone seeking for the truth or trying to fight a battle while battered by the storms of adversity. It may be someone in a position of responsibility who takes courage because your light is always there. Whoever it is, be assured, someone is silently watching you. Your light tells the seeker that you have found the truth and that its oil keeps your light burning. It tells the discouraged that there is purpose in life. It tells the afflicted that tribulation grows patience. They see your light shining and are comforted to know they are not alone in a dark world.

You are responsible to keep your light shining. If you do not, those who depend on your light will wonder what is wrong. They will miss your helping hand, your warm smile, your words of encouragement. They will feel alone in the darkness. But if you gaze continually on the light of the Word, others will not be let down because you will consistently reflect His light and glory.

Now therefore give me this mountain, whereof the Lord spake in that day; for thou heardest in that day how the Anakims were there, and that the cities were great and fenced: if so be the Lord will be with me, then I shall be able to drive them out, as the Lord said.

—Joshua 14:12

Caleb was the only man chosen from the tribe of Judah to join the other eleven men in spying out the Promised Land. Moses gave them clear instructions about what he wanted done. He admonished them to be of good courage.

Caleb took his responsibility seriously. Upon coming home, he gave an enthusiastic report. "Let us go up at once to possess it; for we are well able to overcome it" (Numbers 13:30). But he was hindered by the majority—outnumbered in his desire to go back and take possession of the land he knew God would give to them.

However, forty-five years later, Caleb's strength remained intact. His faith in God was undaunted as he boldly entreated, "Give me this mountain." He knew the giants were there. He had seen them forty-five years before. But he also knew the Lord would help him drive them out.

The Christian faces giants too. You may face the giant of discouragement, possibly because of being unable to accomplish what another may do with ease. Or if you are the one with plenty of ability, you may need to overcome the giant of pride.

You may face the giant of financial worry, asking questions such as, *Can I meet my payment if I take care of Grandpa for a week? Should I pursue my business dream? What will be the outcome of my investment?*

Giants exist in the working world too, such as the stress of pleasing customers or an employer, bitterness at someone else's promotion, or the desire for a different job.

We know nothing of Caleb's battles with the giants or of the times he might have been tempted to let the giants live. He certainly became weary, and he may have had to fight some battles with little help from others. We know that his challenges were great, but his faith in God gave him the inheritance.

Establish Caleb's kind of confidence in God. Then when you face a giant, you, too, can overcome and inherit the land when the battle is over. ✳

January 5

A friend loveth at all times, and a brother is born for adversity.
—Proverbs 17:17

While working on the mission field away from family and well-known friends, I have learned to enjoy new friends. Some of the friendships I've established here have become stronger than some of my former friendships. On one occasion when I was feeling a bit discouraged, one of my mission friends stopped by unexpectedly. My friend shook my hand and said with warmth and sincerity, "God bless you!" Then we chatted for awhile. I felt richly blessed after my friend left, just realizing that someone cared enough about me to let me know!

Loyal friends know your faults, but they keep right on loving you through whatever is happening in your life. Today, thank God for your loyal friends.

And being in Bethany in the house of Simon the leper, as he sat at meat, there came a woman having an alabaster box of ointment of spikenard very precious; and she brake the box, and poured it on his head.

—Mark 14:3

The unbroken alabaster box, however beautiful it may have been to look upon, could not anoint Jesus or fill the house with an aromatic odor. These things happened only after the box was broken and its precious contents poured out.

I am unbroken when . . .

   . . . I am ashamed to witness for Christ.

   . . . I have no encouragement to offer because I feel others should encourage me.

   . . . I cannot rejoice with those who rejoice.

   . . . I pursue my own activity instead of Christian duty.

   . . . I do not pray for someone else's happiness because it means requesting something for her that I also desire to have.

When I am unbroken, I am a closed vessel too proud to spill one drop of myself, so I hide the battles that rage inside of me. The devil deceives me into thinking that this is the way to retain my image and win approval. However, when I am only a vessel filled with my miserable self, I have shut out the Lord and others. It is a lonely existence, and I cannot live joyfully that way.

I can choose to be broken even if it is a painful process. I am broken when . . .

   . . . I am happily convinced that my present circumstance is God's best for me.

   . . . I do not worry about the future but place myself unreservedly into the hands of God.

   . . . I am moved to worship as I meditate on my Saviour's incomprehensible love for me.

   . . . I am not envious at another's good fortune.

   . . . I lay aside the part of me that wants to slink into the shadows; I accept, instead, the duty to which God is calling me, even if I cannot see the outcome.

When I am broken, the peace of God floods my soul. The vessel that I once thought so essential to my well-being lies about me in pieces. But I do not care, because I see that the vessel is not so important; it is the breaking of the vessel that brings goodness. When I am broken, the joy of the Lord comes pouring in as well as out, because there are no barriers. Only the Master Potter can do this as I lay myself into His hands. He, not I, knows where to break me so that the sweetest of fragrances may come forth.

Then Lot chose him all the plain of Jordan; and Lot journeyed east:
and they separated themselves the one from the other.
—Genesis 13:11

Lot faced a choice. He lifted up his eyes and saw the well-watered plains of Jordan. The meadows were lush. The opportunities seemed endless. Lot made his decision and journeyed east.

After he pitched his tent toward Sodom, Lot made a number of choices. However, he was unable to control the results of his choices. Lot chose to live in Sodom, but did he choose his wicked sons-in-law? He chose his friends, but did he choose for them to act wickedly when the angels came? He chose to live in a cave, but did he choose to father the nations of Moab and Ammon?

God allows us to make choices, but His laws do not change. We will reap what we sow. The wages of sin are death. Do you want to live with the results of the choices you are making today? ✳

He riseth from supper, and laid aside his garments; and took a towel, and girded himself. After that he poureth water into a basin, and began to wash the disciples' feet, and to wipe them with the towel wherewith he was girded.
—John 13:4, 5

His eyes were as a flame of fire, and on his head were many crowns; and he had a name written, that no man knew, but he himself.
—Revelation 19:12

Who of us has not sat nervously in the extravagantly furnished office of a professional who does not leave anyone guessing whether he has money and prestige? We listen in bewilderment to unfamiliar terms and expressions and are left in a fog as a highly-educated man speaks professional jargon. Even some seminary-trained ministers speak in theological terms that are difficult for us to understand.

Let us leave the extravagantly furnished, twenty-first-century office and travel back in time to the hills and valleys of Palestine. There we see a traveler trudging the dry, dusty roads. Now He stoops to touch a leper, now He pauses at the cry of a blind beggar and brings hope and happiness into his life. He picks up little children and mingles with the outcasts.

Although He is the Creator of the universe, He is too poor to travel any other way than to walk. Although He owns the world, He does not so much as claim a pillow to lay His head. He left an ethereal home for a life of hardship. He is all-wise and knows seraphic language, but He spoke about birds, the flowers, the seed, and the sower in language anyone could understand. The touch of His hand and love shining from His eyes needed no interpretation. His glory for the most part remained hidden, and He made it plain by the way He lived that His interests were not power and prestige. Because of this, the lowly found in Him an understanding friend.

When His earthly tasks were nearing completion and He knew He was about to receive a glorious kingship, He did not sit around dreaming about it, nor did He boast. Instead, He did that which is unheard of for a king. He stooped to the menial task of washing His disciples' feet.

Such a life merits my highest aspirations! No matter what I know, what I accomplish, or what I have, I must keep my eyes on the fact that I, too, am a servant. I am not on a quest for glory except the Father's glory. I will be successful in my mission as long as I have a servant's attitude both toward God and my fellow man. ◗

....

....

....

....

....

....

....

....

....

....

....

....

....

....

....

....

....

....

Blessed are the pure in heart: for they shall see God.

—Matthew 5:8

Purity is . . .

   . . . a body free of disease.

   . . . honey without wax.

   . . . milk with no bacteria.

   . . . wheat with no chaff.

   . . . gold without alloy.

   . . . water directly from the spring.

   . . . air free of smog.

   . . . a life with no sin.

Purity is all that belongs to something but nothing more. A pure heart has nothing adverse to God in it. A pure life is holy and free from all sin. Is your heart pure?

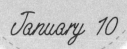

January 10

Strengthened with all might, according to his glorious power,
unto all patience and longsuffering with joyfulness.

—Colossians 1:11

Shelf life, cellophane wrappings, and brightly colored labels do not prove the strength and durability of a product. These qualities can best be measured by putting a product through strenuous testing. After it has gone through repeated testing and refining, it is ready for further service.

An easy life with few setbacks and hardships does not produce the adorning graces of patience and longsuffering. If we pray for more patience, the Lord will honor those prayers—but not by handing out a nicely wrapped package of patience tied with a bow of longsuffering. Instead, He will send it in ways that will give opportunity to exercise patience and longsuffering. You may encounter situations like these:

* The man you asked to repair your roof several months ago has still not come, and every time it rains you have to set out all your buckets to catch the water coming through the ceiling.
* The drain in the sink is clogged again; all your feeble efforts have accomplished nothing and nobody offers to open it for you.
* You need to see a dentist and your car needs repairs, but a note from the bank says you have overdrawn your checking account.

Do not panic or complain. The Lord is answering your prayers. He sees that it is more important for you to learn patience and longsuffering than it is to have the roof, the drain, and the car repaired when *you* think they should be repaired. He wants to correct the flaws in your life so that you will be useful for His service.

Then Agrippa said unto Paul, Almost thou persuadest me to be a Christian.
—Acts 26:28

*A*lmost means "slightly short of; very nearly." The following statements illustrate what *almost* can mean:

The train almost missed the truck, but then it wrecked.

The levee of the Mississippi almost held back the water, but then it broke.

The sick woman almost got well, but then she died.

The book almost got published, but then it was rejected.

It almost snowed, but then it rained.

The plants almost survived the disease, but then they succumbed.

I almost got to church on time, but I was late.

I almost sent a story to the publishers, but then I did not finish it.

I almost wrote Grandmother a letter, but then I read my book.

I almost went to the ladies' monthly sewing, but I was too busy.

I almost invited the strangers to my home, but I was too shy.

I almost baked a cake for my neighbor, but the day slipped by.

I almost sewed a dress for my sister's birthday, but I ran out of inspiration.

Agrippa wanted to go to heaven. He *almost* became a Christian, but almost is not altogether. If Agrippa did not become persuaded later, he died and went to hell—almost a Christian, but still lost.

Our efforts to help others must cross the finish line, or they, too, will be unknown or incomplete. *Almost* is slightly short of the goal. ✳

Psalm 3

Sara sighed wearily. *Will I ever be happy again?* The ache in her heart was almost more than she could bear. With all her heart she wanted to follow the Lord and be content however He would lead. Yet the void within her longed to be filled.

This was not the first time this conflicting struggle of her singleness troubled her. Often it came from only small happenings. But it seemed to be a big problem that threatened to keep her from victory this time. Her sister, who was five years younger, was planning to be married.

Sara knew her attitude was displeasing to God. It was also harmful to her spiritual growth and her relationship with others. Oh, to overcome her fear of remaining single. She knew it was a victory she must gain if she wanted to please God.

She realized that God alone could conquer that fear. In her helplessness, in faith believing, she handed the battle over to the Lord. She yielded her entire life to the Lord, acknowledging the fact that He had a right to rule her life as He chose.

As Sara drew apart to commune with the Lord in the stillness of prayer, she found the inner strength to accept her singleness as God's choice for her. Peace and power were hers as she rested in the arms of her heavenly Father, the source of all good things.

January 13

Sing praises to God, sing praises: sing praises unto our King, sing praises.
—Psalm 47:6

What value does singing have in the Christian woman's life?

Singing gives you strength to finish what you have begun. "So will I sing praise unto thy name for ever, that I may daily perform my vows" (Psalm 61:8).

Singing gives you strength when you face a trial. "But I will sing of thy power; yea, I will sing aloud of thy mercy in the morning: for thou hast been my defence and refuge in the day of my trouble" (Psalm 59:16).

Singing gives you victory over your enemy, the devil. "And when they began to sing and to praise, the Lord set ambushments against the children of Ammon . . . and they were smitten" (2 Chronicles 20:22).

Through song we can express our gratefulness to God for all He has done for us. "Sing unto the Lord with thanksgiving. I will sing unto the Lord, because he hath dealt bountifully with me" (Psalm 13:6).

By our songs we can tell others of God's greatness and sustaining strength. "Sing unto him, sing psalms unto him: talk ye of all his wondrous works" (Psalm 105:2). "So will we sing and praise thy power" (Psalm 21:13). "Sing praises to the Lord, which dwelleth in Zion: declare among the people his doings" (Psalm 9:11).

Singing produces calmness and serenity in the Christian's heart. "Sing praises unto his name; for it is pleasant" (Psalm 135:3).

Keep on singing until the Lord ushers you from this life to one where you will sing heavenly songs. "I will sing unto the Lord as long as I live: I will sing praise to my God while I have my being" (Psalm 104:33).

For ye were as sheep going astray; but are now returned
unto the Shepherd and Bishop of your souls.
—1 Peter 2:25

He was a great one to explore the outdoors, and now his small form was hard to see in the fast-falling snow. I was glad when he started toward home. A feeling of happiness and comfort came over me as he came closer and closer. Finally I saw not only a form but a boy. The distance and the snow had made me apprehensive about his safety.

Is that the way my heavenly Father feels when I wander away from Him? Does the distance that has come between us give Him apprehension about my safety? How He must rejoice when He sees me turning homeward and coming closer and closer.

But why do I wander away? My wanderings and the little boy's wanderings come about for the same reason. The distant places look attractive. The place where he was did not look especially dangerous—it was only an open field. But he could have wandered to the woods beyond and gotten completely lost.

I may think that the places where I wander do not appear especially dangerous either. I do not dabble in "worldly" places, or so I think. But I forget that any thought not in harmony with God is of the world. There is no other category in which to put it. God was lamenting the distance between Himself and the rebellious Israelites when He said, "For as the heavens are higher than the earth, so are my ways higher than your ways, and my thoughts than your thoughts" (Isaiah 55:9).

If I do not return to God with my thoughts, I will also depart from Him with my ways. Much more than my physical safety is at stake. My soul is at stake when I stray from the Father's safe shelter. When I compare the safety of staying close to Him with the lack of safety in the world, I understand why He wants me where He can care for me. 🌀

January 15

For the law made nothing perfect, but the bringing in of a better hope did; by the which we draw nigh unto God.
—Hebrews 7:19

Hope motivates us to visualize an attainable goal. It keeps us going even when odds are against us. The farmer lives through a drought, tills the ground the following spring, and hopes for a better year. Mechanics and secretaries work hour after hour, sure they can find a solution to a problem. Mothers show their daughters how to sew, with high hopes that the growing girls will soon be making garments of their own. Teachers instruct children, expecting them to become something more than they are now.

Our lives are surrounded by hopeful people. Without hope for improvement, life would look bleak. In the same way, our spiritual hope helps us to visualize who we can ultimately become. Without knowledge of the Word, we have no hope beyond our present state. But as we meditate on what God wants us to become, our lives can be perfected.

As Abraham's faith in God took him through the test of giving up his only son, so our hope in God will help us overcome difficulties we face. When we realize that God is in control of our lives, we can entrust the outcome to Him.

Our hope in God gives us boldness to speak to others of our salvation. We know God's Word is sure; therefore, we are not timid to share it. Hope gives us patience with others. They fail, as we also do, but we pray for them and hope they will be victorious in the next battle. We hope the unbeliever will be saved. We hope the immature will blossom to maturity.

Our hope in God gives us lasting joy. We are satisfied that what God has promised will come to pass, and that someday our unseen hopes will become sight.

January 16

> For I say, through the grace given unto me, to every man that is among you, not to think of himself more highly than he ought to think; but to think soberly, according as God hath dealt to every man the measure of faith.
>
> —Romans 12:3

I have often looked up from my work and noticed that I have a light burning unnecessarily. Sometimes the sun has come out while I am absorbed in what I am doing. When I take notice of my surroundings, I see that the sunlight far exceeds the light coming from the ceiling, making the inside light useless. Sometimes basement lights or bathroom lights waste energy when they burn all day for no good reason. Lights are a blessing during times of darkness, but God has also provided the light of day by which we can see.

I am called to be a light and to use my energy wisely. I want to serve where I am needed. Just as a room is flooded with light at the flick of the switch, so I want to be useful at the Spirit's bidding. Sometimes I am tempted to think of myself as the answer to everyone's problems, thinking that I know best or that my help is better than anybody else's. When I fall into that line of thinking, I am like those lights that burn unnecessarily. Just as God has provided daylight when no artificial lighting is needed, so He has given gifts and abilities to others besides me. If I insist on "shining" when I ought not, I will soon be outshone by others who have a more brilliant light because of their humble obedience.

Just as bulbs that burn constantly need to be replaced often, we face burn-out when we try to do too much in every situation. We need to remember that we have an on/off switch that we must allow God to operate, and that God has provided nighttime for a reason. Just as physical darkness is more conducive to rest, so we might be called to withdraw from certain scenes because it is more restful for us.

Today, heed the flick of your own switch through the voice of the Spirit.

....

....

Her sun is gone down while it was yet day.

—Jeremiah 15:9

A person's physical life is sometimes compared to a day. We think of birth as the dawning, the prime of life as the full light of day, and the declining years as the sunset. That is the natural order of things. But because we live in a fallen world, sometimes things happen that are not natural or right. We do not have a promise of how long our personal day on earth will be or when our sun will set. God tells us, "Watch therefore: for ye know not what hour your Lord doth come" (Matthew 24:42).

A sunset in the middle of the day would not seem natural or right, and it certainly did not seem right when the sun set on my sister's life when she was only twenty-six years old. God did not wait until the evening of her life to call; a traffic accident brought on her sunset while it was still day. But through the darkness of grief, we realized that her life had produced rays for a memorable sunset. Even though we were left with only the golden rays of that sunset, we were thankful that the rays left a beautiful legacy as she passed to the land of endless day.

Our heavenly Father is holding the timepiece, the clock of our lives. Just as a sunset at noon would bring a sudden ending to the day, the sun of your life could set quickly. And so, my friend, live this day with the awareness of the brevity of life. If your record would read, "Her sun is gone down while it was yet day," may the rays of your sunset be bright and clear.

My sheep hear my voice, and I know them, and they follow me.

—John 10:27

The Good Shepherd does not lead aimlessly. His goal for His sheep is green pastures and still waters. The pathway to the goal may lead through dry, brown pastures and by turbulent waters. If the sheep become tired and stay in the unpleasant places, it is their fault. They are not listening to the Shepherd's voice as He calls them to move on.

Although this world is not our place of rest, our Shepherd wants us to come to a place of rest in Him. As we pass through struggles and adversities, His calm voice calls us and invites us to rest in Him. When we respond to the Shepherd's invitation, we find the green pastures and still waters in our relationship with Him. The waters of our unsettling circumstances may still roar and uncertainties may still abound, but they become less and less threatening as we listen to the Shepherd's voice.

Other voices may beckon. Some voices tell us to give up or give in, and some tell us we are following the wrong guide because the way is uncertain. But as we keep following, we learn that we can follow the Good Shepherd with perfect confidence even if the way is uncertain. Hearing and following His voice above the roar of the storm always leads to a place of calm.

We must pay careful attention and not allow other things to drown out His voice. If we do, we will be lost in the storm or starve in the dry pastures. But Jesus will lead us to vast green pastures and volumes of still waters when we listen to His voice.

And those members of the body, which we think to be less honourable, upon these we bestow more abundant honour.

—1 Corinthians 12:23

A crew of men from church had traveled to another state to rebuild a house that had burned down. When they came back, they gave a report about their experiences. When Allen talked about his job, he said, "I didn't really do anything important. I talked to only a few men. I was busy marking boards for the others to saw and nail. I wore out a whole pencil on lumber, making marks totaling a half mile."

I could envision Allen's careful labor as he worked in seclusion, meticulously marking boards. He said he had not done anything of importance, but can you imagine the chaos if he had not measured and sawed the lumber to correct lengths? It would have proved very frustrating to the foremen and the crew.

Christ is building His church, and we are His laborers. Are you filling your role with diligence? What you do may seem unimportant. You may not be a leader, and others may take for granted the things you do. Nevertheless, you are required to be faithful in what may seem unimportant.

If no one had measured the boards for the new house, the progress of the building would have been hindered. In the same way, your position in the church is important. Your level of faithfulness in filling your role does affect others. Today, ask the Lord to help you do your part in building His church in whatever role He has for you. ❄

In the multitude of my thoughts within me thy comforts delight my soul.

—Psalm 94:19

O Father, you know why I am alone tonight and why my daughter-in-law is alone. You know why my husband's work was ended at the age of fifty-six and my son's at twenty-seven, only four months later. You know they both loved you and felt your call to special work that would honor you here on earth. My husband saw so much more yet to be done. My son's work was hardly started.

It seemed to me that healing would have been the greatest answer, but that is my human way of seeing things. I know you have said your thoughts and ways are higher than mine—just as heaven is higher than the earth.

You know my husband and my son were committed to your will. You know why they both chose not to prolong earthly existence with treatments that would not really heal. Perhaps in your permissive will, you would have let them live longer with prolonged treatment, but I believe sometimes death is your first choice.

I am a parent, and I know that when I plan something my children will especially enjoy, I am eager for the time to come when I can share my surprise with them and enjoy their delight. Is that how you feel about heaven, Father, and did you welcome their commitment to you as an opportunity to reward them earlier than most?

Your Word says, "Precious in the sight of the Lord is the death of his saints" (Psalm 116:15). Thank you for loving them, and for loving me.

Your Word also says, "In the multitude of my thoughts within me thy comforts delight my soul." Thank you for all your comforts. They are truly delightful.

> Let me look up in faith and smile,
> And let me not be sad,
> For why should I feel sorrowful
> With what makes heaven glad?

I don't know all the reasons, Father. But you know them . . . and I am content.

January 21

The Lord will give strength unto his people; the Lord will bless his people with peace.
—Psalm 29:11

One morning as I was walking to the school where I taught in Honduras, I felt burdened with the challenges I was facing. My heart felt heavy and hopeless. As I walked, I looked up into the sky to breathe a prayer for strength for the day. What I saw just made me stop and gaze. Dark clouds blotted the sky, but above them the sun was shining. All around the clouds was a stunning silver lining. It gave me so much courage—even though I was facing hard times just then, there was hope! I felt strengthened by the thought that it would not always be this way.

Then another thought struck me. *Someone is praying for me.* And I knew who it was—the Holy Spirit was praying for me with unspeakable feeling and compassion (Romans 8:26). With the Lord by my side, I felt prepared to face the day ahead of me.

The Lord will give you strength for today too!

And the king said, And where is thy master's son?

—2 Samuel 16:3

Wherefore wentest not thou with me, Mephibosheth?

—2 Samuel 19:25

Early in his reign, King David remembered his beloved friend Jonathan. Jonathan's relatives were not David's responsibility, yet David wanted to honor his friend. He set out to find someone of the family to whom he could show kindness.

Finally he found Jonathan's son Mephibosheth, who was lame. David sent for him and invited him into the palace to eat at the table as one of his own sons. He also made Mephibosheth owner of all that had belonged to Saul.

But then things changed, and David encountered trouble. His own son was trying to overthrow the kingdom, and David and his servants fled for their lives. While David was going through this time of intense pressure, he noticed that Mephibosheth was not in his company of supporters. He was disappointed; his earlier kindness seemed not to have generated gratefulness and loyalty.

He vented his frustration when Ziba came with provisions. "Where is Mephibosheth?" he asked. Ziba implied that Mephibosheth had stayed behind in hopes of getting back his grandfather's kingdom.

Later, when David personally asked Mephibosheth why he had not come, the story was vastly different. Mephibosheth had wanted to go with the king but his servant had deceived him. His servant had said that he would saddle a donkey so that Mephibosheth could go with the king. But the servant did not perform the task he had promised, and due to his handicap, Mephibosheth could not go with the king unassisted. Then David understood and realized that Mephibosheth had honored him more than he had expected.

Are you experiencing such a blighted hope in a friendship? Someone you loved, supported in prayer, and cared about may seem to have forsaken you. If you are disappointed, learn to lower your expectations of others and give them the benefit of the doubt. Maybe they would like to help more than they are able.

It was not Mephibosheth's fault that David was disappointed. He had not been able to do anything about the report that Ziba had taken to David. Likewise, your friends may not be able to support you in the way they would like to. Turn your disappointment into an opportunity to pray for your friends and help them in their time of need. ✹

....

....

....

....

....

....

....

....

....

....

....

....

....

....

....

....

....

Delight thyself also in the Lord; and he shall give thee the desires of thine heart.
Commit thy way unto the Lord; trust also in him; and he shall bring it to pass.

—Psalm 37:4-5

Excitement surged through the young woman as she thought on the verses she had just read. *It must surely mean that it is God's will for me to get together with the young man I admire. It says God will give me the desires of my heart,* she interpreted. *And this is my desire.*

The friendship she desired never developed. Later, the young woman looked at the verses differently as the faithful Spirit revealed their true meaning. When we take pleasure in the Lord and adore Him, our desire and delight will be to do His will. As we commit our ways to the Lord and allow Him to direct our lives, He will surely bring to pass the blessings and rewards promised to us in this life and through eternity.

Our part is to delight in, commit to, and trust in the Lord. God's part is to give us our truest desires. He will bring them to pass, always blessing and rewarding those who delight to do His will.

January 24

And the King shall answer and say unto them, Verily I say unto you, Inasmuch as ye have done it unto one of the least of these my brethren, ye have done it unto me.
—Matthew 25:40

I rejoice as I notice especially the word *least* in this passage of Scripture. The promise is to those who serve the most unimportant people, and by doing so serve Christ. Who are these people through whom Christ can be served unawares? He mentions the sick, the hungry, the stranger, the thirsty—in short, those who are looked down upon, or those who might be overlooked by a person who thinks she is on her way to performing a golden deed. To serve Christ, we must humble ourselves rather than lift ourselves up.

This truth is evident in the life of Christ Himself. He became poor, hungry, and thirsty. Notice His lifestyle and the people He chose to be around. Notice the sinners, the Samaritans, the lepers, and the lunatics. Indeed He was meek and lowly just as He had said. If He lived that way, why should those who claim to be His followers seek to live any other way or refuse to do acts like He did?

The least are one category of Christ's representatives on earth. They are here to give others an opportunity to serve Christ. What a high calling for them! And what a high calling for those who desire to be like Christ and serve these representatives.

Trust in the Lord with all thine heart; and lean not unto thine own understanding. In all thy ways acknowledge him, and he shall direct thy paths.

—Proverbs 3:5-6

As the schoolchildren were dismissed for the day, I finished up things in the classroom for another weekend. My heart was still heavy with indecision about the school board's request to teach the intermediate grades the following year. As I reflected on the past year of teaching, I knew it had been fulfilling and rewarding, but there was so much more responsibility than I had expected.

Brother Jonas, my co-teacher who also served as the principal, had told me that afternoon, "We would like to meet with you next Thursday concerning your position next year."

"Please pray for me," I begged.

"We have and will continue to do so. God knows best, and He will make His will clear to you," Brother Jonas assured. As he left my room, I cried out to the Lord for wisdom and direction.

"Trust in the Lord . . . he shall direct thy paths." It seemed so simple, yet it was such a struggle. How could one lay aside personal desires and wish to see God's plan? Denying oneself is not an easy task.

I continued to pray as I traveled home, and finally a deep peace settled over my soul. Somehow, I felt assured that God would direct me. My longing was to be as clay in the potter's hands.

Whatever your situation and whatever decisions you face, my advice is to persevere in prayer. With discipline and the grace of God, you can be victorious. God is concerned about your burdens, and He waits to hear your cry for guidance. Trust in Him. Your own understanding may lead you astray, but He is completely reliable.

Now the Lord had said unto Abram, Get thee out of thy country,
and from thy kindred, and from thy father's house, unto a land that
I will shew thee: and I will make of thee a great nation, and I will
bless thee, and make thy name great; and thou shalt be a blessing.
—Genesis 12:1-2

"Why now? Why me?" These words were cried in distress after figure skater Nancy Kerrigan was clubbed in the knee by an assailant. The trials for the U.S. Olympics were only days away. Nancy's future depended on that knee. Without the full use of it, she had to withdraw from the race. She was devastated.

Can you identify with her? Your life finally feels more secure. Your home is paid for. You enjoy your friends and the church. Your sister and her husband have moved close to your house. You enjoy your job. Suddenly, you need to move.

It does not seem fair to you. Other people live on and on in the same community. Why must you move so soon again? Why could it not be someone who is more capable of making adjustments? *Why now? Why me?* But you have no answers.

Abram did not have answers either. But God told him that to be a blessing to others, he must go. God gave him clear direction for his future. He had to leave the country.

You need not fear when God calls you. It may mean giving up the security of the home you're accustomed to. It may mean living with another family and making new friends. But when you feel sure that this change of plans was meant for you, you can step out one day at a time.

You find strength. You make new friends and feel at home. After some time has passed, you thank God many times that He asked you to leave your home. You are blessed with riches beyond what you could have imagined. ❁

....

....

....

Ye are the salt of the earth.
—Matthew 5:13

Salt is used when preparing nearly every dish. We use it to can and preserve foods, and we use it at mealtimes. Salt is important to us. In the Sermon on the Mount, Jesus tells us that we are the salt of the earth. How are we like salt?

Salt seasons food. We notice quickly if food has no salt; it just does not taste right to us. We need to help season this earth by using our talents to influence others for good. We should tell them about God's love and let them see God's love and work in our lives.

Salt preserves life. People would die if they would eliminate their salt intake. Without our prayers and faithfulness to God, the church would soon die. Contribute what you can to the church by praying for each member and the leaders. Pray for lost souls so that the church of God will continue to expand.

Salt has power. One grain of salt alone would not make a great difference in taste. Together, a number of grains can do wonders. The Dead Sea has so many grains of salt that it can keep a person floating on its water. In the church, we members need to stand together, or the church will not have the power to stand or to reach others in the community. We need to strive to do our part to work with others in the church. ✪

And let us arise, and go up to Bethel; and I will make there an altar unto God, who answered me in the day of my distress, and was with me in the way which I went.
—Genesis 35:3

Throughout the past years, I have joined Jacob in "building altars." Each time I pass that "mound of stones" I am prompted to pause and worship there, remembering that "day of distress" and "how God was with me in the way which I went."

My personal altars are my small notations in Bible margins. Mostly the "stones" are dates, some person's name, or other brief notes that instantly remind me how God accompanied me at that time.

May I have your company on a short tour to several altars?

When I wasn't sure if God wanted me in the Northern or Southern Hemisphere: "The meek will he guide" (Psalm 25:9).

My first separation from Mom and Dad: "And [I]will be a Father unto you" (2 Corinthians 6:18).

My baptism: "I know whom I have believed" (2 Timothy 1:12).

A message preached by my father: "Fathers, provoke not . . ." (Colossians 3:21).

After a distressing incident, a minister kindly met me after church and assisted me in building this altar: "Forgetting those things which are behind . . ." (Philippians 3:13).

This one bears a 1981 date. Each time I pass by here I am reminded He is *still* longsuffering: "The longsuffering of our Lord is salvation" (2 Peter 3:15).

Here I have written the date of birth of our small congregation: "All the commandments shall ye observe" (Deuteronomy 8:1).

The date an eleven-year-old boy perished in a fire: "I go to prepare a place for you" (John 14:2).

And aren't all your pathways worn bare to the altar at Psalm 27:14, where I have scratched in five dates? "Wait on the Lord."

Where are your altar sites?

> For ye have need of patience, that, after ye have done the will of God, ye might receive the promise.
>
> —Hebrews 10:36

Patience does not complain in troubles; rather, it cheerfully endures. We are not born with patience, and we need to grow in this character quality and add it to our daily life.

James 5:7 tells us that we need to have patience until the Lord comes or until we take our last breath. "Behold, the husbandman waiteth for the precious fruit of the earth, and hath long patience for it . . ." Even so, as we face trials of accepting God's plan for our lives, we need to be patient and faithfully walk in the pathway God has for us now.

Patience is not instant; we need to cultivate it. Jesus is our perfect example of patience. Romans 15:5 tells us that we have a God of patience who grants us patience. You can rest in that!

But without faith it is impossible to please him: for he that cometh to God must believe that he is, and that he is a rewarder of them that diligently seek him.

—Hebrews 11:6

Institutions and organizations are crumbling, and it does not take long to figure out why. God is pushed aside and left out. Questions are asked and much money is spent on research, but answers are evasive. Again it seems the reason is that God is ignored.

I seem to think a lot about material things . . . but surely I'm not pushing God aside. I have a firm belief in God.

Sometimes I do not sense my need. I do not feel as dependent on God as I had been. I wonder why . . . but no, I'm not pushing God aside. Every time I look outside and see the beauty of the creation, I recognize that God is the Creator of it all.

I feel disturbed and unsettled. I really want a settled peace in my heart. If only . . . but still, I'm not pushing God aside. I read His Word every day, at least a little.

I would not intentionally push God aside or reject Him. But somehow these verses seem to ring in my mind: "Thou believest that there is one God; thou doest well: the devils also believe, and tremble. But wilt thou know, O vain man, that faith without works is dead?" (James 2:19-20).

My problem with materialism shows that I have more faith in what I see than in what I cannot see. I do not have my eyes on eternal things. I must admit that I do push God aside in this aspect of my life.

My problem with feeling self-sufficient might stem from not giving heed to the Spirit's voice in little things because I think I know better. He may see my independence and choose to retreat; He will not force Himself on me. Soon I start feeling as though something has come between God and me. Obviously, I again pushed God aside. I did not have the faith that He knows best.

The problem with feeling unsettled and disturbed—could it come from a lack of trust, from not leaving that disturbing matter to the Lord? Again I lack real faith in His promises.

Are worldly institutions rejecting God? Yes. Do I sometimes reject God? My life makes it obvious. Faith in God means more than believing that He exists. I must have a faith that moves me to live above the present and convinces me that His will is always best. With such a faith, I can experience a restful, trusting life that will not crumble.

January 31

Charity suffereth long, and is kind . . . is not easily provoked, thinketh no evil.
—1 Corinthians 13:4-5

Our family moved to my grandparents' farm when my grandparents were getting older. Grandmother got sick and needed a lot of help and care. Someone always needed to stay with her, so our family was usually separated when we went to church or visited relatives and friends. It was not easy for me to spend so much time helping Grandmother without seeing a paycheck. At times I was tempted to wish she would die so that she would be out of our way.

Then one day Grandmother gave me ten dollars. That was a lot of money in the early sixties! It helped me realize that my grandmother was not taking me for granted. She did appreciate the things I did! The evil thoughts that had tempted me were gone.

And now, years after my grandmother died, I rejoice that I did not continue thinking evil thoughts. What if Grandmother would have died when I wished she would? Would I not still be carrying the regret for that today? Those thoughts would not have been worth all the pain that I would have felt throughout the years since then. But where love is cultivated, no regrets can remain. Praise the Lord for victory!

....

....

....

....

....

....

But to do good and to communicate forget not.

—Hebrews 13:16

God's command to do good and to communicate is very important if we want to maintain proper relationships with others.

Communication starts in your care for other people. You care about the joys and disappointments in their lives. You listen to them and try to feel how they feel as they relate to you.

Communication is sharing your experiences with others. Tell your friends about the trip you enjoyed or the new hobby you've taken up.

Communicating with your friends should go deeper than your everyday experiences. Share the verse that gave you courage this morning. If you feel a need to grow in a certain area, share it and ask for the prayers of your friends.

Communication includes questions. Ask a friend about her day and what she finds meaningful in life. This will show you are interested in what happens to her.

Communication means that you are open to discuss how you feel about issues you are facing.

Communication builds confidence in each other as you share, but only as you keep confidential the personal struggles a friend shares with you. Communication will soon cease if your friend hears that you shared with others what was meant for only you to know.

Seek to obey this important command of God with those you are working or living with daily.

February 2

And why take ye thought for raiment? Consider the lilies of the field,
how they grow; they toil not, neither do they spin: and yet I say unto
you, That even Solomon in all his glory was not arrayed like one of these.
—Matthew 6:28-29

I was worried! Would the low wages from my winter job cover my expensive heating bill? What would happen if I couldn't pay my bills?

Then I saw it. Hanging right above the thermostat was a motto with a message just waiting for me to receive. "But seek ye first the kingdom of God, and his righteousness; and all these things shall be added unto you."

How good God was in guiding me to hang those precious words at that appropriate place, out of all the other places I could have chosen! The winter passed, and I had enough fuel and enough money.

We could have worries and fears about many things. Do you ever worry about the old age that is creeping up faster than you wish it were? Do you wonder who is going to take care of you if you do not have children?

God's promises are for the old and feeble as well as for the young and healthy. They are for all His children who turn their faces heavenward and look to God to have their needs met.

The flowers possess a glory unequaled by Solomon's. We can possess an even greater glory because of the promise that those who gaze on the Lord will be changed into His glory.

Let the world's offers to insure and secure you come and go. May you be found with an upturned face waiting for that greater glory to descend upon you. As your soul rejoices in the sweetness of that glory, your worries and cares will cease to disturb you.

A man's heart deviseth his way: but the Lord directeth his steps.

—Proverbs 16:9

Psalm 33

I was packing my suitcase, looking forward to my flight, when plans suddenly changed. I found out I was not needed at my destination after all, and I was very disappointed.

Another time, my friend and I planned to go visit another friend forty miles away and encourage her, but we found out that our friend would not be at home the day we could visit. We had to change our plans.

You may have had similar experiences—times when your balloon burst or your feelings felt like a flat tire. These things happen to everyone from time to time. The Apostle Paul experienced a dramatic change of plans when God stopped him on his way to Damascus. He was struck blind, helpless to carry out his plans. But Paul was willing to reevaluate his life and make amends. Maybe this was when Paul learned the importance of accepting a change in his plans, because later in life we see him willing to follow God when God again showed him a path different from the one he had planned.

How do we respond when the Lord changes our plans? We can become miserable in our disappointment and make those around us unhappy too. Or we can get on our knees and ask God which direction He wants us to go now.

Sometimes we may not have properly discerned God's will for us. We might have hindered the work of God if we had carried out our intentions.

If we walk close to the Shepherd, He will guide our steps, though He may lead us into pastures different from what we had planned.

Read Jeremiah 29:11. God is not trying to make our lives difficult. He sees the whole path of each life from beginning to end, and He knows how to guide us.

February 4

Consider how great things he hath done for you.
—1 Samuel 12:24

But God, who is rich in mercy, for his great love wherewith he loved [me] (Ephesians 2:4) . . .

. . . hath made me (Job 33:4).

. . . hath been mindful of [me] (Psalm 115:12).

. . . hath looked upon my affliction (Genesis 29:32).

. . . hath regarded the low estate of his handmaiden (Luke 1:48).

. . . hath inclined his ear unto me (Psalm 116:2).

. . . hath attended to the voice of my prayer (Psalm 66:19).

. . . hath sent his angel, and hath delivered me (Acts 12:11).

. . . hath delivered me out of all trouble (Psalm 54:7).

. . . hath redeemed my soul out of all distress (1 Kings 1:29).

. . . hath prospered my way (Genesis 24:56).

. . . hath given me counsel (Psalm 16:7).

. . . hath prepared for [me] a city (Hebrews 11:16).

. . . hath called [me] to glory and virtue (2 Peter 1:3).

. . . hath made [me] accepted in the beloved (Ephesians 1:6).

. . . hath blessed me hitherto (Joshua 17:14).

. . . hath put a new song in my mouth (Psalm 40:3).

. . . hath said, I will never leave thee (Hebrews 13:5).

. . . hath given [me] everlasting consolation and good hope (2 Thessalonians 2:16).

. . . hath given [me] an understanding (1 John 5:20).

The Lord hath done great things for [me]; whereof [I am] glad (Psalm 126:3).

> Then one of the twelve, called Judas Iscariot, went unto the chief priests, and said unto them, What will ye give me, and I will deliver him unto you? And they covenanted with him for thirty pieces of silver.
>
> —Matthew 26:14-15

Judas, do you see the same attitudes in people today as you did long ago? Do you see people taking the same steps you took? Do you see these things in me?

When you betrayed Jesus, you probably did not realize what was going to happen to Him. You wanted the money and thought He could deliver Himself. Even if you had no intentions to have Him crucified and thought He would deliver Himself, did it not matter to you that He would be rudely arrested by a band of ungodly soldiers? Did you not care how He would feel? Ah, yes, I remember. You had your eyes on the moneybag.

Are you pointing your finger at me and saying that sometimes I don't care either what happens to Jesus because I have my eyes on something else? I would have to admit that you are right.

When He asks me to do something for Him and I am reluctant because I do not see my way clear financially, then my eyes, like yours, are on the moneybag and I care more about it than about the Lord.

When I should witness to someone and I am either ashamed or afraid, I care more about what happens to me than I care about what happens to a soul for whom Christ died.

When I think I have to talk and laugh a lot to be accepted, I care more about making an impression for myself than I do about making an impression for Christ.

When I have a long face because I feel I have been mistreated or misunderstood, I care more about my own feelings than I do about overcoming and allowing God to be glorified through my trials.

When I have a wrinkled brow and a blank stare because I doubt and worry, I care more about having my needs met in my own time and way than I do about allowing God to work in His time and way.

When I do these things, I, like you, have no control over the outcome of my actions. Many could doubt the God in whom I claim to believe, and many could be lost. So why do I do these things? Ah, yes, I remember. I have my eyes on myself.

> There is a lad here, which hath five barley loaves, and
> two small fishes: but what are they among so many?
>
> —John 6:9

Each of us is only one person, but we have great power if we are children of God. Through His Spirit, we can accomplish valuable things.

Abraham spent time interceding in prayer for Lot and his family who lived in Sodom. His intercession saved four of his relatives from the destruction of fire.

Nehemiah wept, fasted, and prayed for the city of Jerusalem that was in ruins. Because of his concern, the walls were rebuilt and the enemies defeated. God's people rejoiced.

Because of one little lad giving his lunch to Jesus, more than five thousand people had plenty to eat.

Paul's nephew risked his life for his uncle by relaying a message of the evil intentions of Paul's enemies to the chief captain. Paul's life was spared.

When Dorcas died, the widows showed the coats and garments she had made. They sorrowed for Dorcas because she had loved them.

One person in whom God resides does make a difference. When one is free of personal ambition, God can use him or her to accomplish wondrous things.

February 7

And when he had taken the book, the four beasts and four and twenty elders fell down before the Lamb, having every one of them . . . golden vials full of odours, which are the prayers of saints.

—Revelation 5:8

I was awed as I gazed at the majestic column of thick, white steam rising from the factory into the deep blue sky. It seemed to glisten in the evening light. When smoke pours from a chimney, it's not unusual for it to fall to the ground or be blown sideways by the wind, so how could the cloud of steam keep its vertical position? The answer was obvious. The atmospheric pressure was high and the air was still, so nothing hindered the mass from pushing its way upward.

The sight reminded me of something else that rises beautifully if there are no hindrances. It is our prayers. They are even more beautiful to God than the steam cloud was to me.

Prayers prayed with a lack of faith, in a hurry, without a burden or a sense of need, or while thoughts are wandering, are like smoke that is blown to the ground. The person who prays with a careless attitude has a wrong concept of God. He may become discouraged because his prayers are not answered, but the fault is not God's. The winds that hinder and the "low pressure" in the heart must be dealt with. A satisfying prayer life is well worth the effort it takes to make it so. Prayers rising heavenward through an unclouded atmosphere are a blessing to the one who prays, and they glisten in God's sight.

> Lord, thou hast been our dwelling place in all generations.
>
> —Psalm 90:1

Generally, a dwelling is something with which we are familiar: a treasured abode where we find security, comfort, and rest.

In this prayer of Moses we hear him acknowledging God as his dwelling place—his home base. His earthly dwelling was often insecure and unpredictable. As a baby he was hidden from the public. We can only imagine how much time his mother spent teaching him about God until he was taken by Pharaoh's daughter. His parents must have laid the foundation well. Through all the teaching of the Egyptians, he did not leave his early training.

In young adulthood he attempted to run ahead of God and had to flee for his life. The forty years of exile were proving ground for Moses, and he learned to communicate with God. God tested him and found that He could trust Moses with His chosen people.

How his faith must have been tried when he approached Pharaoh again and again. His dogged determination incensed the Egyptian, but God was in control and Pharaoh buckled. Then came the final exit and another forty years of testing. He depended on his Anchor and it held. When he was denied entrance to the Promised Land, he recognized that God was his dwelling place and not Canaan.

Sometimes God must take us aside to prove and try us. He may have a greater task ahead, or He may continue to give us mundane work. Whatever it may be, He wants us to realize that He is our dwelling place forever.

Many generations have come and gone, and God remains the same: faithful, solid, and unchangeable. He is our refuge today. ◗

But speaking the truth in love, may grow up into him in all things, which is the head, even Christ: from whom the whole body fitly joined together and compacted by that which every joint supplieth, according to the effectual working in the measure of every part, maketh increase of the body unto the edifying of itself in love.
—Ephesians 4:15-16

God often meets my spiritual needs through His people—those who make up the church.

If I have a need for patience in tribulation, I am inspired to patience by observing one who is radiant under trying circumstances.

When I fail in being as helpful and thoughtful as I should be, I can learn from one who is always ready to help.

By listening to someone who has more discernment than I do, I learn to be more discerning and less gullible.

When I battle to keep my tongue under control, I can learn the value of silence from one who is quiet.

When I lack warmth and concern for others, I learn its necessity from the one who warms my own heart.

When I am bowed down with cares, I am inspired to cheerfulness by one who is cheerful in the midst of cares.

When I am hurried and harried, I learn to stay calm from one who is serene though pressed by many duties.

By observing the one who thinks things through before making decisions, I learn not to make quick, unwise decisions.

Someone who could be wrapped up in her own happiness shares her life with others. This teaches me unselfishness.

I am inspired to become more like Jesus by observing the Spirit at work in yielded lives. Is someone inspired by observing the Spirit at work in my life?

....

....

But it is good to be zealously affected always in a good thing.

—Galatians 4:18

Marie bounded up the steps, singing as she entered the room where Anna was working. Anna, whose day had been a normal routine of telephone calls and interruptions, caught the spirit of enthusiasm. The next time a call came in, Anna's cheeriness produced a smile in the caller. The caller passed on her smile, and so the circle of Marie's happiness spread wider and wider.

We cannot normally follow our smiles as we did Marie's in the illustration above. We can be confident, though, that they do have an effect, because we know we are affected by attitudes around us. Let us determine to allow only the good deeds of others to influence us.

"And let us consider one another to provoke unto love and to good works" (Hebrews 10:24). By observing the actions of others, we can determine to be more loving and giving. Maybe you notice how large the mission offering is. When you realize that others are giving much more than you are, a desire may stir in you to give more the next time. Your friend's patience with her handicapped foster child may help you see a need to be more longsuffering with your first-grade student who seems so slow. Another friend with many responsibilities leaves her work to spend an afternoon helping an older lady in the church, inspiring you to help someone in need as well.

How much better if all were affected so positively. But just as positive actions and attitudes are contagious, so are negative ones. It takes a lot of effort to counteract a negative attitude, but with God's help we can overcome.

Realizing that our lives affect others, let us walk carefully and live a life above reproach. ✾

Wait on the Lord: be of good courage, and he shall
strengthen thine heart: wait, I say, on the Lord.
—Psalm 27:14

Fast food. Instant mixes. Microwave ovens. Push buttons. Is the speed and hurry of the world rubbing off on us to the extent that we expect instant answers from the Lord? Is that why we are tempted to be impatient and wonder why He does not answer?

The Lord has not changed with the times, neither has His Word. He still exhorts us to wait. When I flick a switch or push a button, I may forget that the machine is running. But if I have to stay there to see that everything functions as it should, my mind is more likely to stay there too. If the Lord would always give me answers instantly, I could easily forget that I need to depend on Him for both physical and spiritual survival. But when the answer is long in coming, I go to Him continually. I learn how to pour out my heart to Him. I learn to search my life. I grow in faith as I wait, because He has promised to answer—and I know that He will. Our text verse sums up all these things by telling us that our hearts will be strengthened as we wait on the Lord.

Isaiah says, "They that wait upon the Lord . . . shall mount up with wings as eagles" (Isaiah 40:31). Who would not desire to soar spiritually and rise above the storms of life like the eagle does in reality? It is not possible unless you first have a time of learning from the Lord while waiting on Him. You need a source of strength to soar. That strength comes from the Lord and the things I learn as I wait before Him.

If He asks me to wait before He answers, I know it is more important to wait than to receive an immediate answer.

Freely ye have received, freely give.

—Matthew 10:8

What do you have that you have not received? Every day you are a recipient of God's blessings. Do you thank Him? Do you live as though you appreciate His gifts? Do you share with others what you have received?

A clear, sparkling mountain stream feeds the Sea of Galilee. The water is fresh and the sea full of fish. Day and night the water flows into the sea and out again.

When the water flows out of the sea into the Jordan River, it drops downhill fast, over waterfalls, making many twists and turns. Finally it empties into the Dead Sea, which has no outlet. The millions of gallons of water that run into the Dead Sea just lie there in the sun and evaporate. Salt deposits are left behind, and even the fish cannot live in its salty waters.

Do you see the contrast of a living and giving individual to one who only receives but never shares with others? Be like the Sea of Galilee. Pass on the joy of your salvation through your consistent smile, your friendship, your sympathetic ear, and your finances.

Jesus told the disciples to heal the sick, cleanse the lepers, raise the dead, and cast out devils. There was work to do, and Jesus wanted them to share with others the power He was giving to them.

There is much to do today as well. Many people need you. The more you give, the more you will receive so that you can bless even more people. You will find a giving life to be a blessed one. ✳

February 13

Then went the devils out of the man, and entered into the swine: and the herd ran violently down a steep place into the lake, and were choked.
—Luke 8:33

The devils had pled that Jesus would allow them to go into the swine. Jesus gave them their request, but they still ended up in a place they had not wanted to be. The herd of demon-possessed swine plunged into a nearby lake.

The devil has not changed. When he is within the heart of man, he still takes man where he does not want to be and leads him to destruction. Through my thoughts, Satan can get me into places where I never thought I would be. It looks innocent enough to think that life is unfair. But a thought like that is not from the Holy Spirit, because the fruit of the Spirit is faith. Thinking that life is unfair is not trusting the plan of God. If I persist in that thought, it will take me to a dark and destructive place spiritually. An impure, lustful thought is not from the Holy Spirit because the fruit of the Spirit is goodness. That impure thought, when focused on, will take me where I never dreamed I would be. Impatience is not from the Holy Spirit because the fruit of the Spirit is longsuffering. If I persist in impatience, I will destroy people in my care who need God's love.

Lord, hold before me two visions—the vision of the violence brought on by the devil's maneuvering, as well as the vision of the peace and serenity of sitting at your feet, brought about by the absence of the devil.

February 14

Hast thou entered into the treasures of the snow?

—Job 38:22

The view is beautiful, breathtaking, inspiring—altogether lovely. Lacy snowflakes have covered everything barren: mud holes, dried weeds, and dead plants. What I see is pure whiteness. The sun shines on the drifts, and I squint because of the brightness of the morning. The coldness outside has brought a calmness to the world.

I am reminded that my heart was black with sin. I wanted my own way, but I was miserable living for self. Then Jesus came and drew my heart to Himself. He showed me a better way. When I welcomed Him into my heart, He washed it whiter than the snow I am seeing. I became happy and life took on a new meaning. Peace replaced the turmoil I had felt, sorrow turned to joy, and victory overcame defeat.

Sometimes I still fail. At those times I need to ask Jesus to wash me again, which He is faithful to do. Again I can feel clean and white, whiter than anything man has ever seen. Jesus forgives my sin, and I lift my heart in praise and thanksgiving for the pardon. God has a storehouse of grace, a treasury as pure as snow. It is always available for you and me to enter into and partake of its purity. ✸

February 15

There came unto him a woman having an alabaster box of very precious ointment, and poured it on his head, as he sat at meat.

—Matthew 26:7

Ruth lay across her bed, deep in thought. The message that morning at church had deeply impressed her, but she was still unable to conclude how to apply it.

The sermon had explained how Mary had brought very precious ointment to Jesus, breaking the box and pouring it on Him. Jesus called it a good work. Looking at her notes, Ruth reread the challenges the minister had presented. "What do you consider your dearest possession? Are you willing to give that to Jesus?"

What does that mean for me? Ruth was puzzled. *How can I give my family to Jesus? I cannot give my home and car to Jesus. What about my sewing machine or my dishes? Am I really giving them to Jesus just by giving them up and selling them?*

Later Ruth visited with a wise couple named Joe and Anna. She presented her question when the opportunity came. "How can I give my dearest possessions to Jesus?" she asked them. "I need my things. I cannot very well be of service to the Lord without them."

Joe answered, "Well, the Christian life is a surrendered life. Our possessions need to be surrendered to God."

"It might also mean we should not be selfish with our possessions," Anna discerned. "I tend to highly prize some of the dishes I received from relatives many years ago. When my daughter wants to use them for a special occasion, I have struggled with the fear of them breaking. Then I decided it is selfish to value something so highly that I could not part with it."

In the coming days Ruth saw new meaning in the minister's message. She remembered when the church had asked her sister and husband to be among those eligible to be chosen for a two-year term of missionary work. Although they were not chosen in the end, she had cringed at the possibility of them leaving. She realized that she needed to come to a place of surrendering her family to Jesus in that way.

Ruth began asking herself specific questions. *Do I willingly allow others to use my car when they have a need? Is my home open to strangers even when it does not suit me? Do I use my sewing machine to sew for the needy?*

Along with her questions came the realization that Jesus might not need her possessions, but He wanted her heart. Only as she allowed herself to be broken like the alabaster box could her possessions be of any use to Jesus. ✳

And he arose, and came to his father. But when he was yet a great way off, his father saw him, and had compassion, and ran, and fell on his neck, and kissed him.

—Luke 15:20

The parents had been gone most of the day. When they walked in the lane, two happy little girls came running to meet them. The youngest one was quickly swept up into her daddy's arms, where she felt safe and secure. It did not matter that she had fallen that day and skinned her knee. It did not matter if the other little girls had not let her play with them or that one of her toy teacups was broken. Nothing mattered except that her daddy was home and she was with him. The family happily gathered around the table that evening. They felt at peace because everyone was at home.

I am separated from my heavenly Father in the physical sense. Someday I want to see His arms stretched out to welcome me home. It will not matter if I had faced persecution or if my heart was broken and I was disappointed. Nothing will matter except that I am home with Him and safe forevermore. Safe! Safe from all the arrows of the devil. Safe from fears and fighting. Safe from weariness and wanderings. I can picture a happy gathering around a heavenly table. We will rest in complete peace because then all the Father's children will be there—safe at home.

Ye shall not need to fight in this battle: set yourselves, stand
ye still, and see the salvation of the Lord with you.
—2 Chronicles 20:17

Did you ever bring needless stress upon yourself because of your curiosity? Perhaps several people held a conference to discuss some matter and you were not included. You would have liked to know what was said. Or perhaps you know a pleasant surprise awaits you, but you do not know what it is or when it will be. Your curiosity does not allow you to focus on anything else. In these cases, you think you must know and you must have answers. But you really don't. These matters are under control, and you will find out what you need to know when the time is right for you to know. In the past, things turned out right, did they not?

Do you struggle needlessly because you think you must have answers when the devil challenges you? He might ask, "Why did the Lord put you in this place? There is not much opportunity to do anything for Him in your position." Or, "Why doesn't the Lord give you what He does others?" Or, "Why does God ask this of you if He does not ask it of others?" Panic-stricken, you grope for an answer, something concrete to cling to. You think you have to have answers because Satan's challenges keep you from thinking about anything else. But you do not have to have an answer. Ask God to fight for you, and have faith that He will take care of each of your questions. You will see His answers when the time is right for you to know. You can rest in His care.

Let thine handmaid, I pray thee, speak in thine
audience, and hear the words of thine handmaid.
—1 Samuel 25:24

Courageous Abigail was willing to risk her life to calm an enemy who planned to harm her family.

Abigail must have thought a lot before she approached David to make peace. She took time to make loaves, measure out corn, gather fruits, and dress sheep for meat. She realized that David, a man of God, had made an impulsive decision. Her humble approach and gifts soon touched David's heart. He saw his wrong and spared the lives of Abigail's family, allowing God to bring judgment upon the one who had wronged him instead of taking matters into his own hands. Abigail's wise move brought her many blessings in the future days too.

Like Abigail, we may see the need to go to another person to restore peace between us. We need to take her approach to prepare before we meet the other person. In preparation, wait until you are calm. Take time to pray for yourself, asking God to cleanse you of any unloving or unforgiving attitudes. Pray for the right words to speak, and pray for the other person. Then humbly share what is on your mind. Listen as the other person expresses her feelings on the matter. Make right any wrong that she feels you have done to her. Many times as we are willing to open our lives and share our problems with each other, we find a real closeness again. God will bless our relationships with peace as we communicate in the right way.

And Moses said unto him, Enviest thou for my sake? would God that all the Lord's people were prophets, and that the Lord would put his spirit upon them!

—Numbers 11:29

A young man ran into the camp and announced that two men were prophesying. Thinking this was encroaching on Moses' authority, Joshua asked Moses to forbid them to prophesy.

But God's Spirit was with Moses. Although God had ordained him as ruler over all the congregation of Israel, Moses remained meek even in his position of authority. The thought of two more men prophesying did not ruffle his feathers. "Would God that all the Lord's people were prophets," was his reply.

What is your reaction when you see a younger person showing talent in an area you excel in? Do you encourage her? You might be tempted to fear that she will become more gifted than you are.

Meekness will take the opportunity to encourage someone else to excel in heights above what you have accomplished. Moses did not fear his position. He was there only because God had put him there. If his responsibility was to be given to another, Moses would listen to God's voice about it.

Sometimes we are surprised at the results of our encouragement to others. A teacher instructed her student in writing poetry and marveled at the pieces the student later composed. A writer encouraged a beginner to mail her article to a publisher, and it was accepted for publication. A wife encouraged her husband in a project he had not attempted before, and he lived up to her expectations. A father encouraged his daughter's talent, and she was able to be a blessing for many years because she developed her gift.

Though the role of encouraging others may not result in monetary gain, the blessing of helping another accomplish a goal is reward enough. Deflecting the glory from ourselves will bring more glory to God. ✷

February 20

When the ear heard me, then it blessed me; and when the eye
saw me, it gave witness to me: because I delivered the poor that
cried, and the fatherless, and him that had none to help him.
—Job 29:11-12

At the sound of knocking, Sharon opened her door and was greeted by a
pathetic sight. An aging woman stood there, holding a malnourished young
child she identified as her grandson. "Would you please care for him?" the woman
pleaded. "His mother doesn't care for him."

Sharon's heart reached out as she held the thin, unresponsive, fifteen-month-old
boy. Of course she would care for him. *Who couldn't love this little child? Didn't
God tell us to pity the fatherless?*

It took time for the boy to trust her when she talked to him. Finally after several
days he stopped squeezing his eyes shut when she talked to him. He even began
to chuckle at times. With proper food, he soon grew happier and fatter, and he
learned to walk and talk. Sharon spent many happy hours with the child.

Eighteen months later a couple came to adopt the boy. Although the parting
was difficult for Sharon, she was overwhelmed with gratitude to God that parents
had been found to provide a Christian home for this child.

Tears came to her eyes as she opened the gift that the parents had given her for
caring for this little boy, now their son. On the motto were painted the words,
"One caring heart is all it takes to make a difference." She thanked God for His
love that reached through her to this child, who now had a brighter future.

Do you know someone who needs your love and care? Give it freely, whether
the person in need is a child or an older person. Many unloved and unwanted
people exist around us. Pray that God would show you someone who needs your
love today. One caring heart can make a pivotal difference. 🌀

And he said unto me, My grace is sufficient for thee: for my strength
is made perfect in weakness. Most gladly therefore will I rather
glory in my infirmities, that the power of Christ may rest upon me.

—2 Corinthians 12:9

Spending a day with a group of friends can be comforting, heartwarming, and encouraging. It is good and right that we should frequently assemble and fellowship with others. But it takes time alone with a person to get to know that friend intimately. When there is peace and quietness with few distractions, I can focus my attention solely on my friend and really listen to what she has to say. If a close friend invites me for this type of sharing, I am thrilled and delighted beyond words, for I thoroughly enjoy such a privilege. I would be foolish to cancel such an invitation and miss out on the blessings. I might do that, however, if my values are mixed up.

The Lord wants to be my close friend and I want to be His. He frequently draws me aside where there are few distractions and my mind is drawn to Him. He invites me to spend time with Him alone. Here I can get to know Him and listen to the things He says. By making me aware of my weaknesses, He helps me realize how dependent I am on Him. Through my frailties, I am drawn away from my activities and into a position that requires me to be still. I could ignore His invitation, but that would be evidence of misplaced priorities. I would then miss out on the blessings of the insights He wants to share with me.

His way of inviting you to set your attention on Him may differ from the way He chooses for me. Whatever that way is, blessings await you if you accept His invitation.

They fell on their face, and were sore afraid. And Jesus came and touched them, and said, Arise, and be not afraid. And when they had lifted up their eyes, they saw no man, save Jesus only.

—Matthew 17:6-8

The secret to having peace in a troubled world is Jesus. Nothing, however threatening, can touch us if our focus is on JESUS ONLY, the one who is in full control.

A minister once said that fear is like a telescope: it focuses on a specific issue and magnifies it. What we fear becomes oppressive to us and rises to become an authority over us. If we fear people, circumstances, or the future, the fear oppresses us and controls us. Like Peter on the waves, if we focus on our own weakness in the face of overwhelming situations, we will be engulfed and sink.

Fear distorts our vision. It magnifies the problem and minimizes God's unlimited grace and power. In essence, it judges the Almighty God to be incapable and insufficient to control His own creation and to meet our needs.

When we focus on God and remember that He is in control of everything and everyone, our vision will be clear and our fears will be quenched. Let us not look around or within, but up, that we may see JESUS ONLY.

She will do him good and not evil all the days of her life.

—Proverbs 31:12

When we see goodness, we stop and take notice. Good art, such as paintings or photography, makes us look twice and admire. Good craftsmanship and good housekeeping inspire us to do likewise. Goodness is a fruit of the Spirit, and a woman filled with that quality will not go unnoticed. Her value cannot be bought or measured.

The adjective *good* is a broad term. We say the food is good, we are feeling good, the garden looks good, or we had a good time. But the goodness that is part of the fruit of the Spirit is superior to the common usage of the word *good*.

Goodness will enable the daughter of the King to be beneficial to others. While associating with others, her holy life will inspire them to a closer walk with God. Her good deeds will urge others to join the ranks of givers. The books she reads will be unobjectionable. Her thoughts will be pure as gold. Her loyalty to Christ will be unquestioned.

Goodness is unequalled by anything else. It is first class—the best. It is no wonder that when goodness is mentioned in the Bible, it most often refers to God. The good news is that when He lives inside us, we have the power to become truly good.

....

....

....

....

....

....

Delight thyself also in the Lord; and he shall give thee the desires of thine heart. Commit thy way unto the Lord; trust also in him; and he shall bring it to pass.
—Psalm 37:4-5

As you look into the future, you most likely face questions that no amount of thought will ever answer. What would I do if I lost my present job? Who will provide for my financial needs when I am too old to work and make money? Who will take care of me in the event of sickness? Listen to the testimony of the above verses by one elderly single sister.

"I find that the more I delight in laboring for the Lord and helping others, the more satisfaction my heart finds in life. Doing things for the needy, even if it is just cutting out quilt patches for the sewing rather than heaping treasures to myself, brings me real joy. I also enjoy writing to elderly ladies or the disabled through shower announcements.

"It takes discipline to keep my mind on God and off the material things of life. Though I do not have much in this world's goods, I find that God always provides. I want to praise Him for that."

Though you do not know the future, God does. You do not understand how things will work out, but God does. The same God who provided for the widows in the Bible will also provide for you. When you bless others as this elderly sister does, you will make it easier for others to want to help you too.

....

....

....

....

....

> For thou shalt worship no other god: for the
> Lord, whose name is Jealous, is a jealous God.
> —Exodus 34:14

I would be jealous and hurt if a friend with whom I thought I shared a special bond would . . .

> . . . enjoy her time with others more than time spent with me.
> . . . give others the little tokens and expressions of appreciation she used to give me.
> . . . do nothing to keep up her end of the friendship.
> . . . confide in others but not in me.
> . . . not gladly do things for me that she does for others.

God yearns for a special, individual friendship with each of His children. He becomes jealous when He sees one of them . . .

> . . . savor the things of man more than the things of God.
> . . . give glory and affection to others that belong to Him.
> . . . do nothing to keep in touch with Him but have time for everything else.
> . . . hesitate to do things for Him.

God craves an intimate friendship with His children, not only for the joy it brings to Him, but also because He wants to give joy and satisfaction to those with whom He shares a friendship. He can only give it to those who keep up their end of the friendship.

It thrills me to know that God is jealous of me—that He really enjoys my fellowship and does not want to lose it. I do not want to lose it either, because it is too precious for words.

And the bones of Joseph, which the children of Israel
brought up out of Egypt, buried they in Shechem.
—Joshua 24:32

For forty years someone carried the bones of Joseph from the land of Egypt to
Canaan. Whenever the cloud lifted from the tabernacle, somebody, somewhere, was responsible to carry that box of human remains.

"What are you carrying?" I can hear one say to the other.

"Joseph's bones," comes the less than enthusiastic reply. "You would think he
could have let our fathers bury him in Egypt. All this work just because he was
so concerned where his bones are buried. I am embarrassed when someone asks
me what I am doing."

Did God ever show you something He wanted you to do that you could not
understand? Remember, God's thoughts are higher than your thoughts. Be willing to do His will.

God may ask you through another person to do something. You may not understand
the purpose of what they are trying to accomplish, but be willing to help anyway.

Joseph was dead. He would never know whether his request was honored. They
could have buried him in the wilderness after everyone was tired of bothering with
the bones. But they didn't. They saw the job through to the end.

Sometimes you are asked to work behind the scenes. Few people will ever know
that it was you who did the work, but God holds you responsible to see it through
to the end. You might not get it done today or tomorrow, but God wants your
willing heart all the way through your task. ✹

> And he shall bring forth thy righteousness as
> the light, and thy judgment as the noonday.
> —Psalm 37:6

Mordecai was hated, scorned, and envied by Haman. He could have chosen to fight back at Haman in an effort to keep his position. He could have told Haman how he had saved the king's life. But he did none of these, instead allowing the Lord to have His way. God brought forth Mordecai's righteousness and rewarded him justly.

Joseph was hated, sold as a slave, thrown into prison, and forgotten. He could have become bitter, sulking, and vengeful. Instead, he was forgiving, kind, and helpful. He did not make a public outcry about the mistreatment he had received. In His own time God exalted Joseph and made known what a great man he was.

Anna, the aged widow, could have been unhappy and bitter with life. She could have chosen to pine away in self-pity, refusing to help herself and others. Did she? No, she shines as an example of absolute dedication to the Lord's service. God brought out her righteousness, her radiance, by allowing her the privilege of seeing His Son.

Jesus, when He was tried and crucified, could have called for thousands of angels to deliver Him and thus prove to the accusing mob that He was right after all. Instead, He quietly yielded to the disgrace without trying to assert His power to get out of it. His righteousness and judgment continue to be revealed as light and truth. He will do for you today what He did for these people of long ago if you make the same choices they did.

....

....

....

And Mary arose in those days, and went into the hill country
with haste . . . and entered into the house of Zacharias, and salut-
ed Elisabeth. . . . And Mary abode with her about three months.
—Luke 1:39, 40, 56

Mary, a single woman, and Elisabeth, a married woman, found many blessings in sharing together what God had been doing for them. They seemed to enjoy their fellowship with each other, finding they had some things in common.

Too many times single women find themselves uncomfortable with married women. They feel left out as married women talk about their children and husbands. If you are single, you can avoid this left-out feeling if you take time to learn how to share your time and thoughts with the married women in your life.

Many things can be done to help a busy mother. Help her with her canning, washing, or cleaning so she has more time to spend with her children or to do some sewing. Do some sewing for her if you enjoy sewing more than she does. Remember that she has some long days at home with the children while her husband is away working. Stop in for a short visit to let her know you are thinking about her. Offer to do some shopping for her if you are going to town, or take care of her children so that she can go. Take an interest in her children and in the things she likes to do.

As you do things for her, you will develop a relationship in which you can meet each other's emotional needs. Share the blessings you received recently in your personal devotions or the struggle you are facing right now. You may be surprised at how well a married woman can relate to your struggles as a single person. You will find that you have much in common and that you can be a real encouragement to each other. It will help you to see that no matter what one's calling is in life, we all face struggles. Sharing helps us appreciate each other more. This will help you become a caring person and will also help you find contentment in life as a single woman.

> One thing have I desired of the Lord, that will I seek after; that I may dwell in the house of the Lord all the days of my life, to behold the beauty of the Lord, and to enquire in his temple.
>
> —Psalm 27:4

Our deepest desire should be to dwell in the house of the Lord all the days of our lives, to behold His beauty, and to be with Jesus face to face. A relationship with Jesus is a precious gift, inspiring in us a willingness to give Him our talents, time, and lives. And when we allow Jesus to have complete control, our lives become truly blessed.

Walking close to Jesus is a rich experience. When we are close to Him, we have a great longing to spend time reading His Word and praying. Prayer is our vital breath!

Jesus knows and understands us. Prayer is simply a continuation of our walk with Him. When we can escape the noise and hurry of the day and meet with Jesus in a private and quiet place, it becomes even more meaningful. It is wonderful to be able to bring our problems and temptations to Him and lay them before Him one by one. We can then wait in silence with our hearts open before Him, focusing our minds on Him until He speaks to us.

How wonderful it is when He speaks! Sometimes He brings Scriptures to our minds that fit our problems. Sometimes He gives us direction through the counsel of another person. Sometimes just the sense of His presence with nothing to distract us is soothing and comforting to our tried and tempted hearts.

For we dare not make ourselves of the number, or compare ourselves with some that commend themselves: but they measuring themselves by themselves, and comparing themselves among themselves, are not wise.
—2 Corinthians 10:12

The fabric turned out to be a disappointment. When the lady compared it with the other bolts of fabric in the same row, its color had appeared satisfactory. But the store had not been adequately lit, and when she examined the fabric outside in the sunlight, she found it hardly suitable for a dress. Seeing the fabric's true color and knowing that money had been wasted was a big disappointment.

We sometimes fall into the same trap in a spiritual sense. We compare ourselves with others in a short-sighted way. We compare our clothes, our speech, our deeds, our prayers, our reverence to God—in short, our whole lives—with the lives of others. We do this when our hearts and minds are only dimly lit, and we think that our lives are satisfactory—just as good or even better than others.

With permission from a salesperson, the fabric buyer could have taken her choice outside, where the true color would have shown. Perhaps she was in too much of a hurry, and since it appeared all right when compared with the rest, she took it, only to suffer disappointment later.

It is not wise or safe to presume that my spiritual life is in better condition than those with whom I compare myself. As long as you compare your life with another lady's, you will not rise any higher than she does. You have a higher, nobler calling than this.

You must take time to view your life in the light of God's Word. If you don't, you will suffer a disappointment at the end of your life far greater than your disappointment over a piece of fabric.

Now faith is the substance of things hoped for, the evidence of things not seen.

—Hebrews 11:1

What is the substance of something you hoped for? Substance is existing physical matter. When you hold something in your hands, you have received the substance you had hoped for. What is evidence of something you have not yet seen? Evidence is proof. In court, without showing evidence you could hardly expect to prove anything.

Substance and *evidence* are words used to describe faith. Faith is so strong that it is like the substance of what we don't yet have and like the evidence of what we haven't yet seen.

The writer of Hebrews was contemplating what faith had already done for those who had believed. Abel's faith compelled him to offer a sacrifice. Enoch's faith became reality when he was carried to heaven. Noah built an ark to prepare for a flood that nobody but his family believed would come. Abraham moved, not knowing the future. Sarah bore a child in her old age. Isaac, Jacob, and Joseph foretold events. Moses chose to live with God's people in spite of the consequences. Rahab's faith produced prompt obedience.

Then the writer seems overwhelmed. Time would not allow him to write about Gideon, Barak, Samson, Jephthah, David, Samuel, and the prophets. Their faith subdued kingdoms, produced righteousness, obtained promises, stopped the mouths of lions, quenched fires, rescued them from the sword, strengthened them, overcame their enemies, and raised the dead to life again.

Notice the difference from verse 36 on. The people referred to here were not miraculously delivered. They were mocked, scourged, imprisoned, stoned, sawn asunder, tempted, killed, afflicted, tormented, and left homeless. Their faith did not spare them from hardships, yet they remained true to God, even to death. They believed in a life beyond what they were experiencing at the moment. Their faith gave them strength to stay with their decision, just like Abraham, Sarah, Rahab, and all the rest.

So when hard times come into your life or your prayers are not miraculously answered, do not feel discouraged and think that your faith must be weak. It may take greater faith to endure affliction than to experience miracles. It takes a lot of courage to keep on when you see no results—but that is faith. ✸

That I may know him, and the power of his resurrection, and the fellowship of his sufferings, being made conformable unto his death; if by any means I might attain unto the resurrection of the dead.

—Philippians 3:10-11

How can I expect to know Him if I do not have an interest in Him? And how can I have an interest in Him if I spend little time thinking about Him and even less time reading about Him? I cannot expect to know the power of His resurrection if I have not died to myself, and I cannot know the fellowship of His sufferings if I do not suffer. If I cry out in indignation over the least hurt, I will likely not recognize the suffering that will bring me into fellowship with Him.

If I refuse to learn to know Jesus, to die to self, or to suffer, I cannot expect a spiritual resurrection. I can only expect to remain spiritually dead.

I must recognize that when deprivations, persecutions, and hindrances come my way, I can use them as opportunities. It is impossible to conform to His death if the flesh never has to die. Knowing Him and the power of His resurrection makes it worth dying to my flesh. Knowing the fellowship of His sufferings is knowing true fellowship with Him. Suffering and dying for Him, whether physically or to the flesh, will prepare us for eternal fellowship with Him.

March 4

Anna, a prophetess . . . served God with fastings and prayers night and day.

—Luke 2:36-37

What things were happening in your life seven years ago? Seven years is only a short span of time, but much can happen in that amount of time. It is long enough for an established routine to become a part of you.

Anna, the prophetess, was married for seven years before she was left a widow. She faced the world alone, keenly aware of her loss. Though alone for many years after that, she made herself available to God's service. As with other widows in the Bible, God seemed to have a special role for her to fill, because she was willing to let God use her.

Anna's dedication to the Lord was not sporadic. She served God night and day, fasting and praying. Is it then a wonder that God chose to reveal baby Jesus to her?

She spent much time in the temple. How many people she must have met over the years! What a lifetime of influence! What a difference her prayers and encouragement must have made!

Children, youth, parents, and grandparents were used to seeing her in the temple. So when Anna saw Jesus and knew He was the Redeemer of Israel, she could not keep it to herself. She had spent time in prayer, and now her heart was prepared to serve as a missionary to these same people. Most likely the ones she had cared about were now willing to listen to her message. They had noticed the intensity with which she had worshipped God. Now she had an audience to tell the good news of Jesus' birth.

We have only a few verses to tell us about Anna's long lifetime. We know so little, yet we know what was important about her life. Her example still inspires us today. ❀

And let the peace of God rule in your hearts, to the
which also ye are called in one body; and be ye thankful.

—Colossians 3:15

Several major projects were waiting to be done. I had a dress to make and spring cleaning to do. I did not feel like starting these. I felt disoriented, confused, and out of control. I knew why: too many small things were cluttering my mind—little jobs that I had seen waiting day after day, week after week, and perhaps even month after month. There was the loose binding on the blanket that needed repairing and the leaking hose that I needed to tape. Each new day, I thought I would order a part for an appliance, but I still had not done it. The list seemed endless: a flower to transplant, a baby gift to buy, apples to use before they would rot. The thought of all these unfinished tasks sapped my strength and left me feeling incapacitated. When I finally took care of those little things, my mind felt clear and organized once again, and I could move on to other things with greater energy.

Are there little things hindering your peace and wholehearted service to the Lord? A half-truth, perhaps, that you need to confess to a sister in the church? The garment you bought at a yard sale and still haven't altered to comply to the church's standard? The letter of apology to write to someone you have wronged long ago? The habit of hasty, shallow devotions on busy days? That one area still not surrendered? You will have much peace when these are taken care of, along with fresh zeal to go forward to greater tasks!

And they that passed by reviled him, wagging their heads, and saying,
Thou that destroyest the temple, and buildest it in three days, save thyself.
If thou be the son of God, come down from the cross.
—Matthew 27:39-40

Do you have to see miraculous, sensational things before you believe? Do you shake your head at the things you do not understand? Do you desire immediate deliverance from the distresses and perplexities of life?

Jesus' vision was higher and deeper than the present moment. Had He accepted immediate deliverance, there would have been no resurrection, no triumphant victory over death. Heaven would be stilled of the glorious victory notes of "Thou art worthy . . . for thou wast slain" (Revelation 5:9).

If you chafe under the cross, dissatisfied with your lot in life, you will attempt to deliver yourself from your present circumstances. But like the butterfly that must struggle slowly out of the cocoon to become what it was created to be, you will live to your full potential only if you courageously face whatever trial God is taking you through. When you trust Him, prepare yourself for blessings and miracles. They happen as you patiently wait for Him.

Consider the faithful saints who did not accept earthly deliverance in order to "obtain a better resurrection" (Hebrews 11:35).

Use hospitality one to another without grudging.

—1 Peter 4:9

My parents taught us at a young age to thank our overnight hosts for their hospitality when we went on trips. One time the hostess asked me if I knew what hospitality meant. Of course I knew! Or at least I thought I did.

Years later hospitality took on a new meaning. When I shared my home with another girl, I discovered that true hospitality involves much more than a desire to be friendly. It meant doing some hard work and creating a relaxing and welcoming environment.

Hospitality meant being willing to entertain guests even when the lawn was not mowed or the windows had not been cleaned. Hospitality for us meant welcoming other singles into our home even when they were strangers. It meant we had an overflowing houseful of girls during fellowship meetings or ordinations, and they might arrive and leave at all hours of the night. Hospitality meant giving up our plans or including our visitors in them. It meant a higher grocery bill that month. Hospitality meant putting forth our best efforts to make our friends' husbands feel at home when they dropped by.

When we did all this and more without grudging, we were blessed by increased friendships. We hoped our friends enjoyed the time with us and wanted to come again. Beyond the satisfaction of friendships, though, we knew we had pleased God by showing hospitality. ✳

He that findeth his life shall lose it: and he that loseth his life for my sake shall find it.
—Matthew 10:39

I did a foolish thing when I left the lounge chair outside, exposed to the elements of winter. I had reasoned that it was better to leave it outside than to put it in the basement where it might rust, but I was wrong. Since the chair was not built to withstand the pressures of cold weather, one end tore loose from the frame and sagged to the ground, leaving an ugly gap. In an attempt to shield the chair, I had only exposed it.

Sometimes I do a similar foolish thing in my spiritual life. I stay in a place of temptation or in a struggling position rather than asking someone to pray for me. I reason that it is better to keep my public image than to reveal what is going on inside of me. But I was not made to withstand all the blasts of the devil by myself. Without the help and protection of others, I begin to sag under the weight of spiritual struggle. Where I was once useful, I now have a gap—emptiness that cannot support anything or anyone. Trying to shield myself, I only exposed my lack of spiritual health.

When I had considered where to store the lounge chair during the winter, I had thought only about the damp, cool part of the basement and not about the warm, dry part. My chair would have been well preserved in the dry part. When I have spiritual struggles, I fear what others will think if I tell them what I am going through. I tend to forget the tremendous power of others' love and prayers. But when I think about that power, I choose to open myself and come under the protection of people who will care for me and can help me.

For who hath despised the day of small things?

—Zechariah 4:10

Who thought the temple would ever be finished or amount to anything in Ezra's day? The enemies had mocked and despised the work. Likely many of the Jews had also given up and looked on, thinking it was too great a task. But slow, daily perseverance paid off. This was God's work, and He chose not to use great people or impressive tools. Rather, He chose to complete His work through faithfulness in the small things.

God chooses weak people and small instruments to accomplish great things. Though the beginning may be small, God can make the latter end increase greatly. A grain of mustard seed may become a big tree. The day of small things is precious, and it will eventually be known as a day of great things.

David used an everyday sling and a common stone, and by them God won a great victory. A lad gave his lunch to Jesus, and Jesus blessed that small sacrifice and fed five thousand people. A poor widow gave her few mites and Jesus took notice. Sometimes we may wish to do great things, but Jesus notices the little things. Even when we offer just a soft, tender word or a cup of cold water, He says we have done it unto Him. We do not need to feel discouraged—God is looking for those who are faithful and willing to be used by Him in small ways.

March 10

And Jabez called on the God of Israel, saying, Oh that thou wouldest
bless me indeed . . . And God granted him that which he requested.
—1 Chronicles 4:10

Desires can be difficult to deal with. Many of our desires are not wrong, but we still need to submit them to God and bring them under His lordship. It is instructive to notice the desires of Bible characters and the outcomes of their desires. Some were good desires and some were evil. Some desires were granted, while others were not.

Abraham desired a better country.

Achan wanted the forbidden articles from the spoils of Jericho.

Lot wanted the well-watered plains.

Caleb longed to conquer a mountain.

Job wished that his thoughts were written down.

Haman wanted to get rid of Mordecai and the Jews.

David desired another man's wife.

Absalom wanted to make a name for himself.

David wanted to build a house for the Lord.

Elijah wished to die.

Hannah desired a son.

Ahab coveted Naboth's vineyard.

Hezekiah requested a longer life.

Solomon asked for wisdom to guide the people.

Elisha wanted a double portion of Elijah's spirit.

Lazarus desired the crumbs from the rich man's table.

The rich man later pled for a drop of water.

Mothers wanted Jesus to bless their children.

Zacchaeus wanted to see Jesus.

Martha wanted Mary to come help her serve.

Paul's desire was that Israel would be saved.

Paul requested that his thorn in the flesh be removed.

The eunuch wanted to be baptized.

The thief on the cross asked Jesus to remember him.

Jesus' desire was to do the will of His Father.

What do *you* want?

....

....

....

....

....

....

....

....

....

....

....

....

....

....

....

....

… knowing that the same afflictions are accomplished
in your brethren that are in the world.
—1 Peter 5:9

Snow was falling from the sky and covering the ground with a beautiful blanket. Many of the flakes did not fall directly to the ground but were driven to and fro and up and down before they finally reached their destination. As I gazed over the landscape with its even cover of snow, I could have thought each flake had gracefully fallen from the sky and landed directly below its starting point. But since I had watched the flakes coming down, I knew this was not the case.

On my way from earth to heaven, I experience trials that remind me of a snowflake's journey to earth. Many times I am buffeted and tossed by the winds of adversity. I am driven this way and that, and I almost despair. But I take courage from seeing others persisting in their race as they encounter all kinds of pressures. I also think of those in the past who persisted and reached their destination. Remembering them also spurs me on in the course. I may be blown hither and yon, but with perseverance I can inspire others along the way and arrive safely at my destination.

Jeremiah 18:1-6

A potter's house contains ugly, gooey masses of clay, a wheel, the messy hands of the potter, and a furnace. All of these intriguing elements work together to make beautiful, artistic vessels.

God is a potter. There is none other like Him (Isaiah 46:9). He is the one who can fashion lovely vessels, but He cannot do it without the clay, the wheel, and the fire. You and I are the ugly, gooey masses of clay—nothing attractive. We are sinners who must yield our lives to the Master Potter and allow Him to shape and refine us into vessels He can use. The potter's wheel can be likened to the scope of life's circumstances, joys, trials, disappointments, and heartaches.

We, the clay, can yield to the Almighty Potter and allow circumstances of life to mold and shape us into something beautiful, or we can resist the Potter's work on the wheel and become marred. If we chose the latter, we will become a castaway, a vessel the Master cannot use.

Some of us will need to submit to the wheel again and again, but the Potter knows just what we need to make our lives fulfill His best purposes. God allows individuals to experience many different circumstances, both of joy and pain, so that He can form useful and beautiful vessels. Our cheerful submission and radiant testimony can be likened to the paints the skillful artist applies to the vessel: the more fully submitted, the brighter the glow.

At some point in our lives, we may think God is finished with us and no more turning is necessary. But in this life, God is never finished with us. A vessel is not complete until it has gone through the fire. The all-wise Potter knows just how much heat is needed for each vessel. Unpleasant experiences, disappointments, and pain are turned into times of spiritual growth if we learn to submit to the skillful hands of the Potter. As we yield our whole life in submission to His plans, we will be "a vessel unto honour, sanctified, and meet for the master's use" (2 Timothy 2:21).

March 13

The glory of the Lord shall endure for ever: the Lord shall rejoice in his works.
—Psalm 104:31

A wonderful way to begin a new day is to look around you and notice God's glory. Fix your eyes on the lush, rustling leaves. Tune your ears to hear the merry birds, chirping frogs, or other little rejoicing creatures. Breathe deeply of the expansive atmosphere surrounding you. Are not all of these something glorious from God? Each new day that He gives you should be for serving and praising Him. When we take our eyes off ourselves and focus on God, our spirits are lifted. No matter how gloomy the day may seem, there is always some place where we can see God's glory shining through if we look for it.

Dusty, dingy windows do not let in as much light as sparkling, clean windows do. The brightness of our day will depend on the way we look at our surroundings. Are you looking for God's glory, or are you focusing on self? The glory of God is all around you. Take time to praise the Lord for the good things He gives to you.

He healeth the broken in heart, and bindeth up their wounds.

—Psalm 147:3

I looked down at my hands and was appalled. My skin had dried out to the point of looking crumbly. Painful cracks opened when I flexed my fingers. I realized this had happened because I had failed to regularly apply healing lotion to my hands. I resolved to more diligently apply lotion, remembering that even when my hands appear to be all right, they still need that protective layer.

My spiritual life is like my hands, falling into an unbelievable state when I do not daily apply a healing remedy. Even when I think I'm living in victory and peace, I must continue building my relationship with God. If I have a habit of neglect, my soul will become dry and parched, and sin will appear. I will worry and fret because I have not lately been reminded that God will provide. I will become bitter, seeing only the dark side of life, because I have not been meditating on the love of God. I will have a negligent attitude toward the commandments of God because I do not study them. I will neglect prayer, not realizing the depth of my need. These factors will cause life to become painful and joyless.

It takes awhile for me to rub lotion into my hands, and it is often inconvenient. Because I do not want to do household tasks with oily hands, it is easy for me to wait for a more convenient time. But too soon I see the dryness and cracks appearing. When I do take time to keep my hands well maintained, I am rewarded with smooth, useful hands.

It takes time until a spiritual truth is firmly fixed in my mind and applied to my life. Other things often vie for my attention, tempting me to postpone my communication with God until a more convenient time. But suddenly I realize how many sinful tendencies have crept in. When I do take the time to develop my relationship with God, I am well rewarded with purpose, joy, and a useful life. ❧

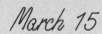
March 15

While the earth remaineth, seedtime and harvest, and cold and heat,
and summer and winter, and day and night shall not cease.
—**Genesis 8:22**

The move from Tennessee to New York was not exactly what I preferred—I don't revel in long, cold winters. But I decided to move closer to my relatives, especially since I am single and getting older.

During the long winter months, as snowstorms keep blowing in and foot after foot of snow accumulates, one might begin to wonder whether warmer weather will ever return. Even in March while it's still cold and the ground is covered with snow, I eagerly read letters from farther south that tell of spring-like weather. Will spring come back to New York too?

Then God reminds me of the above promises. Yes, I am sure that spring will be back. The Bible says it will! God did not say it will come to our state as quickly as it does to Tennessee, but He did promise that it would come back. Happily I watch as the temperatures again rise into the fifties.

This verse means more to me than the promise of warmer weather. It reminds me that all of God's promises are sure. His Word never fails. We must believe His promises so that we can witness to those who feel they cannot believe.

Do you live as though you believe all of God's promises? Claim them for your own today. Just as sure as I am of the return of spring, so you can be sure that all of God's promises are true.

....

....

....

....

March 16

It is better to trust in the Lord than to put confidence in man.

—Psalm 118:8

"One of the worst struggles I have with being single," Aunt Anna confided to me, "is the fear of taking the horse and buggy away from home. If I would have a husband to take charge of that, I could sit back and relax in the buggy like other women my age do. Instead, every time I get into the buggy, things seem out of my control because I am afraid of what the horse will do."

I knew Aunt Anna's fear was real, and I could identify with her. Though I had a car, my teaching position away from home necessitated some traveling alone. I often thought, *What if something happens between two exits on a long stretch of highway halfway home?* I needed to pray often and trust the Lord.

After I married, my fears of traveling alone subsided because my husband was with me in the car. However, I discovered that God was not finished teaching me to trust Him. Due to complications while I was pregnant with our first child, at times we feared for the life of our baby. The uncertainty caused some anxiety. We took our concerns to God, but I discovered that, although my husband could encourage me, he could not give me trust in the Lord. He could assure me that all would be well, but he did not know what the outcome would be. I needed to avail myself of God's strength. In that trying time, I could only trust in the Lord because the situation was out of man's control.

So, no matter what our circumstances in life, God wants us to see our helplessness and trust Him. Humans are limited, and when we trust only in people, we will be disappointed. God desired Aunt Anna's trust, and He wants mine too. We can never get away from our need of God, no matter who we are or what we are doing. ✸

March 17

Having then gifts differing according to the grace that is given to us, whether prophecy, let us prophesy according to the proportion of faith; or ministry, let us wait on our ministering: or he that teacheth, on teaching.

—Romans 12:6-7

Budding fruit trees with their green tips are an encouraging sight after a cold winter. The blossoms that burst forth afterward and perfume the air are even more thrilling. But the buds and blossoms must wait for the proper time. When the sun shines brightly and the air is warm, they sometimes begin the bearing process too early. I want to tell them, "Wait, little buds! I know you have a mission to fulfill, but you must wait for a while yet. Even though you think it is time for you to be out, the weather could turn cold again, and much damage could be done to you."

I would like to warn the buds because I know what might happen to them if they do not wait. I think sometimes my heavenly Father tells me to wait for the same reason. Before I proceed on any mission, I must make sure the time is right. Those things I call detainments might be God telling me to wait. Perhaps there are things He wants me to learn before I move forward. He sees that if I proceed too soon, more damage than good will be done, and the bountiful harvest I envisioned may not come to pass. There is no need to become impatient and fretful just because others are moving forward. I must wait for God's signal to me.

Notice the many times the Scriptures speak of waiting. The godly people of old were those who waited, prayed, and moved when God commanded, while the ungodly were those who lived for the here and now.

If there an immediate need and the Spirit says "Go," it is time go without delay. But a child of God must also recognize and follow His voice when He says "Wait." When you patiently wait, your labors will result in a bountiful harvest.

> The water that I shall give him shall be in him a
> well of water springing up into everlasting life.
>
> —John 4:14

The Jordan River is a type of living water, signifying our lives as we give ourselves in service to others. Mt. Hermon's springs and the snow-capped mountain peaks melting in the summer fill the river with fresh, life-giving waters that irrigate the Jordan Valley plains. A fertile strip of land thirty miles wide at some places is just waiting for the blessing these refreshing waters bring. Beyond the reach of the precious water, only barren desert and scrubby hills exist. The rich, fertile fields can tell of the miracle that transforms them.

Jesus, the Spring of Living Waters, will fill our lives with cleansing, life-giving streams as we drink deeply of God's Word. The rich streams of grace and salvation can flow forth to enrich the barren fields of our lives. We can bless others with refreshing streams as we give of our time, talents, or labor. "I beseech you therefore, brethren, by the mercies of God, that ye present your bodies a living sacrifice, holy, acceptable unto God, which is your reasonable service."

The Spirit of God and His grace, which will never fail, replenish our spring of living water so that we can continue to help others become fruitful and joyful. Eternity only will reveal where all the streams of blessing have reached when we gave our lives in loving service and shared the Living Water.

O Jordan River, type of God,
With thy mercy flowing free,
O let thy water o'er me roll,
Till I am pure and clean
Then let my life to others flow,
That more of Christ may be
Spread on this dying, sinful world,
And more may trust in thee.

Through God we shall do valiantly: for he it is that shall tread down our enemies.
—Psalm 60:12

Today I face numerous enemies. One of them is the cold and drizzly day, combined with my fatigue and loneliness. I could choose to let my mood match the circumstances. But I have Jesus, and in Him is fullness of joy. He treads down the enemy of gloom and gives me radiance. Through Him I can do valiantly even on a dreary day.

Another enemy towering mightily above me is a big task assigned to me. I could choose to shrink back in fear as I view its magnitude. But I have Jesus, in whom are hid all the treasures of wisdom and knowledge. He treads down the enemies of unbelief and cowardice, and He gives me faith. Through Him I can do valiantly in the face of a seeming impossibility.

I am also aware that the enemy of fear seeks to gain entrance. I am afraid of what others think. Do they think I have made a wrong decision? I could choose to let fear of man dominate my life—but I have Jesus, who tells my heart not to be troubled. He treads down the enemy of the fear of man and gives me peace. Through Him I can do valiantly, regardless of what others think.

....

....

....

....

....

....

March 20

By him therefore let us offer the sacrifice of praise to God continually,
that is, the fruit of our lips giving thanks to his name.

—Hebrews 13:15

The other day I met up with a friend who is living like the thankful former leper. She struggled with a physical problem for several years, but God walked with her through the issues and eventually brought her healing. Since then, she makes a conscious effort to tell people how grateful she is.

A talk with my friend never results in the usual "what I did today" conversation. Rather, she tells me the opportunities she's had lately that have inspired her—the chance to decorate a building for a ladies' event, the joy she gets from her seasonal job, and the way God is providing for her husband to exercise his musical talents in nursing homes and churches. "I feel as though I've come out of a really dark period in my life, and God is just pouring out blessings and opportunities on me," she says with an excited smile.

Is my friend living in reality? Is she dishonest if she does not mention any trials she may have? I don't think she ignores the realities of this sin-cursed earth; rather, she chooses to focus on God and the reasons she has to be grateful. Choosing gratefulness is a way to ward off anxiety, fear, depression, and temptation. It is a way to live in intentional obedience to our faithful Gift-giver.

March 21

For, lo, the winter is past . . .
—Song of Solomon 2:11

Spring! It is a thrilling word. As the last bank of snow disappears in the warm sunshine, the winter blizzards fade into dim memory. Daffodils push their green blades through the soil, and before long the first crocuses blossom. The spring peepers strike up a chorus from a nearby pond, and spring birds return and sing their songs.

Has springtime come into your heart? Do not let the failures of yesterday or last week keep you from the joy that can be yours today. Perhaps the cold winds and storms of an emotional winter will help you more fully appreciate the sunshine of today.

Winter is over—it is now springtime. Refresh yourself, drinking in the blessings all around you. See the flowers bloom in your life—a result of reading the Word. The ability to sing like a bird is the result of a rejoicing heart. Like the coo of a turtledove, your words can bring calmness and comfort to others. Do others notice the fruit of the Spirit in your life? That fruit can grow only through dedication and attention. Is your life giving off a sweet fragrance like the spring blossoms? Only a heart cleansed by the blood of Jesus can emit a fragrance that others will enjoy.

Springtime can be a daily experience in the heart of every believer! ✳

As for God, his way is perfect.

—Psalm 18:30

Sara was babysitting her four-year-old niece, Justina. They were riding in the car on their way to pick up Justina's older siblings at school. Justina had fallen silent and seemed to be thinking. As they neared the school, Justina looked at Sara and smiled softly. Then she asked, "When do you want to get married?"

Sara smiled back. She did not feel nervous or upset by the question. Justina had noticed, even at her young age, that most grown-up girls got married. Sara did some fast thinking, although she knew what her basic answer would be. Her heart glowed with love for this little girl and for the opportunity to share truth with her.

"I do not know, Justina, when I will get married. Maybe I will someday, but maybe I will never get married. God does not plan for everyone to marry. Some girls and some boys never get married, but they can still be happy. Although most people get married, it isn't wrong if they don't." Sara breathed these words prayerfully into Justina's tender heart with the desire that they might take root and blossom in a life yielded and surrendered to God's choice.

Sara bowed her head as they reached the school. "Oh, Lord, thank you for the privilege of sharing about your sovereignty in guiding our lives. I always want to be open to following your will. Bless all the little girls who have questions about marriage. Help me to view marriage as high and holy, but not bigger and better than life itself. In Jesus' name, Amen."

And it came to pass, as they were much perplexed thereabout, behold, two men stood by them in shining garments: and as they were afraid, and bowed down their faces to the earth, they said unto them, Why seek ye the living among the dead?
—Luke 24:4-5

Why did the women make that unnecessary, early-morning trek to the tomb? Jesus had told them He would rise again. Why did they not remember it sooner? Was it because they were heartbroken and worrying about what would happen now that their beloved Lord was killed? They could have saved themselves much grief had they not been so slow to believe.

God may view scenes from our lives with the same kinds of thoughts we have as we think about the scene at the tomb. Does He see that the women of today have not changed much from the women at the tomb?

Who of us has not had doubts about our salvation? We doubt in spite of the promise, "Him that cometh to me I will in no wise cast out" (John 6:37). Who of us has not felt anxious when we saw a difficult circumstance ahead? We are anxious in spite of His promise, "I will never leave thee nor forsake thee" (Hebrews 13:5). Who of us has not worried about material needs? We worry in spite of the promise, "Your heavenly Father knoweth that ye have need of all these things" (Matthew 6:32).

We have the same Lord as the women at the tomb had. His promise to them was fulfilled, and He will fulfill His promises to us as well.

And the same day Pilate and Herod were made friends together:
for before they were at enmity between themselves.

—Luke 23:12

Relationships are the glue of life, and when bonds are broken, they should be repaired. You have potential through your words and actions to help or hinder relationships of others. When you encounter opportunities to help mend broken relationships, it helps to remember role models from the Bible.

Jesus, the Prince of Peace, was accused as a malefactor yet became the reason for a friendship between two former enemies. Jesus had been a peacemaker throughout His ministry, so it comes as no surprise that the day of His death was likewise.

After the Apostle Paul's conversion, he wanted to become a friend to those he once hated. He was not accepted at first in this new society. Barnabas used this opportunity to tell the disciples about the change in Paul's life. After that, the disciples were no longer afraid. What if no one had stood in the gap and Paul had been rejected from the church?

Paul may have remembered this act of kindness years later when Onesimus needed to return to his master. He beseeched Philemon to accept his former slave since he had changed and was now a brother in the Lord.

Sometimes our efforts at restoring a relationship do not accomplish much. Jonathan spoke well of David to his father Saul. For a time Saul's anger was appeased, but later he tried to kill David again. It seemed that Jonathan's efforts had been in vain.

Did Rebekah ever realize how her conniving affected the relationship between Jacob and Esau? Her sons' lives were torn apart because of what she had done, and it seems they never spent much time together after that.

What are you doing about broken relationships? A word of appreciation about one person to another may restore their relationship, but a backbiting tongue and self-preserving spirit will only widen the gap between would-be friends. ✵

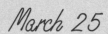

But Naaman was wroth, and went away, and said, Behold, I thought, He
will surely come out to me, and stand, and call on the name of the Lord
his God, and strike his hand over the place, and recover the leper.
—2 Kings 5:11

Poor, disillusioned Naaman. Even though he was a mighty man of valor and
the captain of Syria's army, he had a few lessons to learn. He needed to learn
that great things sometimes happen in ordinary ways, and not always dramati-
cally or instantaneously.

God provides opportunities for us to learn similar lessons. If He would take
away the pain immediately when I ask Him to, I would not learn all the lessons
that can be learned only through pain. That is why the Lord does not always
provide an instant, glorious deliverance from a problem, a perplexity, or even a
temptation that I long to be delivered from. If the Lord would instantly provide
a way out of every unpleasant circumstance, I would not learn to trust Him to
see me through. If the Lord would immediately hand me everything I ask for, I
would not learn contentment. If He would provide instant victory in every trial, I
would not learn to wait on Him. If He would always give me on-the-spot answers,
I would become proud and arrogant. If I never felt the weight of burdens, I could
not help others bear their burdens.

Naaman needed to learn that the answer to his problem lay in his obedience,
not in his prestige. We also need to realize that. In addition, we need to realize
that at times we need to go through a learning process more than we need an
instant answer.

The Lord is my shepherd; I shall not want.

—Psalm 23:1

A small girl once asked me, "Do you have girls?"

"No," I answered.

"Do you have boys?" she asked.

Again I said, "No."

Then she asked a thought-provoking question. "Well, who do you have?"

A brief feeling of loneliness and a bit of self-pity swept over me as I rather feebly replied, "I have nieces and nephews."

Later I pondered her question and was consoled as I thought of those I have who are real blessings to me. I have parents who love me with a deep love and give the security of good counsel. I have brothers and sisters and their spouses who care about me. I have nieces and nephews who bring me much joy and satisfaction. I have Christian friends, married and unmarried, with whom I can share. They are an encouragement to me.

Above all, I have God—my heavenly Father, my constant Companion and Counselor. I have God the Son, Jesus, who understands me. He was tempted in all points as I am. He is my Saviour and He is interceding for me. I have God the Holy Ghost, my Comforter and Guide who leads me into all truth.

Thank you, heavenly Father, for all those who belong to me.

For the hope which is laid up for you in heaven, whereof ye heard before in the word of the truth of the gospel; which is come unto you . . . and bringeth forth fruit . . . since the day ye heard of it, and knew the grace of God in truth.
—Colossians 1:5-6

A child holding his father's hand might pull back fearfully when they near a big dog, but he does so needlessly. He does not trust that his father knows the dog isn't mean. His progress is impeded because he does not rely on the sufficiency of the larger hand. He has no idea what it can do for him.

Many Christians do not trust God in a practical way. They are not becoming more fruitful because they do not know the grace of God in truth. They may know that it was the grace of God that brought them out of darkness, but they do not trust His grace to carry them through difficult circumstances. When faced with the unknown, they look at their fears instead of at the grace that will carry them through. They shrink away when they are called to a difficult task. Rather than being an inspiring example of faith and trust, they become an example of one who does not know God.

The only way for the child to learn the ability of his father's protecting hand is to allow himself to be led by that hand. As long as he draws back, he will not experience his father's protection and guidance. Likewise, the only way for the Christian to experience the grace of God in truth is to allow God to lead him. It is not in the easy, pleasant circumstances of life that grace is learned. To see the vast storehouse of grace, one must feel a need to draw from it again and again. Partaking of this grace instead of being overwhelmed by the perplexities of life brings forth fruit.

....

....

....

> Now there are diversities of gifts, but the same Spirit. And
> there are differences of administrations, but the same Lord.
>
> —1 Corinthians 12:4, 5

One spring when the flowering trees were blooming brilliantly, I saw one that inspired me. It was not the biggest and brightest tree that left its imprint on my brain. It was a little, thin thing, hardly even a sapling, that taught me a lesson. The lesson was this: *it did what it could.* I did not require it to have more flowers or to be as showy as a bigger tree. It was obviously performing according to its capabilities.

You may identify with either the smaller or the bigger tree. If, like the big tree, you have been called to produce many "flowers," you may have many gifts to give to the world. You are quick to sense needs, and you rush to meet them. The caution for you is to not possess zeal without knowledge. You may need to ask yourself whether your act of mercy is appropriate at the moment and whether you are going about it in an appropriate way.

God does not look down on anyone lacking a certain gift. He does not give the same gift to everyone. You are not required to possess the same abilities as someone else; likewise, other people are not required to possess the same abilities as you do. If all of us exercise our gifts with wisdom and prudence, there will be no lack. We can learn from each other and perhaps grow in something we do not think is our natural ability, but if we push each other, we will do more harm than good.

Some people excel in doing "quiet" things, and they are no less blessed than those who perform "showy" deeds. It does not matter if you are like the little tree or the big tree. If you do all you are able, someone will be helped and God will be glorified.

March 29

Who humbleth himself to behold the things that are in heaven, and in the earth!
—Psalm 113:6

Observing God's creation humbles us as we realize that He is infinite. God's power knows no limits. Even if we studied nature all our lives, we would never be able to know everything there is to know. When the heights of the universe and the depths of the ocean are searched out, man only discovers that he has more questions than he had before he began his search.

All the wisdom of the world cannot come close to being able to do what our Almighty Creator accomplished by His spoken word. Even with the money and technology that we have, we can never discover all there is to discover.

Roaring water cascades over rocky ledges. Millions of gallons of water plunge over the falls into deep ravines. Day and night the water keeps on flowing, yet the source does not run dry. Streams flow into the rivers and rivers into the ocean, yet the ocean is held within its boundaries. Tons and tons of water crash into the rocky shores only to be pushed out to sea again.

Have you ever stopped to consider how much effort and expense it would take to recreate a sunrise? Yet every day this miraculous happening takes place right outside our door at no cost at all. God also has perfect timing. Today the sun will rise only a minute later than it did yesterday, and tomorrow it will rise a minute later than it did today.

Then there are multitudes of other awe-inspiring sights that no artist could ever completely reproduce. The growing plant unfolds leaf by leaf. The rainbow arches across the sky. A great blue heron swallows a fish whole and then stoops to gulp some water. From the tiniest deep-sea lantern fish to the tallest redwood tree, we see God's handiwork. When we take time to notice, we can only say, "Praise ye the Lord!" ✹

For they that say such things declare plainly that they seek a country.

—Hebrews 11:14

In the spring of the year, farmers prepare the soil with an obvious goal of harvesting later. Some children going to school make it obvious that they have graduation in mind. The lives of young people may show that they have marriage in mind. Middle-aged people may be thinking of retirement. What a person's mind is set on proclaims a message about what he or she is seeking.

The Christian woman's habits show that she has eternal life in mind. Her decisions, her attitudes, and her walk of life declare plainly that she knows she won't always live on this earth. She seeks another home. When disappointments come, she takes them calmly because she knows this life is only temporal. She does not seek to have the most, the finest, and the best, because she knows that material possessions will pass away. She is not overly concerned when she hears thoughtless remarks directed toward her. Instead of allowing them to settle in her heart and cause bitterness to spring up, she rejoices in the fact that her name is safely recorded in the Book of Life.

Yet she is also aware of a battle within her. Because she lives and moves in this world, she is caught in the struggle between good and evil. That is why she feels nearly torn to pieces at times. Her spirit reaches for the things of God, while her flesh struggles with earthly habits and attitudes. The battle is not enjoyable, yet the fact that there is a battle is another reminder of the heavenly home to come. If this earth were her only home, there would be no battle. And so she continues to seek her eternal home and to fight the good fight, knowing that the forces of this world will assuredly be defeated by a stronger force. A home in a heavenly country is being prepared for her!

Thou therefore endure hardness, as a good soldier of Jesus Christ.
—2 Timothy 2:3

While teaching school in a community away from home, a woman made the trip back home to visit her parents. One day after her visit, she picked up her Bible. While paging through it, she found the above verse marked and the following words written by her father.

> *Dear Daughter,*
>
> *As you face the issues of life, the unknown future, and the challenge of teaching these precious souls, keep looking to your heavenly Father, to the face of our loving Lord. Remember His Word and His precious promises. Keep near to the cross. Die to self daily. Experience the joy of salvation and that of being in His service. The Lord bless you richly, watch over you, and keep you in His care. We pray for you daily even though we are many miles apart. Pray for us too!*
>
> *With love and concern, Dad*

That father never knew how precious that verse became to his daughter. That little piece of yellow paper was often a reminder to her to endure the battles of life as a good soldier. It was only a small piece of paper, only a few words penned by a caring heart, but the strength she received from that verse could not be measured.

Have you ever desired to accomplish great things for God like the Apostle Paul, Conrad Grebel, or the ministers in your church? Ask God for inspiration and find someone who needs a little piece of yellow paper in her Bible. It might help her endure hardness as a good soldier through the battle she is fighting. ✳

And the boys grew: and Esau was a cunning hunter, a man of
the field; and Jacob was a plain man, dwelling in tents.

—Genesis 25:27

Quietness and peacefulness are certainly more desirable character traits than
roughness and self-will. One seems to portray a godly character, while the
other does not. Like Rebekah, we tend to admire those who are quiet and peaceful.

But Rebekah did not reckon with the fact that her peaceful son Jacob still lived
up to the meaning of his name: *supplanter, schemer*. He still had Jacob's heart,
Jacob's mind, and Jacob's will. He was a schemer until his encounter with the angel
at Jabbok. There he became a changed man. He humbled himself and became
willing to bow before another rather than to seek his own advantage.

A quiet nature is no substitute for a born-again nature. Let us make sure that we
are admiring a Christ-like nature and not one that is hiding self-will. A Christian
nature will be like Christ through and through, doing the things that Jesus would do.

The real Jacob hid behind a quiet nature. The real Pharisees hid behind a conservative nature. The real Ananias and Sapphira hid behind a generous nature.
Regardless of how quiet, how kind, or how conservative these people were, they
were not accepted by God in their unconverted state. Only when a person has
the nature of Christ is he accepted by God.

April 2

When the enemy shall come in like a flood, the
Spirit of the Lord shall lift up a standard against him.
—Isaiah 59:19

A flood causes panic and confusion. Churning, swirling floodwater has tremendous power. It can sweep away buildings and change the appearance of the landscape. It can take lives.

Goliath confronting the Israelites is a striking example of what we face today when the enemy comes in like a flood. Because of his massive size and his bold words, Goliath seemed to be in control. His continued appearance brought alarm. The weapon he carried appeared too frightening for anyone to challenge.

Goliath came in like a flood, bringing confusion and fear. The Israelites' eyes were on him instead of on God. The people saw the gigantic form and panicked. Goliath caused them to think he was in power.

Satan often acts like our Goliath. His speech is bold and he throws out words such as, "What will people think? The Lord is keeping something from you. You will lose something of great value if you make that sacrifice. Just a little bit will not matter." He is not shy and he appears repeatedly. His appearance, however, is no cause for panic if we meet him with unmovable faith. The children of Israel lacked faith, which is why the appearance of their enemy brought fear and panic into their camp.

The enemy's power is not what he portrays it to be. He is defeated already. He is no match for God, and he will flee when we confront him in God's power.

....

....

....

....

But my God shall supply all your need according to his riches in glory by Christ Jesus.

—Philippians 4:19

God created women with emotional capacities and needs. Originally, these relational capacities were intended to complement the man, allowing the woman to become a help meet for him. This gift also helps the woman to nurture and care for others in all the relationships God gives her.

But where does the single woman find her emotional fulfillment? She does not have what God originally intended—the balance of the man. She can find a measure of fulfillment in relating to her father, but sometimes that is not possible. Especially as she grows older or lives away from home, the single woman may find herself grasping to fill her emotional needs.

If this is the case with you, you need not despair. God has made you and He will not forget you. He wants to fill your emotional needs, and He understands them. He is able to meet any need you have; as the Creator, nothing is impossible with Him. He knows you inside and out and wants to be your security and stay. "Trust in him at all times; ye people, pour out your heart before him: God is a refuge for us" (Psalm 62:8). Tell Him what you need. Let Him be all to you. Listen to His words in Isaiah 66:12-13. Let Him soothe and comfort your spirit and your tired emotions. Turn them over to Him; He is near, and He wants to help. Sometimes He will do it through His Spirit and sometimes through the church, but He will never let you down.

Read the book of Isaiah. Claim for your own the many promises of His personal care. Also remember the Apostle Paul's commendation of those who are wholly dedicated to God without the distraction of family affairs. "He that is unmarried careth for the things that belong to the Lord, how he may please the Lord. . . . The unmarried woman careth for the things of the Lord, that she may be holy both in body and in spirit" (1 Cor. 7:32, 34).

I believe the promises of God,
I can trust His never failing Word;
When earthly hopes shall fail,
And hosts of sin assail,
I rest upon the promises of God.

April 4

> Not that we are sufficient of ourselves to think any thing
> as of ourselves; but our sufficiency is of God.
> —2 Corinthians 3:5

None of us can boast that we are able to get along in life with no help from others. We enjoy companionship, and we are not sufficient of ourselves. We need someone with whom to share the joys and sorrows of life, someone to help us make decisions in our business affairs. If you find yourself a single woman or in a marriage that is less than ideal, you may long for someone intimate with whom to share each thought and struggle, someone who truly understands you. You think you would be happy then.

But even an intimate relationship cannot meet all our needs; even good relationships carry disappointments. Our sufficiency, trust, and confidence need to be solely in God. Our every thought needs to be subject to Him in order for us to be a blessing to others. As we find our sufficiency in the Lord and yield our lives fully to Him, we can have a joyful life, something worth sharing with others. We will find He always keeps His promises and is able to meet our every need as we serve others from the position He has called us to in life.

We have a "friend that sticketh closer than a brother" (Proverbs 18:24) with whom we may always share everything we face. What a great blessing! Sometimes we tell Him only about our problems and struggles, but we share more than that with close friends. We tell them about the things that bring us happiness, and about anything that we're interested in. Jesus will listen to that too. He wants us to know that He has a listening ear.

As you find your sufficiency in the Lord, He will provide faithful men and women from whom you can seek counsel and share life's experiences. Ask Him— and then wait expectantly for what He will graciously give you.

April 5

I beseech you therefore, brethren, by the mercies of God, that ye present your bodies a living sacrifice, holy, acceptable unto God, which is your reasonable service.
—Romans 12:1

A sacrifice is the forfeiture of something highly valued for the sake of something else considered to have a greater value or claim. When we consider it our "reasonable service" to give our bodies as a living sacrifice to God because of what He has done for us, we can agree with the dictionary definition. But when we turn the definition around and think that our sacrifice is more valuable than the cause for which we are sacrificing, we will not think of it as reasonable. We will start having a "martyr complex" and a self-pitying attitude.

One hindrance to making a complete sacrifice is a lack of faith. You might not always understand why God is asking you to sacrifice a plan, a vacation, or a secure position. *I would gladly relinquish my plan if I knew that something better would happen,* you might think. But often you don't know that there is something better. You feel caught in midair with nothing to cling to—nothing but faith that whatever you are forfeiting is not as valuable as the Person for whom you made the sacrifice.

When Shadrach, Meshach, and Abednego sacrificed their reputations and positions by not bowing to an image, they did not know what the outcome would be. They simply gave their bodies as a living sacrifice because they knew there was One who had a greater claim on their lives. And in the midst of the fire, that greater One, who had been right beside them all along, revealed Himself to them. We will always find that the presence of God is more valuable than whatever we sacrifice for Him.

April 6

Psalm 119

Before I was introduced to black sponge mushrooms, I did not realize what I was missing. But ever since my first taste, I have not been able to get my fill of them. They are not easy to find, however. One happy day I stumbled across one in the woods near our home, and soon I found several more near it. Since then, every April holds a special importance as I head for the mushroom patch.

Even when it is raining, my friend and I search for those hidden crowns as we shield ourselves with umbrellas. Even when our schedules are busy, we take the time to search the woods. Our thrill does not lessen whether we find the fifth or the fiftieth one. Perhaps this is because the little black peaks are often nearly hidden by leaves, like a well-kept treasure. We walk carefully so as not to step on and crush even one. It may take hours to search out the territory to find enough for a few meals. We have also run across a big, black snake that scared us away—but only until the next April! One year health did not permit me to do much mushroom hunting, but I took a lawn chair along so I could rest between rounds of hunting. Determined, you say? Yes, and richly rewarded!

I am challenged to ask myself if my daily hunger for the Word is that great. Do I search through the Bible, concordance, and dictionary to discover new truths? Am I willing to spend hours if necessary to read and pray to discern God's will for my life? Do I find time for the things of God, or is my schedule too full? Is it easy to skip my time with God because I do not feel well today? Am I led away from the Word when Satan comes with other allurements?

When I keep going back to God and His Word, many rich blessings await me. I am filled with the fullness of Jesus, fed and satisfied. And I eagerly look forward to the next time I can go back to find more treasures from His Word. ✻

April 7

And a man shall be as an hiding place from the wind, and a covert from the tempest; as rivers of water in a dry place, as the shadow of a great rock in a weary land.
—Isaiah 32:2

My friend Margaret reminds me of a river of water in a dry place. She has a perpetually cheerful spirit that always inspires me. I am comforted in knowing that she prays for me a lot. I know that she has an answer if I have a problem and an encouraging word when I am weary. She often has a jewel of truth from the Word that she wants to share. Yet she has had many difficult experiences in her life. Amazingly, she has not allowed those experiences to make her bitter.

What is behind her tranquility that enables her to live above her weakness and loneliness and reach out to others? It is that stream of living water that flows in and out of her. I am drawn to that beautiful stream because I, too, want to experience refreshment in times of trouble.

Attaining this stream of blessing may prove less difficult than maintaining it. I know that if I want to have clear streams of living water flowing from me, I must be free of the pollution of self-centeredness and self-will. If I do not obey the voice of the Spirit, the stream will be cut off, leaving barrenness where abundance once was. If I neglect to meditate on the Word and obey it, I tend to seek satisfaction from polluted sources such as wrong reading material or entertainment that does not feed my soul. I might seek it in outward adornment, desired because my soul is not being adorned properly. I may use superficiality in my speech to hide the emptiness inside.

The flow must be maintained at all costs. I must avoid polluted sources so that I can remain an unblocked channel, abounding and overflowing with blessings. I want to bless other weary pilgrims as I have been blessed, refreshing them on their journey to heaven.

> Thou art worthy, O Lord, to receive glory and honour and power: for thou
> hast created all things, and for thy pleasure they are and were created.
> —Revelation 4:11

I memorized this verse at a young age, but the depth of its meaning did not sink in until I was a little older. We were created for God's pleasure and not our own. Christ did not come to please Himself, so why should I want to please myself?

Even after I realized this, desires for things I didn't have kept filling my mind. One of the biggest desires was to get married. I wrestled with that, wondering what it means to give God 100 percent of my life, submit my desires to Him, and live only for His pleasure. Finally I realized that if God gets the most glory, honor, and pleasure from my life if I serve Him in celibacy, then that is what I want. I have no peace and joy when I continue to pine away for what He has not seen fit to give me. When I am tempted to be jealous of a married friend's lot in life, I remember that my lot is God's unique choice for me. In that I can rejoice. I can also rest in God's wisdom, because He knows my life from beginning to end.

Full submission brings joy and causes me to praise my Lord more. As I commit my ways to Him and trust Him for all things, His presence in my life feeds my desires, and they are purified. His direction is always better than my own reasoning.

April 9

But unto Cain and to his offering he had not respect.
—**Genesis 4:5**

Since 1937, day and night, good weather and bad, a guard has watched at the Tomb of the Unknown Soldier in Washington, D.C. A guard must undergo critical inspection before beginning his shift of duty. His uniform and weapons must be in perfect condition. A guard may not speak to others or change his strict military behavior except in extreme circumstances.

Those who visit the tomb stand in awe as a new guard takes his position. He covers the distance on the walkway in exactly twenty-one steps. Then he faces the tomb for twenty-one seconds, turns, and pauses twenty-one seconds before retracing his steps. If he is given an order, the guard will reply crisply, "Orders acknowledged."

God also gives orders. He told the first two sons to offer sacrifices; however, God could not respect Cain's fruit offering. Maybe it was the best of all his fruit, but it was not what God had asked of him. He had asked for the best of the flocks. God could not respect Cain's offering because Cain did not meet God's criteria.

Are you doing today exactly what God is asking you to do? Can God hear your heart acknowledging His orders? God will not tell you in an audible voice what He wants done, but He will speak to you through prayer and His Word. You will know what His orders to you are. You will know exactly how many steps to walk in which direction. When you follow Him in everything, those who watch your life will be able to say, "She has acknowledged God's orders." ✳

....

....

....

> That we should be to the praise of his glory, who first trusted in Christ.
>
> —Ephesians 1:12

It was not an example of good advertising. The jug containing expensive detergent was dirty. Had it been given a good washing with what it claimed to contain, it would have been sparkling and attractive. Dirt, although sometimes unavoidable, is always unattractive. If you constantly find it in places where it should not be, you might make remarks such as, "I never want to eat there," or "How could anyone live in a house like that?"

Slovenliness in natural things is bad enough, but when it shows up in spiritual matters among those who claim to live for "the praise of His glory," it is a tragedy. Like the detergent jug that should have reflected the quality of the product it contained, so the Christian should reflect the glory of God in such a way that He will receive praise and that others will be attracted to Him.

People are watching those who claim to have God's glory. If, instead of seeing that glory, they see dirt such as pride, constant struggling, complaining, an unforgiving spirit, or selfishness, they will make remarks such as "I didn't expect her to be like that," or "If that is the way Christians are, I never want to be one."

Temptations to let spiritual dirt settle a bit are sometimes unavoidable. But the temptations do not have to bring on slovenliness. That only happens when we succumb to the dirt and avoid cleaning it away. But we have power to become clean because of what is inside us: the glory of God.

Casting all your care upon him; for he careth for you.
—1 Peter 5:7

A young son repeatedly disappointed his parents. He did not mean to be bad, but it just seemed to happen often. "Son, you need to ask Jesus to help you do better," his father gently admonished.

"I have asked Him so often before," the penitent son replied. "I think He is too busy to help me."

Obviously this son had a wrong concept of our help in time of need. But how do we respond when we are in need? Do we ever feel that God must be tired of helping us? Maybe the problem is that we are tired of asking God for His help. Is it any wonder our prayers are not answered? God invites us to come, not timidly or doubting, but boldly, believing that He will help and answer.

Sometimes we are disappointed or angry in a given situation. God wants us to come to Him in prayer and tell Him just how we feel. When we leave the problem with Him, we can then go on with peace in our hearts, knowing the answer is up to Him and He will give us the grace we need.

"But without faith it is impossible to please him: for he that cometh to God must believe that he is, and that he is a rewarder of them that diligently seek him" (Hebrews 11:6).

For if ye forgive men their trespasses, your heavenly Father will also forgive you.

—Matthew 6:14

The mother was near exasperation. Her efforts to prepare a delicious soup for her family's supper were not producing what she had envisioned. In desperation she kept adding different ingredients, hoping to make it more delectable. Finally the moment came when she had to place it in front of her hungry family. To her amazement, they ate it with relish and actually enjoyed it!

Sometimes my life seems like that soup. I feel like a failure. I talk too much, but sometimes not enough. I procrastinate. I fail in seeing needs as I should. Finally the moment comes when I must confess to God. Amazingly, He forgives! When I repent, His peace floods my soul.

Even though the family mentioned above liked the soup, they could have found fault with it had they been picky. Even so, God could find fault with my life if He chose to do so. He could grudgingly forgive me. But that is not what He chooses to do. He chooses to cast all that aside, give me another opportunity, and thrill my heart anew with His presence and peace. God forgives with such great love!

Peter denied identity with Christ. Paul persecuted the church. David committed adultery. The jailor beat Paul and Silas. God freely forgave them all.

Unthinkingly, someone hurt my feelings. Someone overlooked me. Someone forgot to meet my needs. Someone made a mistake. Can I forgive with God's love?

The Lord hath his way in the whirlwind and in the storm, and the clouds are the dust of his feet. He rebuketh the sea, and maketh it dry, and drieth up all the rivers.
—Nahum 1:3-4

When Hurricane Andrew hit Florida and the surrounding areas in 1992, nothing on earth could control the 200-mph winds. Buildings toppled, lives were lost, and property worth billions of dollars was obliterated. People could only flee or find cover.

During the flood of the Mississippi River in 1993, men's efforts to keep the rushing water within its banks were futile. Millions of sandbags were filled to hold back the strong currents, yet the water roared over the man-made levees. Lives and crops were lost as hundreds of acres of land were flooded. Men stood helplessly by, watching and waiting out the storms.

In 1994 an earthquake hit California. Tremors shot through the hearts of the people as the ground heaved beneath them. Bridges and buildings collapsed. Some lives were lost, while others were miraculously saved. Humans had virtually no control over that situation either.

Catastrophes such as these can remind us that One stronger and mightier than man controls the natural forces. No power compares to God's. We may feel like the situation is out of control, but we must recognize that just because it is out of our control does not mean that it is out of God's control.

Humans have made mindboggling achievements in recent years. Architecture, technology, and communication are very advanced. Yet all that is nothing to God. In a moment of time, He can destroy what has taken man years to build. Man can design a great deal, but it is trivial when compared to the creation of God. Who can comprehend the vastness of the universe? Today, ponder God's power. "He hath shewed his people the power of his works" (Psalm 111:6).

We have seen his star in the east, and are come to worship him.

—Matthew 2:2

I had fallen asleep with a heavily burdened mind. My life seemed like a network of complexity, and I wondered anxiously what the future held. My greatest desire was to be in God's will and to be used in His service for His glory. But I felt hampered by circumstances and bound by physical limitations. Why was my life so fettered, so opposite of how I wanted to serve God?

Around midnight I suddenly awoke, turned my head, and opened my eyes. I blinked, dazed by an unexpected blaze of light streaming through the narrow strip at the bottom of my east window. A big, bright star! Was it real? I had never before been able to see any stars through that slit. As I gazed in awe, it slipped up past the edge of the carport roof that overshadowed my window. A moment of afterglow, and then all was dark again. But the message had reached my heart, and now its precious truth flooded my soul. It was not chance that had guided all those minute details together into one precious moment. It was God! My heart was comforted and full of worship in knowing that my life in God's hands was planned, guided, and timed with as much precision as the star.

Sometimes in my zeal and desire to be used by God, I make the mistake of trying to limit God to my way and time. But God has a set time as well as a set purpose, and all He needs is my yielded self. If I am in God's will, every person I meet, every circumstance and experience, is a part of His all-wise plan.

If you have any doubts of divine guidance in your life, go outside on a cloudless night and begin counting the stars. Count until you are overwhelmed with the unsearchable wisdom and power of God. Then come with a humble, yielded heart and worship your Lord. ☻

The eternal God is thy refuge, and underneath are the everlasting arms.

—Deuteronomy 33:27

My nine-year-old friend and I took a walk after the sun had set. Because I am not sure-footed on unfamiliar ground in the dark, he allowed me to lean on his arm—or rather, to hold onto it. It was not quite strong enough to lean on as I would on an adult's arm, yet I was touched by his willingness to meet my need. He did help me to keep my balance, but I knew he could not keep me from falling.

I live in a dark world, and I need help to live a godly life. I appreciate the examples of other Christians. I appreciate their perseverance and the fruit coming from their lives. They are a big help and they keep me balanced, but they do have weaknesses. Because of the human tendency to fail, I cannot lean only on them.

I appreciate the blessing of freedom of worship and the privilege to gather to hear the Word of God. This inspires and spurs me on, but it has limits. Between attending services, I need encouragement and reminders too.

I appreciate reading accounts of individuals who performed acts of kindness and generosity, or who stood unyielding on an issue of moral principle. But their lives may also hold inconsistencies, so I cannot follow their example in everything.

Where, then, is somebody or something to lean on safely as I travel through the dark? The Lord invites me to lean on His arm. It does not fail. It is always available and has no inconsistencies. It is revealed in the Word, so I can use that as a safe guide. That strong arm seems to be around me as I read excerpts from His Word: "He giveth power to the faint . . . They shall run, and not be weary; and they shall walk, and not faint . . . I will uphold thee with the right hand of my righteousness . . . For I the Lord thy God will hold thy right hand . . . The joy of the Lord is your strength."

Heaviness in the heart of man maketh it stoop: but a good word maketh it glad.

—Proverbs 12:25

Have you ever had a day when you felt pressure from people all day long? All you wanted to do in the evening was to get away alone to rest, think, and relax.

On one such occasion I had my exit out of a church service planned, but because several visitors were near the door, I felt I should meet them before I left for home.

To my surprise I learned that one of the visitors had faced a hard situation like the one I was going through. When I left some minutes later, my outlook had changed. My heart had been stooping, but a good word had helped to lift the load. Most likely this sister never realized what she had done for me.

We do not need to say much. When our actions show one of the following statements, the message will be understood:

I understand.
I care.
I will pray for you.
I went through that too.
I love you.
I appreciate what you do.

His lord said unto him, Well done, thou good and faithful servant:
thou hast been faithful over a few things, I will make thee ruler
over many things: enter thou into the joy of thy lord.
—Matthew 25:21

Did you notice that the servant was called good and faithful because he was faithful over a *few* things? We often get this twisted and allow the influence of many years and many voices to tell us just the opposite: if we have many things and responsibilities, we are doing well.

God says we can be assured of His blessing if we are faithful with even just a few responsibilities. In His mercy, God distributes gifts according to our various abilities. If He would put a responsibility upon me that I could not carry out, I would be an unprofitable servant. If He would give me more than I could take care of, I would be a poor steward. Having less, and even by appearance doing less, will not disqualify us for heaven like unfaithfulness will.

Being discontent with my little can cause me to become unfaithful. When I wish for more, the devil has blinded my eyes, making me believe that my acceptance with God lies in how much I do or have. But the truth is that my acceptance is directly related to how devoted I am to God and how much I've allowed Him to take control of my life. When God has captured all my attention and interest, I will be so busy serving Him that my little will become much because I am occupied with His joy.

Little deeds have inspired and challenged me as much as great sermons. When I taught school, I was touched when little people willingly shared small things like a sheet of paper or a crayon. A man stopped to do a kind deed by closing the car door for me. A student brought me a drink because she heard me saying I was thirsty.

The children and the man on the street were perhaps unaware of what it means to be faithful in little things. How much more should I as a Christian be aware of the value of being faithful in a few things?

If a man therefore purge himself from these, he shall be a vessel unto honour, sanctified, and meet for the master's use, and prepared unto every good work.

—2 Timothy 2:21

When I wear a Sunday dress, I am usually careful not to get it dirty. First, I try to stay away from dirty places; but if I need to go to a dirty place, I try my best to leave the dirt there. If dirt manages to get onto my dress, I am careful to wash it well. Then when I need a dress, it is a pleasure to find one crisp, clean, and ready for service.

Committed believers will continue in the lifelong process of sanctification. They will choose other godly people as their primary friends. They will not rationalize unwholesome choices, because they do not want to be stained. They will carefully rid themselves of unsanctified influences before the influences blot their character. Thoughts and desires will have to pass the test of sanctification before their minds will dwell on them.

Whether or not we have visible spiritual stains, we do have constant contact with our sinful natures and worldly influences around us. No substitute will cleanse like the Word. The more often and thoroughly it is applied, the more beautiful will be the result. God is pleased when He can find a person who submits to being sanctified; God is able to use her in His kingdom.

All these things require diligence. At times there will be misunderstandings and even alienation because of the choice to remain sanctified. But the reward of submitting to sanctification is the ability to present to the Master a pure, spotless garment.

This poor widow hath cast more in, than all they which have cast into the treasury.
—Mark 12:43

A boy who loved his teacher wanted to give her some flowers.

One day he had an inspiration when he was shopping with his mother. "Mom," he began eagerly, "may we buy one of those for my teacher?"

Looking around, his mother was puzzled until she realized what her son was referring to—the showy wreaths used to decorate tombstones. "Oh, no, son," she said, smiling. "People use those for the graveyard, not to give to friends. If you want to give your teacher some flowers, why don't you go out in the lawn and pick a bouquet of spring beauties?"

"Oh, Mom, those flowers are so tiny. I wanted to give my teacher a big bouquet like the one on her desk. Do you think she would like my spring beauties?"

"Yes, I am sure she would," his mother assured him.

She was right. I was delighted with the delicate flowers.

Later, after my teaching career ended, I was laid up for a while. My doctor ordered rest. As days turned into weeks, I began to feel useless. I felt unable to serve others as I had enjoyed before. I could not visit others who were sick. I could not cook or bake for others; they were needing to do it for me. I felt frustrated because I could not accomplish the things I felt needed to be done. Then one day I remembered a young boy who had brought much joy to me with his bouquet of spring beauties. I also remembered the widow who gave all her living, although it was almost nothing.

The Spirit reminded me that I could do small things such as pray, write letters, and send cards while in bed. I knew I could not do big things, but since I did not have a large bouquet of flowers to give, I knew the Lord wanted my spring beauties.

April 20

> A faithful man shall abound with blessings: but he
> that maketh haste to be rich shall not be innocent.
> —Proverbs 28:20

I thank the Lord for friends so kind,
Who give me worthwhile things;
For warmth of home and friendly smiles
That help my heart to sing.

For health and strength and joy today,
Ability to read,
Promises of heaven, my home;
I want to meet my Lord indeed!

The above poem was the inspiration of an elderly, single sister who lives alone. Though I do not know her well, her letters bring enthusiasm into my life. They are filled with deep thankfulness that she is still able to care for herself, while many her age live in nursing homes. She finds many reasons to rejoice in her blessings. She is thankful for the youth in her church who sing for the elderly. She does not get bored because she stays busy doing small things for others. She expresses time after time how happy she has been throughout the years because she has accepted the will of God for her life.

She challenges me to be faithful and to count the blessings that abound in my life. ❀

....

....

....

April 21

And if I send them away fasting to their own houses, they
will faint by the way: for divers of them came from far.
—Mark 8:3

I see the needs constantly. A look of sadness replaces the usual smile and cheer
on a sister's face, and I wonder what circumstances are oppressing her. Crowds
of people conformed to this world walk past me into the supermarket as I wait
near the entrance, and I am struck with the thought that each individual has an
eternal soul. A friend whom I meet occasionally seems unsettled, dissatisfied,
and troubled with her life. A woman in the waiting room of the doctor's office is
troubled about the deteriorating condition of American society, but she believes
that humanistic efforts can stop this deterioration and bring the world to near
perfection. My doctor wants to know the difference between my beliefs and those
of a related group. I get onto the subject of assurance of salvation and he asks,
"What do you mean by being saved?"

Am I going to send these people away fasting and fainting when I could help
them in their need? Maybe I feel I have needs myself and have nothing to give.
In the account from which our text is taken, Jesus and the rest of the people had
not eaten for possibly three days. Jesus still gave what He could because He had
compassion. I must pray for compassion, first to see and then to meet in some
way the needs of those who fast and faint.

....

....

....

....

....

Why art thou cast down, O my soul? and why art thou disquieted in me?
hope thou in God: for I shall yet praise him for the help of his countenance.
—**Psalm 42:5**

People in Bible times struggled with troublesome emotions and sinful attitudes just as we do today. Picture Ahab, king of Israel, when he requested something he could not have. Depressed and displeased, he lay on his bed, turned his face to the wall, and refused to eat. Jezebel, his wife, called it sadness of spirit, but it was none other than self-pity. He was pouting because he could not have what he had set his heart on.

The Lord used Elijah mightily. The prophets of Baal were killed. People recognized God as Lord. Yet when Jezebel placed a death sentence on him, Elijah was afraid and ran for his life. He sat under a juniper tree, discouraged. His world had caved in, and he wished to die.

The adversary does not care whom he attacks with self-pity. To the unmarried woman he whispers, "No one needs you!" To the busy mother he says, "You have too many duties." To the childless he may say, "You are a failure." To the teacher he comes with the suggestion, "Give up." To the sick he intones, "No one cares." Whatever he whispers to you, be aware of his temptations, and do not believe what he tries to convince you of.

First, get refreshed by resting as Elijah did. Then listen for the still, small voice of God directing you for the next step. You may be surprised at how soon you will feel relief from the despair that preyed upon you. God may even bless your life with another friend as he did Elijah after he moved on from the valley of depression (1 Kings 19:19). ✳

For God doth know that in the day ye eat thereof, then your eyes shall
be opened, and ye shall be as gods, knowing good and evil.
—Genesis 3:5

Techniques. Anyone who works at a profession over a period of time develops them. Work flows more smoothly and efficiently when proven methods are used. The carpenter learns how to cut a board in such a way that his saw does not bind. A gardener learns that mowing down thistle patches constantly causes them to die. Teachers learn that when teaching a new concept to a slow learner, it is better to teach it gradually in several brief sessions than to try to get the message across in one long session.

The devil, too, is a master of technique. He found one that worked the first time he used it, and he is still using it today. It is the deception that disobedience is wiser than obedience. It has worked so well that it is often not just whispered in the ear but also spread abroad in open teaching. This teaching indicates that man himself may decide what is right and what is wrong. We see that sorrow and confusion result when man thinks he is his own god.

As a child of God, I do not believe this teaching. I do not hear the devil say to me that I am my own god. But he tells me other things in a more subtle way. He tells me to think suspiciously about people. He tells me to be jealous. He tells me to grumble and pout. He tells me to think of myself more highly than I ought to think. God has forbidden me to do these things, and if the devil can get me to do them, I will have made myself a god by obeying my own desires.

Eve learned the hard way that disobedience does not make one a god. Rather, it brings banishment from the presence of God. The devil is a liar from the beginning. The techniques he employs may be tried and proven, but they bring only darkness and confusion. I am joyful only if I obey God and recognize that His commands are for my happiness.

Aperson may leave home and family to move to a new community for a number of reasons. Some eventually move home again, but others make a more permanent move. Whatever the case, leaving home is not an easy venture. It requires you to sever family ties to some degree, learn new customs, and make new friends. Upon arrival in a new community, you may feel like a ship adrift in unknown waters. You may be unsure where you belong in this new community that is already running smoothly without you. It takes courage for you to try to fit in with the other people. But you can find hope in the story of Ruth, who faced these problems and triumphed.

Ruth knew she wanted to serve Naomi's God and live with Naomi's people. It meant leaving her own country, home, friends, and even religion. That first morning when Ruth went out to glean, she was well aware of the fact that she did not belong. She called herself a stranger when Boaz spoke to her. She reminded him that she was not like his handmaidens.

However, Ruth had courage. When she was told to eat with the other hand-maidens at mealtime, she did just that. She could have gone off by herself and felt inferior, but she took courage and associated with the others even though she was new.

Later when Naomi gave her instructions to go to Boaz, she obeyed. The custom may have seemed strange to her, but she did what she knew to do to become a part of God's people.

In time Ruth belonged. No longer was she considered a stranger. The women rejoiced with her when her son was born. It takes time to become part of a community, but you will find a place to belong if you take courage and live virtuously, as Ruth did. 🌼

April 25

But Simon's wife's mother lay sick of a fever . . . And he came
and took her by the hand, and lifted her up; and immediately
the fever left her, and she ministered unto them.
—Mark 1:30-31

After Simon's mother-in-law was healed, she served and ministered to others. Like her, I have been healed too, both physically and spiritually. Many times when we have found a healing remedy, we are quick to share it with others. I have a responsibility, now that I have been healed, to share my remedy with others.

The same remedy that healed the woman with the fever is my remedy too—Jesus. He did the same for me as He did for her—He lifted me above my circumstances and helped me to focus on Him. Now I can serve in my home or any other place. Serving the Lord means doing His will, and I can do that wherever I am.

I can minister to others by making a point of telling them what God has done for me. When He provides an answer through a certain passage of Scripture, I can share that passage and give encouragement to search the Scriptures for answers. When He gives me victory after sharing my problem with someone else and asking for prayer support, I can minister to a friend's need by encouraging her to do the same. When my burden is lifted through prayer and fasting, I need to share about it. It might be just the remedy someone else needs to find victory.

Ministering to people can take many forms. I do not know what all of them are; all I need to know is that I have been healed to serve. God will help me to find ways to do His will.

....

....

....

....

For if there come unto your assembly a man with a gold ring, in goodly apparel, and there come in also a poor man in vile raiment; and ye have respect to him that weareth the gay clothing, and say unto him, Sit thou here in a good place; and say to the poor, Stand thou there . . . are ye not then partial in yourselves, and are become judges of evil thoughts?

—James 2:2-4

We tend to evaluate and judge others by the first impression we get of them. We set a standard and form our opinions by it. But when we give ourselves time and opportunity to become better acquainted with others before classifying them, we stand a much better chance of establishing friendships.

It is a Christian virtue to be neat and clean, but features of the body and looks are not all in our control. Physical handicaps should not make us hesitate to speak or associate with a person.

Rich blessings can be ours if we take time to visit with the elderly grandmother, though she is hard of hearing and we may need to talk louder than usual. We may discover that we have similar interests as the handicapped teacher at the teachers' workshop. Helping the blind brings rewards, though it does take extra time. The stranger may not be the shy person you think she is if you make special efforts to make her feel welcome.

Be aggressive in meeting people. Pay special attention to those others tend to avoid. Consider every person you meet as someone special, someone from whom you may be able to learn something. After all, when we lay aside our "titles," we are all on the same level before God.

And he passed over before them, and bowed himself to the ground seven times, until he came near to his brother.
—Genesis 33:3

Poor, lame Jacob! How could he hope to make a favorable impression on Esau and his troops in such a weak, deformed condition? What would happen when the lame and the mighty met? Would there be revenge and bloodshed, war and turmoil? Had it not been for Jacob's experience at the brook Jabbok, war and bloodshed would likely have resulted. Humbled and lame, he was now willing to give up. No more was he scheming for himself, but he was willing to give of himself and his possessions to another. The history of this meeting may have been different had Jacob not been lame.

When Jacob was made lame, he became a better man—a humble and caring man, a surrendered man. Being made lame is not usually an honorary distinction, but in the life of Jacob it produced the peaceable fruits of righteousness.

Maybe you feel that you have been "made lame." You are not recognized and popular like some other people. Maybe you are poor or afflicted. Your desires are denied, your longings unfulfilled. This lameness does not appear to be an honor, but it is the touch of God on your life. If you accept it, you will become a better person in various ways. The history of your life may be different if you would not be "lame."

Set me as a seal upon thine heart, as a seal upon thine arm: for love is strong as death; jealousy is cruel as the grave . . . Many waters cannot quench love, neither can the floods drown it: if a man would give all the substance of his house for love, it would utterly be contemned.

—Song of Solomon 8:6-7

A mutual, loving friendship is a great blessing. Best friends feel they will be the most special persons in each other's lives forever. Sadly, that is not always the case. Friendships drift apart at times, and sometimes misunderstandings cause large rifts in a once stable relationship.

Perhaps right now you find yourself experiencing a broken friendship. You may feel hopeless and forsaken, with sorrow and bitterness threatening to take over your life. If so, may you feel your Saviour's loving arms surrounding you, comforting and supporting you. Allow God to use the same love you had for your friend to keep you loving and patient now. Do not allow despair to overtake you. Remember that "all things work together for good to them that love God," and you can accept this experience in your life as something that God has allowed for your good. May you share with your heavenly Father the same loving relationship that you shared with your friend. He has set you as a seal upon His heart and desires that you keep Him as the most special person in your life.

Allow the Lord to bless you today with renewed strength to face the future, knowing that He cares deeply for you.

April 29

Therefore they sacrifice unto their net, and burn incense unto their drag; because by them their portion is fat, and their meat plenteous.

—Habakkuk 1:16

A fisherman has had a successful morning. With satisfaction he looks at the pile of fish he caught in his net. Promptly he builds an altar and burns incense to his dragnet because this tool brought him plenty of income. He worships the tool, believing it is the bearer of wealth.

How foolish, you think. The net was only *used* by skilled hands. Had God not blessed, or had the fisherman not put his tool to proper use, no fish would have been caught.

Do you ever find yourself giving to man the honor that belongs to God? How do you respond when you hear an inspiring message or read an encouraging book or article? Much prayer probably went into its preparation, and God gave the inspiration. Man was only a vessel through which God presented Himself. While compliments are in order, remember to glorify God.

Do you thank God if something you have done has been a success, thereby giving Him glory? You are thrilled when your prayer is answered. Do you share with others that you prayed about your problem, or do you take glory that you figured it out yourself? Mention God's goodness to those around you.

When others compliment you for something well done, be humble. You are only an instrument God is using in His work. If you take glory to yourself, you might as well offer a sacrifice to the fishing net for the wealth it brought you.

....

....

....

....

But we all, with open face beholding as in a glass the glory of the Lord, are changed into the same image from glory to glory, even as by the Spirit of the Lord.

—2 Corinthians 3:18

The tabernacle with its covering of goats' hair may have appeared unattractive to those who were not Israelites. But to those who understood its meaning, it was precious. It was a gift from God and a sign of His presence. Likewise, those who do not understand the essence of Christianity may find it unattractive. I wish they could feel its heartbeat and witness its beauty as I have.

My heart thrills as I bask in the joy of living in a community of true Christ-followers. I am privileged to witness the Holy Spirit at work, and nothing is more beautiful. He prompts a person's heart, and a loving deed is done—not out of compulsion but out of an eager heart. It is not the routine thing to do; rather, it requires extra time and special effort. The Holy Spirit is at work, and I see pleasant smiles and glowing faces. He brings peace; therefore, I hear no obnoxious music coming from the homes I visit or the cars I ride in. He blends and unifies; therefore, I have sweet fellowship with God's people. Because He is kind, I find understanding hearts in which to confide. Because He shares, I receive in abundance. Because He controls and sanctifies, I hear controlled tongues.

From my vantage point within the tabernacle, I see and hear this sacredness, this presence of God. I experience it and am encouraged, blessed, and thrilled. From their vantage point within the tabernacle, others are seeing things in me too, though I am unaware. What do they see in me? *Please, God, may it be your presence. If it is not, I do not belong in this holy place. But then make me fit to be here, because there is no other place on earth where I would rather be.*

May 1

But my God shall supply all your need according to his riches in glory by Christ Jesus.
—Philippians 4:19

My car had problems and I was shopping for another one. Nothing I had seen had fit my finances. In essence I prayed, "Lord, I need a miracle."

One afternoon our deacon and his wife accompanied me in making the final selection. When we arrived at the dealership, I told the dealer the condition of the car I was hoping to trade in, as well as my financial range. The dealer was eager to make a sale and tried to convince me to spend more money than I had decided to, but I had left no margin for bargaining. I hung on to my price, and eventually they accepted my offer—almost half the original price. I was dumbfounded.

Almost immediately I was bombarded with feelings of guilt. Had I been deceptive or too stubborn? In a daze I went ahead with negotiations. I knew my feelings showed, but I could not explain them even to myself. I even felt a bit shaky as I got in my car and drove off, only marginally relieved about my new purchase.

The guilty feeling hung on. Midnight came and went. Finally I questioned myself. I then realized I had been honest with the dealer, and I had not asked him to lower the price. I had not been set on that car and had offered to look at others. Then why the guilt? Philippians 4:19 came to mind. There was the answer! I had asked God for a miracle, and He had supplied. Satan, the deceiver, had tricked me, disturbed my peace, and put doubts into my mind. I rebuked him, thanked God for His providence, and fell asleep.

....

....

....

....

I press toward the mark for the prize of the high calling of God in Christ Jesus.
—Philippians 3:14

A mother and her children were on a hike to the woods. To get there, they needed to scale what looked like a small mountain—not unusual in the hills of Kentucky, but not an easy task either.

The mother tired out. "Oh, children," she sighed aloud, "this hill is almost too steep for me."

Her young son answered, "Mom, you can do it. See me? I am still going up." There he was on his hands and knees, crawling up the hillside. He had his eyes on the top of the incline not very far away. One way or another, he was going to get there.

Ah, yes, the mother thought, getting fresh courage after her brief rest, *my son reminds me of our journey through life. The climb is uphill. There are stones in the path, and strength is ebbing away. Heaven is in view, but our feet hardly let us take another step.*

If you find yourself climbing a steep hill in your spiritual life just now, take time to rest; refresh yourself in God's Word. Commune with your Lord. Then, revived, you can press on to victory.

If your goal is to have your devotions first thing in the morning but you find yourself unable to accomplish that, set aside a time in your schedule when it will suit you, and stick to your goal.

Maybe you have a problem of constantly criticizing others. You must confess it as wrong and ask God to help you overcome your habit. Make a conscious effort to seal your lips when the temptation comes to speak evil of another. Think kind thoughts instead.

You may wish to give more money to the Lord, but you find little left at the end of the week. Set a goal to give to the Lord first, and then trust Him to supply your needs.

It is not always easy to obtain our goals. Ask God to help you set realistic goals, and then determine to reach them—even if it means on your hands and knees!

And let us consider one another to provoke unto love and to good works.
—Hebrews 10:24

Recently I cleaned my oven. It was not a task I had planned or wished to do; it's the sort of thing I can easily push off because it is not a pleasant task. What prompted me to clean it was the influence of someone else who mentioned that she would like to clean her oven. Because she had the idea and told me about it, I became inspired to do the same, and I'm glad I did it.

In a spiritual sense, we are to inspire each other to godliness. If I overcome, I show by my life how much more pleasant it is to have a victorious life than one that reveals defeat. If love flows from my heart, others will desire that kind of life too. If I find joy in serving, others will desire to do the same. If I am radiant in serving the Lord, others will seek after that radiance.

The person who said she was going to clean her oven did not tell me that I had to clean mine too. But she told me what she was going to do, so I began to think how nice it would be to have a clean oven myself. The Christians who have inspired me to godliness did not do so by sitting down and giving me detailed lessons in holiness. It was so evident in their lives, so magnetizing, that I wished for the same.

Had the idea about cleaning the oven remained only a thought instead of a verbal sentence, it would not have provoked me to do the same. My oven might still be dirty. If I only *think* about gaining victory, putting love into action, and more earnestly serving God, I will provoke no one to love and good works.

Hannah was struggling to accept God's plan for her situation. She was loved by her husband, yet she had bitterness in her soul. Because she was barren, she felt misunderstood as a woman—and even worthless.

Hannah decided to pour out her heart to the Lord. While she prayed and made a vow to the Lord, only her lips moved. Eli, the priest, noticed her actions but heard no words. Thinking she was drunk, he rebuked her for her drunkenness.

Hannah had a choice to make. She could have quietly left the temple, feeling hurt because she had been misunderstood. She could have nursed her hurt and held a grudge against Eli. She could have left for home and not mentioned her request to him. Instead, she briefly explained her actions, speaking respectfully to Eli but correcting his accusation. Then Eli blessed her. When Hannah left, she no longer had a sad countenance. Later, her prayer was answered.

Similarly, at times our actions may be questioned. Others may misunderstand us because our situation is a bit different from another person's. If we, like Hannah, have appropriate opportunity to express the reason for our actions, we might do so. But we must be careful, lest we appear to justify ourselves.

Meekness is a fruit of the Spirit that should be evident in every Christian woman's life. Taking offence and feeling hurt when we are misunderstood tends to tear down rather than build our relationships with friends.

Most important, let us not be unduly alarmed if we are misunderstood. The situation might possibly look different to us if we were not as directly involved. ✹

And Peter answered him and said, Lord, if it be thou, bid me come unto thee on the water. And he said, Come. And when Peter was come down out of the ship, he walked on the water, to go to Jesus. But when he saw the wind boisterous, he was afraid; and beginning to sink, he cried, saying, Lord, save me.
—Matthew 14:28-30

With the assurance that Jesus had called, Peter stepped out of the boat and started out to meet Him on the water. All was well until he noticed his threatening surroundings, at which point he became unstable and started to sink. But Jesus' call was no less valid during that time than it had been earlier. The wind and the waves had nothing to do with the voice of Jesus, but Peter allowed the elements to overpower that call. Fear replaced faith, and he lost his assurance and happiness in seeing the Master.

Jesus calls every Christian. He may not call us to walk on water, but He will call us to step out in faith to do His bidding. He constantly longs for us to come closer to Him. When we hear His call, we go forward with assurance and joy because He means so much to us. Then because we do not trust Him enough, we look at our frightening circumstances, at the magnitude of the task or the cost, and we become unstable. Fear replaces faith and we no longer have the assurance we once had.

The size of the task and the cost to our flesh have nothing to do with the voice of Jesus. Focusing on those things causes us to lose power and sink emotionally. But keeping our eyes on Jesus gives us power and victory.

....

....

....

....

....

....

> Not that I speak in respect of want: for I have learned,
> in whatsoever state I am, therewith to be content.
> —Philippians 4:11

As I think of Joseph's life, I am challenged by his example of contentment. For children of God, the secret of contentment is to accept that whatever life hands to us is God's plan for us. Can we visualize Joseph in prison, sulking in a corner and having a pity party? He could have thought life just wasn't fair as he recalled how he was mistreated by his older brothers, sold to foreigners, and brought to a strange country. Then to top it off, he was put into prison for doing what was right.

But Joseph knew he was not alone. Not only was God with him, but He also showed mercy to him. The Lord gave Joseph favor in sight of the prison keeper. Joseph did not fold his hands obstinately and decide there was nothing for him to do in prison. The prison keeper saw that Joseph was honest and trustworthy, so he put Joseph in charge of the other prisoners. No doubt Joseph was a good leader, sensitive to his fellow prisoners' needs.

Later he could have taken vengeance on his brothers for the way they had treated him. But instead he said to his brothers, "Fear not: for am I in the place of God? But as for you, ye thought evil against me; but God meant it unto good" (Genesis 50:19-20).

Do we at times find ourselves in a prison of undesirable circumstances or situations? What is our attitude? Do we blame God or others, letting a root of bitterness rob us of our peace with God? Or do we see that God has allowed such circumstances and situations for good to bring about His will? We cannot have a more fulfilling life than being content where God has placed us, whether married or unmarried, and doing the work to which He has called us, whether it's working with children or with the elderly, on the mission field or at home.

Let us be content with our calling, not wishing it were different than it is. "Let every man abide in the same calling wherein he was called" (1 Corinthians 7:20). 🕊

May 7

Every branch in me that beareth not fruit he taketh away: and every branch that beareth fruit, he purgeth it, that it may bring forth more fruit.

—John 15:2

Mr. Walters had his own special apple tree. One day a friend came along who also enjoyed growing fruit trees. Mr. James listened to the story of how Mr. Walters had acquired his special tree. Then, noticing its bushy branches, he kindly replied, "Mr. Walters, your tree must be pruned if you want to get more fruit from it." So Mr. Walters asked him if he would like the job, and Mr. James accepted.

The day Mr. James came to trim the tree, Mr. Walters watched the process from the sidelines. He was astounded at how much of the tree his friend cut off. Finally he exclaimed, "Mr. James, I want something left of that tree to provide some shade too." But Mr. James was envisioning apples from this tree, not shade.

God is planning your life in detail as He prunes you. His goal is "that [you] may bring forth more fruit." You may not understand why God takes away your biggest branches, the ones you feel are providing shade for others. You may wonder why God takes away your health, your money, or a relationship you have shared with someone. Without these things, you feel that instead of having something to contribute to the world, you now have to depend on others, constantly receiving instead of giving.

But whenever God takes a branch out of your life, He has your fruit in mind. He is able to make you more fruitful. Perhaps you can also then offer shade after new growth has sprouted from your life!

And Simon answering said unto him, Master, we have toiled all the night, and have taken nothing: nevertheless at thy word I will let down the net. And when they had this done, they inclosed a great multitude of fishes: and their net brake.

—Luke 5:5-6

Many times I have thought I knew how something should be accomplished. I labored to get others to see my point of view. My way of changing the situation sounded logical and right; therefore, I clung to it stubbornly and tenaciously. Even after the Lord showed me that it was better to remain quiet and allow Him to control the situation, I did not completely relinquish my hold. Like Peter in the text, I had doubts that it would work. Time and again I would try to "help the Lord," only to feel defeated and frustrated. Finally I stopped banging my head against the wall, confessed my sinful tendency, and handled the situation His way. The odds seemed to be against me, but I took Him at His Word and allowed Him to be in control.

And then—mightily, majestically—the Lord worked! I stood in awe watching Him work in ways I never could have. Blessings so great I could not contain them flooded my soul. Now I understand. Since He "worketh all things after the counsel of his own will," He does not need my nearsighted, unwise meddling. After this, when He wants to spare me and make the burden lighter, I will step back and watch Him work.

"And the work of righteousness shall be peace; and the effect of righteousness quietness and assurance for ever" (Isaiah 32:17).

And be ye kind one to another.
—Ephesians 4:32

When I was working for my sick grandmother, several of her nieces came to visit her. They brought some fruit for Grandma as a gift of love. But that wasn't all—one of the nieces also had something for me. She said, "This is for you for what you do for your grandmother." It was only a candy bar, but I will never forget what that deed of kindness meant to me. Knowing that she remembered me, the one who was taking care of Grandma, touched me.

Showing kindness to the ones who are in charge of caring for the sick and the disabled is one way to obey the command in Ephesians 4:32. Often they need just as much encouragement as the person who is being cared for, because their role can be stressful. God will bless your obedience as you creatively show kindness to those who are sometimes overlooked.

And who knoweth whether thou art come to the kingdom for such a time as this?

—Esther 4:14

Though God is not mentioned in the book of Esther, His plan for the Jewish nation beautifully unfolds in its pages. How was it that Esther, a Jewess, came to play a vital role in the kingdom? It is not likely that Mordecai, who raised Esther lovingly after her parents died, would have volunteered Esther for the position of queen. The king's servants may have taken her by force.

Whatever the circumstance that brought Esther to the palace, she leaves an impression of obedience after she left home. Mordecai charged her not to tell the others that she was a Jewess, and she adhered to this command. Chapter two says she obeyed Mordecai just as did when she was brought up by him.

Even years after Esther left home, her respect for the one who had taught her continued. Just because she was not living at home did not mean that Mordecai had ceased to be her authority. His word was final.

After Esther became queen, she heard one day that Mordecai lay in sackcloth and ashes. After she inquired into the matter, she received difficult orders from Mordecai. To be sure that Mordecai understood the magnitude of what he was asking her to do, she sent a message to him saying that the king had not called her in for thirty days. It was dangerous for her to approach the king without an invitation. Mordecai understood the risk, yet he was firm. He reminded her that she may have been called to the kingdom for just such a time as this.

Esther was satisfied. Submissively she said, "If I perish, I perish." She trusted the wisdom of the older authority in her life, and she would do as he had requested even though she feared for her life.

Mordecai trusted Esther to work out the details of his plan, and she did not disappoint him. She knew clearly what he wanted done, and she wisely proceeded with prayer and fasting.

Later Mordecai and Esther worked together on confirming the days of Purim. Because of their mutual trust, they were able to continue accomplishing important tasks together. ✳

May 11

But to do good and to communicate forget not:
for with such sacrifices God is well pleased.

—Hebrews 13:16

So, do you have a co-worker who rubs you the wrong way? And to make matters worse, do you have to live with her too?

Though she has more experience in her job than you, she mumbles vaguely when you ask advice. But when you make a mistake, she can be very specific. You are pleased with your latest project, but she only points out a few details that could have been better. You go shopping for groceries and she wants to buy only the cheapest brands. She hints in a subtle way that you are not doing your share of the duties, such as starting the morning fire. You are ashamed to tell her that you do not know how, because you have always had gas heat. You rearranged your bedroom, but she does not come look at it for a long time. You come to the conclusion that she is jealous of your abilities.

Life looks like one big problem, and you feel you cannot endure. What misery!

But you can take heart. All these things and more happened to me. Yet this lady and I worked together for many years and became close friends, almost like sisters. You may already be asking, "What was your secret?" Simply this: we learned to communicate!

Thankfully we never spoke unkindly to each other, even when that would have been the easiest thing to do. We learned to express our thoughts, and finally we were able to see how miraculously things worked out.

In later years when we went shopping, she was more liberal in spending than I was (I'm not sure who changed). She had been vague with her advice because she assumed I knew more than I really did. She had not realized the adjustments I needed to make in this job.

By talking things over, I learned that she had not come into my room to look at my arrangement because she was hurt that I had not invited her and shared my idea with her. She was more than happy to teach me how to build a fire. In later years, I did more than my share of the chores because she was physically handicapped. As we communicated, we learned to understand each other. Not only did I survive each day, I could hardly wait for the next one.

Now the friend with whom I shared so much of my life has passed away. How miserable my memories would be if I had years of bickering to regret! I am thankful that we learned the value of communication. 🌑

May 12

And we know that all things work together for good to them that love God, to them who are the called according to his purpose.
—Romans 8:28

We usually do not look forward to changes, yet change is inevitable. When the Master Designer is weaving the tapestry of our lives, He sees the final picture. If the threads were all dark or all light, we could not see the relationship of darkness to light that makes the delightful picture in the final scene. We can see only the strand the Master is weaving in our lives today. We are called to trust that His plan is best for us. He uses changing scenes in our lives to form in us a likeness of Himself. He also knows that changes will increase our knowledge, enabling us to better reach out to strugglers beside us on this journey called life.

Not until I lost my dear sister through death by cancer did I know how painful death is. Since these dark threads have been woven into my tapestry, I now feel pain for others in a different way than I ever did before. Would I have chosen my sister's death so I could reach out better to others? Absolutely not! But did the Designer see where He was going with my life? I trust He did, even though my own plans did not unfold.

Change is not all negative. Our friends increase when we are called to serve in another community far from home. A new occupation, although it can create apprehension at first, may be just the thing for which we were made.

Change will happen—let's go with the flow. When we don't resist our Designer's stitches, He will redeem each circumstance and turn our lives into something beautiful. ✺

....

....

....

For all the promises of God in him are yea, and
in him Amen, unto the glory of God by us.
—2 Corinthians 1:20

I hope this scrapbook will be a blessing to my uncle, I thought as I worked happily. I cut out a flower to fit into a corner and arranged a clipping to give the page a neater appearance.

"Isn't it about time you stop for the evening and have your devotions?" questioned the Spirit.

"But it's too early for that," I argued. "Besides, I *am* doing something for the Lord. I even included a few pages explaining the plan of salvation, so this is the Lord's work too."

Still the Spirit persisted, but I reasoned, "I really should get my share of the pages done so that I can pass it on to my cousin when I see her next week. I won't have time to work on it tomorrow, because I plan to bake bread along with all my other work."

"Seek ye first the kingdom of God and his righteousness, and all these things shall be added unto you," the Spirit reminded me.

For a little while I worked on, but not as enthusiastically or as comfortably as I had before. Shortly I put my things away and sat down with the Bible. I became more and more inspired as I meditated. When I closed the Bible, I was thankful I had heeded the voice of the Spirit. I was so inspired that I decided to call a friend and share the treasures of the Word with her. During the telephone conversation, she mentioned that she was planning to bake bread the following day.

"So was I," I remarked. "I have sometimes wondered whether it would be wiser for me to buy bread since I have to take time off from my job to bake."

"Why, I'll give you some of mine," my friend offered quickly. "I'm baking anyway, and I'll bring some to prayer meeting for you."

True to her promise, she shared two loaves of delicious brown bread with me. When she baked again later, she kindly shared another loaf.

When I was obedient to God, I experienced the blessings that go with obedience. This strengthened my faith and helped me to see that the devil puts great emphasis on what it will cost to obey. He does not tell about the rewards of obedience nor about the peace and satisfaction that come from yielding to God. Once again I see that he is a liar—and that God's promises never fail.

....

....

....

....

....

....

....

....

....

....

....

....

....

....

....

....

> I will lift up mine eyes unto the hills, from whence cometh my help.
> My help cometh from the Lord, which made heaven and earth.
>
> —Psalm 121:1-2

Lisa's eyes mist over with tears as she bites a trembling lip. Her aching heart overflows with the longing for someone to turn to—someone wise and practical who cares particularly for her. As she kneels beside the bed, her weary body and mind cry out for a strong shoulder on which to pour her troubles. She envisions someone with masculine strength and a sunny, confident smile assuring her that things are not as bad as they seem.

But help is on the way. The faithful Spirit reminds her of the great Lord. Talk about strength! Talk about being capable! And as for wise, did you ever see anyone compare with the Creator of the ends of the earth?

Earthly beings have their limitations. Even strong men become weary and perplexed at times, but the strength of our God never fails. A woman needs to find strength and renewal by casting her burdens on His strong shoulders and leaving them there. As we bring our longings and insufficiencies to God, our hearts are calmed and strengthened. We can smile again after our tears. Someone loves us dearly!

May 15

I will greatly rejoice in the Lord, my soul shall be joyful in my God; for
he hath clothed me with the garments of salvation, he hath covered
me with the robe of righteousness, as a bridegroom decketh himself
with ornaments, and as a bride adorneth herself with her jewels.
—Isaiah 61:10

Who makes you complete? Is there any circumstance or any possession that will make you more fully a woman?

When I was single, I felt I needed a husband to be a complete and whole person. After I was married, I felt I needed a child to be a real woman. I had to wait awhile before some of my desires came to pass. The Lord was very real to me during the times of waiting, and He taught me many lessons. Isaiah 61:10 became alive for me during those times. God clothes me and pays meticulous attention to me.

Imagine with me the careful preparations of an excited bride and groom on their wedding day. Their hair is clean and neatly arranged. They are freshly bathed, and not a spot of dirt is allowed to mar their garments. Their hearts are filled with eager anticipation of spending time together.

Friend, this is how God clothes you with His salvation and righteousness. This clothing is more pure and clean than any earthly clothing we will ever wear. He loves you so much! Yet His attention and love are pure and free of selfish motives. Go forth today with a restful heart. You are complete in Him, and as tenderly cared for as any bride.

And his allowance was a continual allowance given him
of the king, a daily rate for every day, all the days of his life.

—2 Kings 25:30

When I was twenty-one years old, a young man desired my friendship. I did not know him very well, yet he seemed to be a gentleman. He was friendly and a member of a Scriptural church.

I sought counsel from my ministers, and they did not try to discourage me. Yet I felt something holding me back. I wondered if it was God, but I didn't know why He was cautioning me. I liked this young man and enjoyed being around him. How could I tell him no and then face him every week? I felt sorry for him. I confided in my parents and they joined me in seeking the Lord's will through prayer. Then a verse in Psalm 84 stood out clearly to me: "No good thing will he withhold from them that walk uprightly." I did not like that! Was this young man not a good thing? I struggled. But God kept speaking to me through the verse, and I saw that to retain my peace with God, the answer must be no. It was not a pleasant experience, yet God's grace was sufficient. I felt peace even when I did not understand.

Later there were times when I struggled with the thought of spending all my life as a single person. The tempter seemed to say, "You will be so lonely. How awful that God has done this to you!" But I discovered that I was lonely only as I allowed myself to be.

After numerous years spent as a captive in prison, Jehoiachin king of Judah was given a reprieve. The king of Babylon decided to treat him more humanely than before, and he began to provide amply for Jehoiachin (2 Kings 25). Like Jehoichin, I began to experience God's provision in my loneliness. His grace was "a continual allowance . . . a daily rate for every day." One day at a time He supplied my needs. He gave me many friends and experiences that I would never have had as a married person.

This young man then married another woman in the church, but several years later they made some choices that did not appear wise. It seemed they were allowing themselves to drift from truth. My mind again goes to the verse in Psalm 84: "The Lord God is a sun and shield . . . no good thing will he withhold from them that walk uprightly." Truly, He is my shield, and I praise Him! ◗

> And he said, Blessed be the Lord God of my master Abraham, who
> hath not left destitute my master of his mercy and his truth: I being
> in the way, the Lord led me to the house of my master's brethren.
>
> —Genesis 24:27

Abraham's servant was asked by his master to carry out a difficult mission. He was to leave familiar faces and places behind and travel to a strange land to people he did not know. He was not doing this for personal gain or benefit, but because his master had sent him on an errand. How could he ever do it? Because he had learned to love and trust his master, he started on the long journey, the outcome of which he could not foresee. But his journey was not in vain. Its success hinged on his triumphant testimony, "I being in the way, the Lord led me."

My journey from earth to heaven will be successful only as I am in a way that the Lord can lead me. Sometimes He asks me to do things I do not understand, and I may not be able to see the outcome. He might ask me to give a certain amount of money that I feel I cannot spare. He might ask me to write a letter or help someone else when I have work that desperately needs my attention. He might ask me to take a job that may leave me in a dubious financial position. He will ask me to die to myself—to give up that which I thought was so necessary for my reputation and my life. How can it ever work out? I have learned to love and trust my Master. I know I can trust Him to lead me so that I, too, can say, "I being in the way, the Lord led me."

And Jesus, when he came out, saw much people,
and was moved with compassion toward them.

—Mark 6:34

Jesus was moved with compassion toward the needy around Him. Here were more than five thousand hungry people, and He had only five loaves and two fish with which to feed them. To the disciples it seemed hopeless to even begin feeding all these people, but Jesus used the little He had to meet all their needs.

As we look around us, we see many people facing trials and discouragement, and those who do not know the peace which comes through faith in Jesus. We might be unable to reach many people, but we can watch for opportunities in little things like giving a smile to those we meet, singing songs as we go about our duties, or writing a letter to a lonely or struggling person. We will receive blessings for faithfulness in the little things the Lord prompts us to do. God is able to bless each small deed done for Him, just as He blessed those five loaves and two fish that supplied the needs of many people.

Today, Lord, help me to sense the needs of those around me, and to do well the little you have for me to do.

....

....

....

....

....

....

....

> Thus saith the Lord, Set thine house in order; for thou shalt die, and not live.
>
> —2 Kings 20:1

When Hezekiah received the message from Isaiah regarding his impending death, he turned to the wall and pled to the Lord for his life. The Lord heard and answered his request and granted him fifteen more years to live.

But the next fifteen years of his life were not all prosperous. Hezekiah fell into sin and God was going to punish his descendants for his sin (2 Kings 20). Perhaps if Hezekiah had submitted to God's initial plan for his death, his sons would not have needed to suffer for his sin.

I fear for the life of the unborn child I am carrying—the baby that is becoming more precious to me as time goes on. I am experiencing some complications, and I know that without enough development, this baby will not live. I weep, wanting to ask God to save this dear one's life, wanting one day to hold in my arms the life that has already begun. But I think of the future. I will not insist on the life of this child. It may mean that the child will have to live with a handicap should God answer my request. I will not insist on life on earth, if God's plan is life in heaven instead.

My heart is heavy, but I still want to pray, "Thy will be done." I do not know the future, yet I know God's will is best. He will be with our family throughout the future.

***

Several months after this article was written, the Lord saw best to bless our home with a healthy son, even though he was born almost six weeks early. We often thank God for the way He chose to answer our prayers. We also continue to pray, "Thy will be done," for the unknown future. ❋

But we were gentle among you, even as a nurse cherisheth her children.
—1 Thessalonians 2:7

Hands can become skilled at many things such as building structures, painting pictures, typing speedily, or making pie crusts. But when my niece experienced a difficult hospital stay, hands that knew these skills were not of much use to her. The only hands that helped her through this trying time were the gentle hands of the nurse. The nurse was trained to know what was needed, and she tenderly administered love.

Gentleness must be part of every Christian woman's life, because many hurting people need her ministrations. A woman who is cultivating gentleness in her life will exhibit several defining characteristics. While others are easily perturbed at difficulties, she will not allow herself to wallow in frustration. If an angry person crosses her path, the gentle woman will remain composed. Though saddened by anger, her spirit is not ruffled. She is not quickly offended by the thoughtless remarks or attitudes of others.

When a gentle woman faces pain, she finds composure to master her feelings. She does not blame God for her situation. A gentle woman is neighborly, welcoming both stranger and friend into her home. A gentle woman is tactful when another person's fault needs to be dealt with.

Children enjoy the presence of one who possesses gentleness. The atmosphere is calm, her words quiet, and her patience obvious. She does not need to raise her voice or get angry to prove her authority. She will be able to meet many needs, because she has learned to cherish people. She will be fondly remembered. ✳

She hath done what she could.

—Mark 14:8

I was having a busy day in the classroom. The last few weeks of school were always challenging. Final tests had to be administered and graded. Some students were done with their books, and I needed to find extra work for them to do.

One day I looked out the window and noticed that someone had just arrived on the school grounds. She was a friend from church and a former teacher. I was surprised to see her because she had not been well, and it took effort for her to leave home. When she came to my door, she saw that I was busy, so she called one student out and then left. After I finished story time, my student handed me a note and a gift. This is what the note said:

> Last year a first grader brought a bouquet of spring beauties to me. He thought it too small a gift. He wanted a bigger bouquet . . . How often this has been a lesson to me this winter. I cannot do great things anymore, but I can do little things for God. So today amidst the discouragement I feel because of not feeling well again, I noticed the spring beauties all over my lawn. So I give these to you because I care about you. I know the adjustments of closing school are not easy. I understand and I care.

Tears surfaced as I looked at the little vase with all the spring beauties it could hold. I remembered the words Jesus had said about Mary, who anointed His feet. "She hath done what she could."

My day was brightened and I found courage to keep doing my best in the schoolroom until the closing day. I thanked God for this dear sister who had done what she could and let me know she understood and cared. To me that vase of spring beauties was not just a small thing. It was with a sense of regret that I emptied the vase of wilted flowers a few days later. But the challenge will always stay with me. Am I doing what I can to lift others' loads? 🍂

May 22

Speaking to yourselves in psalms and hymns and spiritual songs,
singing and making melody in your heart to the Lord.
—Ephesians 5:19

When you feel weary or downcast, try singing a favorite hymn or two. If you can't think of one from memory, take time off your work, get a hymnbook, and find a song of praise to the Lord. Even when you feel so blue that you let out a big sigh and think, *I can't sing; it just takes too much effort,* take a deep breath and try it. Before you know it, you'll be done with the first verse—and then you'll finish the song. I have found that I can change my thought patterns more effectively when I use a book than when I sing from memory.

When undesirable thoughts plague you, fill your mind with psalms and verses from the Scriptures. When God seems far away, singing spiritual songs can help you feel nearer to Him. He is not the one who moved away from us; we are the ones who drift. Praise can create a proper frame of mind, allowing God to fill you again. "Draw nigh to God, and he will draw nigh to you" (James 4:8).

Speaking to ourselves in psalms and hymns and spiritual songs is a form of worship to the Lord. Thus we can worship the Lord even when we are all by ourselves. With a song in our heart, we will more easily reflect the state of mind in Ephesians 5:20: "Giving thanks always for all things unto God and the Father in the name of the Lord Jesus Christ."

The unmarried woman careth for the things of the Lord … but she that is married careth for the things of the world, how she may please her husband.

—1 Corinthians 7:34

Maria had been asked to teach a women's Bible class. Did she have time? As she pondered that question, she was impressed with the thought, *Of course I do. There isn't any reason why I cannot spend one evening a week studying.* Her thoughts ran on: *When my husband was living, my activities revolved around his. I could not plan an evening for myself; he might have needed me to help him with something. When the children were small, I knew very little about uninterrupted time. But everything is different now. I am alone. I can plan and usually carry it out if I choose to do so.*

The reality of that possibility seemed to Maria like a luxury, something that had existed only in her dreams. It had not been wrong for her to spend most of her time caring for her family. She had felt confident that God, who established the family, also gave women the special insights and skills needed to carry out the many details involved in homemaking. And it had been right to please her husband and make the home a pleasant place for the family.

But now God was giving her time for study and meditation—the luxury of uninterrupted time. And in a new way she understood what her single friends had enjoyed for years. God sees the many details of His work that married women do not have time for because they are caring for their families. So in His wisdom He placed unmarried women in strategic positions where they can attend to aspects of His work that might otherwise be neglected or carried out less efficiently.

Maria was reminded of the saying her friend had sent her: "God never closes a door but that He opens a window." Living alone had not been her first choice, but now it was God's choice—and He intended for it to be meaningful and productive. One period of life had closed, but another was opening. Both right and good, both with pleasures and problems, but both in God's will. And one just as important as the other. ●

And we desire that every one of you do shew the same diligence to the full assurance of hope unto the end: that ye be not slothful, but followers of them who through faith and patience inherit the promises.
—Hebrews 6:11-12

Do you feel that your calling and gifts are inferior to that of others? God in His wisdom has given you special talents and has placed you where you are. You can fulfill your calling because God has enabled you to do His will. He does not intend for you to live selfishly, but rather to give yourself for others and for His glory.

When we feel inferior, we are often easily hurt by what others do or say. We also tend to get angry when we don't feel the respect we think we deserve. The way to avoid these pitfalls is to stay focused on God's desires and goals for you, believing that He will enable you to accomplish them. When you are focused on your mission, you will have great peace in fulfilling your calling. That is victory! Commit the small details to your Guide, and you can rest assured that He will lead you safely today, tomorrow, and forever.

A grateful spirit will help you focus on your mission. Are you faithful in giving God the praise that is due Him, or do you take for granted the many blessings you enjoy each day? Think of them intentionally, and learn to be grateful for things you may never have thought of before. As you cultivate gratefulness, you will not have time to think about comparing yourself with others—rather, you will be filled with the knowledge that God has chosen you, and you will find the desire and energy to follow His call.

Do all to the glory of God.
—1 Corinthians 10:31

Susan was spending the day in the home of a married friend. Margaret was a busy wife and mother but still found time to make Susan feel like a welcome guest. They had been discussing things Susan dreamed of doing in the coming years.

"The impression I get from you is that just because you are single today, at thirty-five, you have embraced singleness as a lifetime status, which may not be God's plan at all," Margaret chided gently. "He may someday lead you to marriage. Are you open to Him should this be His will?"

Susan thought about her friend's question. She did not feel hurt by it, but she also felt Margaret had not been completely accurate in her assessment. After a moment of reflection, Susan began to reveal her conviction.

"I want to be open to whatever the Lord has for me. I am not of the mind that I will never marry. I try to rest in God's will. Right now being single is His choice for me, so I rest content in that. For my own mental health and my spiritual well-being, I cannot do anything else. Life would be miserable, and it would be wrong for me to live in the hope that someday, surely someday, I will be privileged to marry. It would not be wrong to ask God to lead to a marriage union if it is His will, but it must be done with an utterly committed and yielded will. Paul speaks about being content in whatever state I am, and to me, that also includes being single."

"You are right," Margaret replied. "As we yield our lives to God, we should rest content in whatever He chooses for us and do all to the glory of God. I think you are on the right track in your thinking."

Susan felt grateful that God had shown her how to express her beliefs accurately, and she thanked God for meeting many of her needs through her caring and understanding friends. ◗

May 26

Neither do men light a candle, and put it under a bushel, but on a candlestick; and it giveth light unto all that are in the house.
—Matthew 5:15

I was searching for flowers
To make a bouquet
That would cheer and bring joy
To a lonely one's day.

I saw sweet little flowers,
So white and so pure,
But whether they'd look right
I wasn't quite sure.

For I had seen these flowers
With their petals closed;
Their glory and beauty
Were unexposed.

So I passed by these flowers
For I couldn't depend
That they would stay open
With the others to blend.

Am I like these flowers—
Closed and unwilling?
Is that why I find life
Is so unfulfilling?

And perhaps like these flowers
I, too, am passed by,
And others are chosen
More willing than I.

A dependable flower,
Lord, make me, I pray,
So I can be useful
In your beautiful bouquet.

....

....

....

....

And he gave them their request; but sent leanness into their soul.

—Psalm 106:15

I listened closely while Becky shared her feelings about being eighty-three years old and single. Eighty-three years seemed like a long time to me. Somehow I was sure that, at some point in her life, Becky desired special companionship just like every woman seems to desire.

"In earlier years I also would have enjoyed having a partner and a home of my own. But the Lord did not lead that way, and I felt it was much better to accept His will than to want my own way.

"I had two friends who really wanted husbands. They wanted to be mothers; somehow they felt their lives would be wasted if they did not raise families. So they decided to pursue their dreams and find husbands. They both found young men to marry and had the opportunity to raise families. But both of these women had many hardships. They ended up raising their families mostly by themselves.

"The older of the two became ill with cancer. While she was sick, her husband found pleasure in other women, and she knew about it. Now she had the double blow of cancer and an unfaithful husband.

"The younger woman's husband was not always pleasant to be around. In the end he committed suicide. Life had been difficult for both women.

"Then I contrasted my life with theirs. I realized that with Jesus as my friend and knowing I am in God's will, I have had a much easier life even without a husband and my own children.

"So, young sisters, if the Lord does not provide a companion for you, be satisfied with what He shares with you. When I was young, I made a promise to God that if He did not give me a companion, I would be satisfied with His will. I have had a happy and blessed life. Though I do not have much in this world's goods, the Lord has always provided, and His grace has always been sufficient."

We can still, like the Israelites, demand things of God that He will allow us to have—but with our demand, He may send leanness of soul.

Jesus could have selfishly called for twelve legions of angels while He was being nailed to the cross. But where would we be today had He demanded deliverance? Instead He prayed, "O my Father, if this cup may not pass away from me, except I drink it, thy will be done."

When we follow Jesus' example and give up our wills for our Father's, we will be able to say we lived a happy and blessed life, as Becky testified.

May 28

> Trust in the Lord, and do good; so shalt thou
> dwell in the land, and verily thou shalt be fed.
> —Psalm 37:3

This verse was precious to me as I thought of leaving my dear family and friends to go to the mission field to teach school. It meant so much to know the Lord would be with me after I had left the others behind.

When I trust in the Lord, I will be fed both physically and spiritually. Day by day the Lord will lead me and feed me with His sweet manna. Those who "hunger and thirst after righteousness" will have that blessed promise: "They shall be filled" (Matthew 5:6).

As I adjust to my new surroundings, the weeks and months ahead look long. Yet I know that, as I take one day at a time, I will experience grace enough for each day. I plan to serve the Lord happily here as long as He wants me in this location. I think of the saying, "The will of God will not lead me where the grace of God cannot keep me." He will provide.

For God so loved the world, that he gave his only begotten Son, that whosoever believeth in him should not perish, but have everlasting life.
—John 3:16

How much did God love? He loved so much that *He gave.* God did not just say, "I love you," and then remain unmoved about our sinful condition. Giving is the supreme test of love. There are many ways to give. Perhaps one of the most difficult things to give—the sacrifice that most strenuously tests our love—is time.

Do you have time to listen? To write? To help? To meditate on God and His Word? To pray? If we have given our bodies a living sacrifice, we will make time for these things. We will see things from God's perspective, and He will fill us with love. And remember, love *gives.*

The devil likes to clutter our lives with varied distractions. Giving time takes effort. The fruit of holiness forgets self and goes on to help others. I have yet to experience a dearth or a calamity because I spent time for someone else.

Are your relationships satisfying? If your answer is no, perhaps you think that fulfillment in relationships is found in getting and not in giving. Are you almost ready to cross that friend off your list and class her as unfaithful because she doesn't write? Why not write to her once more? Maybe she has struggles and needs encouragement. Do you feel sorry for yourself because no one invites you to Sunday lunch? Why don't you invite someone? God did not wait to give, invite, or share until someone else did.

The palsied man who was let down through the roof to Jesus did not get there by himself. He was borne there by four kind people who were moved by his weak condition. Where love is, there is a willingness to bear the weak to God in prayer and fasting.

Giving may require sacrifice. Jesus sacrificed when He gave, and through that we experience untold blessings. When God moves us to give and we act in obedience, the giver as well as the receiver will experience abundant blessings.

> We spend our years as a tale that is told. . . . For it is soon cut off,
> and we fly away. . . . So teach us to number our days.
> —Psalm 90

If I would be told that I had but a year, or maybe even only a month to live, what more would I wish to accomplish? Of all my endeavors, which ones would have top priority? Would I have time for Bible study and church services? Would I find time to pray, or would I need to finish my work first? Would I have time to visit the sick and write the lonely, or would I feel the need to earn all the money I could for my savings account? Would the hurts I nursed seem as important as they do now? Would I feel right about holding grudges, or would they suddenly seem sinful? Would my family and friends receive more affection than before, and would I think to speak more kindly to them? Do my friends really know that I care about them? Am I showing them that I am concerned? If I were suddenly taken from this life, would I have done everything that actually needed to be accomplished?

These are questions I have been asking myself. We have no promise of tomorrow; death is more sure than life. I want my house to be in order and my relationships to be up to date. ✳

Rest in the Lord, and wait patiently for him: fret not thyself . . .
—Psalm 37:7

Is there anything a child of God desires more than peace and rest? If you are unmarried, you probably struggle at times with God's choice for your life. Most likely, you long to rest in the Lord, but you have questions. Rest in the Lord when human wisdom points to a fairer way? Rest in the Lord when true fulfillment is supposedly found in serving God in marriage?

Yes, dear heart, rest your whole being in the Lord. Yield to Him all you possess and ever hope to own. We can find rest only by surrendering, not by fighting. When we yield our desires, talents, time, and wills to Him, allowing Him to lead us into whatever or wherever He sees best, we will find rest for our souls.

We do not always understand the path our Lord has chosen for us to travel, or know in what area we are to serve Him. We must ever bear in mind that our main purpose on earth is to live for God's glory and to prepare for eternity. For some, His glory is best exhibited through marriage. For others, God is best glorified through singlehood. Therefore, we need to be constantly surrendered to Him, praying through our every battle as we wait for Him to lead us in the way He knows is best for us.

There is no need to fret. As you rest and wait, there is no room for that. When you rest securely in the arms of your heavenly Father, His will becomes your will. When you are tempted to fret, take heart—your Saviour stands beside you, ready to help you. He spent His life on earth as a single man whose sole focus was to do His Father's will.

These verses are a pillar of strength and encouragement to me as I seek to obey His will. I am happy in the Lord and in His choice for my life.

But if ye bite and devour one another, take heed
that ye be not consumed one of another.
—Galatians 5:15

Hummingbirds are fierce fighters. In spite of their tiny size, they defend their rights at my hummingbird feeder. They use their long pointed beaks not only for sucking nectar but also for stabbing each other's heads in their fight over food. The battle rages with much dashing, darting, and whirring of wings as each one determines to get his share of food and not allow another to get more than his share. I long to tell them that their squabbling is unnecessary; there is plenty of food. Life would be much more enjoyable and peaceful if they could learn to take turns at the feeder and willingly share the food.

But since I cannot teach them this, I will take heed to what they teach me. Their fighting reminds me of the fight that sometimes goes on inside me as I covet someone else's position. Sometimes I struggle with envy because someone else has a talent that I think is better than mine. And when others buy things I cannot afford, I have to fight against bitterness. All this is unnecessary because God has a treasure in store for me. There is no reason to covet someone else's position, because He will shower His abundant blessings upon me if I allow Him to use me where I am. Instead of envying the person who has the talent I would like to have, I can learn from her. In that way, I can be blessed. While living on a limited income and trusting God to meet my needs, I learn about the richness of contentment.

The hummingbirds fight over their food because they are creatures with a wild instinct. But the children of God possess the nature of God. They see that there is an abundance of blessings for everyone, and there's no need to fight over them.

June 2

I am the Almighty God; walk before me, and be thou perfect.
—Genesis 17:1

This verse etches the trim along the ceiling in my office. It always inspires me and meets a variety of needs.

"I am"—the eternal, ever-living One. When a trusted helper fails, He remains. When a supervisor is not available to direct me, He is. When it looks as though all my efforts were wasted or I have caused a major frustration or expense to someone, He is still my God. His heart goes out to me.

"The Almighty God." One day, plagued by temptations in my thought life, I rested my eyes again on that ceiling trim: "Almighty." He can do what I cannot do. He has power to deliver me from sinful thoughts. "Almighty God, help me!" I whispered. "I need power beyond my own." My intercom promptly rang, and somebody was asking details about the schedule of the book I was working on. By the time that conversation ended, another co-worker was at my door, needing an art sketch. That job was interrupted by the arrival of a proof for me to check, which was interrupted by a phone call from a customer with a question. When I finally got back to my job, I realized God had used this flurry to help me. The power of evil had vanished! Praise flooded my being as I thought about the care of the Almighty God.

"Walk before me." This is a reminder when I begin to let wrong motives sidetrack me in my work. Yes, I honor and obey my employer and give good, honest service. But I do not do it for praise or promotion. I am not competing with my co-workers for attention and credit. My highest motive must be God's glory. I do my work for Him to see. I walk before Him, *in His sight.*

"And be thou perfect." This seems to be an exacting command, but Jesus does not ask us to be perfect through our own strength of will. While I cannot excuse slothfulness or poor quality work, God grants me a gentle assurance. Having ordered my steps before Him, I am accepted as perfect. Just as "wash and be clean" does not mean to wash *and then do something else* to become clean, neither does His charge to walk before Him mean that I must frantically search for ways to become perfect. When I concentrate on walking openly before Him, He makes me perfect. I can rest in His power to make me holy.

June 3

That ye might walk worthy of the Lord unto all pleasing, being fruitful in every good work, and increasing in the knowledge of God; strengthened with all might, according to his glorious power, unto all patience and longsuffering with joyfulness.
—Colossians 1:10-11

What attributes are evident in a woman who is longsuffering?

Strengthened by God's might, such a woman remains joyful when someone makes a mistake. Her heart reaches out in pity instead of judgment. With a heart of compassion, she lends a listening ear and desires to help people out of trouble. Her sympathy is recognized by young and old alike.

A longsuffering woman speaks with tenderness and wins the confidence of those she wants to help. Though she is understanding when others make mistakes, she has no tolerance for sin. But when someone is repentant, she cannot help but have mercy and give her another chance.

She is a friend to the discouraged and wishes them well. She feels the grief they are going through. She is touched with the feelings of others and offers condolences.

A longsuffering woman recognizes all the patience God has had for her; therefore, she is moved to help others with a patient spirit.

> Sing, O barren, thou that didst not bear . . . For thy Maker is thine husband . . . but with everlasting kindness will I have mercy on thee, saith the Lord thy Redeemer.
> —Isaiah 54:1-8

Have you ever envied your friends or others younger than you because life seems so easy for them? They begin their courtship, which seemingly passes without any problems, and soon they are happily married. For you, on the other hand, life is a different story. You may have begun courtships several times, only to find your dreams shattered each time. You may even be suffering from such a heartbreaking experience right now. You cannot understand why God allows these things to happen in your life.

Does it seem as though God has forsaken you? Does life seem unfair? Always remember that no matter how forsaken you feel, God will *never* forsake you. He loves you and wants only the best for you. The Saviour is touched by your sufferings; He understands your sorrow.

God knows exactly how you can serve Him best. Perhaps He knows that you can fill His plan better if you are single, or maybe He still has someone who can better serve as your partner. Trust your future to Him and fill the place God has for you right now, the place of joy and contentment, even while you are single.

These verses in Isaiah 54 bless me in my single life. They have helped me to find satisfaction in the life that is God's will for me right now. God wants to fill a husband's place in my life, and He loves me even more than a husband could. Also, many children have found special places in my heart—more children than I could have borne naturally.

May you find the everlasting kindness and mercy of God real in your life as you commit today and the future to Him.

June 5

And the officers shall speak further unto the people, and they shall
say, What man is there that is fearful and fainthearted? let him go and
return unto his house, lest his brethren's heart faint as well as his heart.
—Deuteronomy 20:8

When you are fainthearted or fearful, God does not want you to give up the battle in your Christian life. Neither does He want you to discourage your fellow man, possibly snuffing out his last spark of hope. The Lord desires that you encourage yourself in thinking about Him, for your own good and your fellow Christian's good.

God wants you to demonstrate courage. With a smile you can brighten a lonely person's day, or by some curt remark you can make that same person sink deeper into depression. You can help the discouraged by words of praise, or you can belittle an endeavor and crush any enthusiasm a person may have had. When you listen to a young person's struggle on her way to maturity, your attitude can be detected. Are you concerned or are you critical? It may mean the difference between that person becoming bitter or continuing to battle for victory.

Do not faint in your Christian life, and do not dishearten others in the battle either either. Remember that because Aaron and Hur held up Moses' hands, Israel did not plunge to defeat. ✸

....

....

....

....

....

....

I have learned, in whatsoever state I am, therewith to be content.

—Philippians 4:11

What produces the highest degree or state of contentment in your life? The Apostle Paul, in the cold, damp prison cell at Rome, was condemned for preaching the Gospel. Yet he could say that he had learned to be content. How could he write this beautiful testimony to the Philippian church when his circumstances were so discouraging? But Paul continued writing, "I know both how to be abased, and I know how to abound: every where and in all things I am instructed both to be full and to be hungry, both to abound and to suffer need" (v. 12). Paul's life had been a hard one, not a bed of roses or an easy path, but he had learned through life's experiences the source of true strength. Strength is feeling the Solid Rock under us when trials and temptations come. It is having faith and confidence in Jesus. Then the test will pass and we will still stand firm in Christ who strengthens us. True contentment is when, no matter what the circumstance, our satisfaction is unshaken in our heavenly Father, the source of true contentment.

One day I went to visit my friend Mary, a community lady who had to be in the hospital for a while. As I talked with her, she began recounting her past life with an unfaithful husband and raising her family alone. A shadow fell across her normally expressive face as she described her trials honestly but without self-pity. Her life had been depressing and discouraging until she began going to church and found the Lord. As she related the change in her life, her eyes took on a new sparkle. She laid her hand on her chest and said, "Now I's happy, I's content with Jesus in here." She continued telling how her friends now ask her why she doesn't get another husband. But Mary said, "I don't listen to them. Since I have Jesus, I's content—I's satisfied now!"

Mary knew the secret to contentment, and her joy influenced my state of mind as well.

June 7

And let the Lord do that which is good in his sight.
—1 Chronicles 19:13

A mixture of yearning and contentment fills my heart tonight. Ever since that letter from my friend came in the mail this morning, I have been reminiscing and reflecting. If I could speak to her right now, this is what I would say:

Yes, my dear friend, I have often thought about your daughter already turning eighteen this year. Why? Because it seems like just a few years ago since you and I were that age. What dreams we had—as I suppose most growing girls do. When your special friend came into your life, I was glad for you and hoped that in God's own time He would give to me what He had given you. But He had other plans.

What God seems to give so naturally to most everyone, He chooses to withhold from others. After several years of struggling, I was able to surrender my desire for marriage and accept God's will. I finally realized that He has the right to choose how He blesses the lives of His children. I regretted that I had not learned this when I was young. All I needed to do was yield my life to Him and accept His choice, although it was not as simple as it looks in print.

Despite my reluctance to follow God's choice for me, He was patient in teaching me lesson by lesson how to be free of my self-will—free to rest in His choice for my life.

How could I know then that by yielding my life to the sovereignty of God, I would embrace the deepest joys and truest fulfillment that a child of God can know?

....

....

....

....

....

And Jesus saith unto him, The foxes have holes, and the birds of the
air have nests; but the Son of man hath not where to lay his head.

—Matthew 8:20

Sometimes a sudden longing comes over me—a longing to be more independent. I have to depend on others for so many things. I need financial help. I
need a lot of advice. I need a stronger hand to make repairs. My list is long and I
am tempted to be discouraged; I feel reduced to a parasite. Then I think of my Jesus.

When it was time to pay taxes, He did not have any money; God provided some
for Him. If He slept in a bed, it was one that belonged to someone else. If He ate
a meal inside a house, it was never His house—He did not have a house. Women
ministered to Him, which required humility especially in that era of history. The
colt He rode upon belonged to another man. The grave He was buried in was
not in a family burial plot.

The thought of what others are thinking tortures me frequently. Do they wonder if
I am lazy or wasteful because my medical bills land in the church's lap? Do they look
down on me because my job does not require much intelligence? Have I joined the
ranks of the less fortunate because my dwelling is old? Then I think about my Jesus.

Others had their thoughts about Him. He was called a winebibber and a devil.
By some He was not considered very intelligent because He was a carpenter's son.
He lowered Himself to mingle with sinners. He wept unashamedly over the death
of a friend. He gave Himself into the hands of unrestrained men to be treated like
a beast. He died like a criminal, disgraced and rejected.

My heart cries. I am moved. "Jesus, you were rich; you owned the universe.
You were intelligent; your wisdom exceeded that of the doctors and lawyers and
anyone else on earth. You were perfect; you did not deserve to have your flesh
pierced so that your blood flowed.

"But you were willing because this was the Father's will for you. You allowed others to think what they would about you. You were willing to be thought of as poor,
dependent, and unintelligent. You were satisfied. Why shouldn't I be?"

For in Jesus Christ neither circumcision availeth any thing,
nor uncircumcision; but faith which worketh by love.

—Galatians 5:6

Is the faith you claim to have doing something for you? Is it transforming your life? Today's text shows us that unless a life is motivated by faith and love, the works that come forth are dead, producing nothing of eternal value.

A fruit tree that is planted and nourished in proper soil conditions will bring forth nutritious, valuable fruit. Similarly, faith that is grounded in a love for God will bring forth beneficial fruit: a Scriptural walk of life.

Jesus condemned the hypocrites who thought they were doing great works by casting out devils and prophesying in His name, because these things did not come from a love-based faith. In contrast, He commended little acts of kindness. God is love, and a faith based on His love will act like Him. A faith that works by love does not act out of desire for fame or applause; rather, it recognizes the moving of Him who said, "I will guide thee with mine eye" (Psalm 32:8).

He that dwelleth in the secret place of the most High
shall abide under the shadow of the Almighty.

—Psalm 91:1

Standing on a cliff overlooking the Pacific Ocean, I watched the antics of a sea otter with fascination. Waves came crashing toward the rocks along the shore, but the otter played on in the churning water. From my perspective, the waves looked dangerous. I was afraid they would dash the otter onto the rocks. Then I noticed something unique. Whenever a wave came near him, he quickly disappeared under the water. After the wave had passed, he would resurface and continue his antics.

Later I learned that it is possible to swim underneath a wave, allowing it to pass over you. I was intrigued that the sea otter could either see the wave or feel its pressure in time to dive underneath the surface, deep enough to allow the wave to pass over.

As we sail on the sea of life, we face times when the waves become boisterous and stormy. We see waves coming. We feel pressures and we see the rocks just ahead. Unless we find hope, we could perish.

"Abide under the shadow of the Almighty . . .
Keep me as the apple of the eye, hide me under the shadow of thy wings . . .
Therefore the children of men put their trust under the shadow of thy wings . . .
He shall cover thee with his feathers, and under his wings shalt thou trust . . .
Under his shadow we shall live . . ."

These phrases from Scripture remind us of a truth: we have a refuge in God. We do not need to feel perturbed when we feel the pressures of life. We can escape their powers by hiding under the shadow of His wings. There we will not be overwhelmed nor crushed in discouragement. And when the pressures have passed over, we will be able to resume life joyfully. ✸

June 11

If I do not the works of my Father, believe me not. But if I do, though ye believe not me, believe the works: that ye may know, and believe, that the Father is in me, and I in him.
—John 10:37-38

I am skeptical when an eight-year-old tells me he caught a sixteen-inch fish. Even when he goes into graphic detail about the catch, I remain skeptical. Only when he produces the fish do I believe. The little boy's words have meaning because he can produce evidence—and who can deny evidence?

Jesus challenged the people of His day that if they could not believe because of what He said, they should believe because of His actions. Even the hardhearted Jews could not resist evidence. Nicodemus pointed that out when he said, "We know that thou art a teacher come from God: for no man can do these miracles that thou doest, except God be with him" (John 3:2). Jesus' life stood the test of observation. He could open His life to scrutiny because of His surrendered will—His total obedience to the Spirit. This produced a beautiful, unruffled consistency. Do you remember that when they were seeking a reason to crucify Him, they resorted to false witnesses to accuse Him? This was a glaring reminder of His innocence—that He was not a liar or a pretender, and that His walk measured up to His words.

Whatever you claim to believe in must be backed by convincing actions. Do you say you believe God loves you? If so, your actions must exhibit the security of knowing you are loved. Do you say you are grateful? If so, your speech should have no hint of whining. Do you say that being single is a heavenly calling? If so, people will only be convinced if you live joyfully. Do you say that you respect your husband? If so, you should never complain about his faults to others. You will show that you are not a hypocrite if your walk measures up to your talk.

I commend unto you Phebe our sister . . . that ye assist
her in whatsoever business she hath need of you.
—Romans 16:1-2

Phebe is mentioned very briefly in Paul's letter to the Romans. Much more could have been written about her service to the church at Cenchrea. As a succorer, what was her mission? Literally, *succorer* means "one who stands by in case of need." She must have been an alert sister in the church to notice the needs of the poor, the widow, the lonely, the tired, and the discouraged.

Whatever it was that she took notice of, her compassion also included Paul. By letting our imagination expand, we see Phebe caring for the sick, preparing meals or carrying messages for Paul, and writing letters to those who needed encouragement. She may have done the market shopping for the elderly and the crippled, or helped a busy mother keep her house in order. Wherever she went, she stayed busy.

Notice that Paul admonishes the brethren to assist Phebe in her good works. She needed the help of others. Perhaps there were needs that she knew about but was unable to meet by herself. Paul trusted her judgment in knowing which needs were important.

We need more Phebes in our churches and communities. Even one woman can do a lot for God's people. If you feel called to follow her example, you may encounter opportunities that you cannot fill alone. You may be able to encourage a more capable person to do it. You cannot pay a huge hospital bill for a friend, but you can send a small amount and tell others about the need. When you remember a lonely grandfather, you can send him a card and put his name on the bulletin board at church so that others can send him one too. You may hear that the teacher and her students have the winter blues at school; do something on a Friday afternoon for them that helps them think about something cheerful. Pass out scrapbook sheets for someone who is hurt. The list could go on and on.

Remember, though, that not all deeds of encouragement are seen by others. Little things done behind the scenes sometimes mean more than the noticeable ones. You can bless your church by being another Phebe. ✳

June 13

Beloved, let us love one another: for love is of God; and everyone that loveth is born of God, and knoweth God.

—1 John 4:7

No matter how young or old, everyone craves love. When God fills us with His love through family, friends, or communion with Himself, that love can overflow to others. Love-starved people are everywhere. In my job as a childcare worker, I encounter numerous opportunities to feed emotionally hungry young people.

My experience with five-year-old David illustrated that a child without love will become bitter, hostile, and withdrawn. He constantly caused trouble in his class by destroying other children's papers, hitting, and disobeying his teacher. One day as he was sitting on his chair for punishment, another teacher noticed him. She lived near David's house and knew about his home situation. She told us that his parents acted as if they didn't like him, but they adored his older brother. David was often left to roam the streets, wearing shabby clothes. Once aware of the problem, we made a special effort to love David. In a few weeks he was completely different, exhibiting a desire to obey his teacher and be kind to others.

Love can change anyone. God is love, and He wants all His children to experience His love. As the saying goes, "Love in your heart wasn't put there to stay—love isn't love 'til you give it away." Pour it out for Jesus!

> There they made him a supper; and Martha served.
>
> —John 12:2

Because Jesus rebuked Martha for being cumbered with much serving, we often tend to criticize her. Mary is set up as the ideal, sitting at Jesus' feet. Jesus praised Mary for listening to Him, saying that she had chosen the most necessary activity. But Jesus loved Martha as well. His reason for rebuking her was that she had begun to fret.

If all the women had spent all their time sitting at the feet of Jesus, who would have provided for His physical needs? Jesus was not condemning Martha's role. Yet He did not want her to complain. He wanted her to realize that if she spent time at His feet, she would then be prepared to face her duties with calmness.

Jesus had nowhere to call home, no place to lay His head. So we must conclude that when He came to Bethany and was welcomed into this house, He appreciated Martha's efforts. Surely He enjoyed being in a clean home and eating hot food. It took effort on someone's part, and Jesus was not ungrateful. The hospitality of this home made people feel welcome.

All of us should strive to improve our homemaking and hospitality skills. I know of two single women who are especially talented in these areas. Becky and her sister do not have the responsibility of caring for husbands and raising families, yet they are busy with household duties. They dress chickens and churn butter to sell. Every week they make cheese, bake bread and pies, and make coleslaw and potato salad. They raise vegetables and sell buttermilk.

We need women in the church with the ability to manage—women who can plan menus and think ahead. During weddings, fellowship meetings, and ministers' meetings, much help is needed and appreciated. As with anything else, though, the Lord does not want us to fret about our duties. By approaching our work with prayer and thanksgiving, God's peace will keep our minds calm in the midst of duty. ✳

June 15

Be ye followers of me, even as I also am of Christ.
—1 Corinthians 11:1

When you draw lines to complete a dot-to-dot picture, you will likely not have straight lines between the dots unless you use a ruler. And likely, if your lines are not straight, the picture will not end up looking accurate.

Our lives can be likened to a dot-to-dot picture. The journey of following Christ moves along the path between the dots. The dots are our fellow Christians. When we have come to the end of our lives, the picture that we made will be evident. The ruler is Jesus. When we follow Him in everything we do, our lives will create a beautiful picture that makes sense at the end.

We can choose to focus on the example of others and follow in their paths, but above all, we must follow Christ as our guide. Only as other lives align with His are they safe to follow.

It may be that someone is using your life as a "dot" on her way to the goal. If that is the case, as is likely, it becomes doubly important that your life is patterned after Christ's. It is important that you have an attitude of trust instead of fear. It is important to pattern your life after Christ's in humility and obedience.

When you have a ready testimony and speak freely about Him, you will point others in the right direction, helping them to become beautiful pictures of God's grace. You should never leave the impression that it is safe to follow only your own example. You are only safe to follow as you follow Christ.

For who hath despised the day of small things?

—Zechariah 4:10

Our God delights in using the small, simple, and humble things to do His work. When His Son was born in Bethlehem, a stable became a royal palace for the King, and a lowly manger became a lordly crib. Mary, a humble virgin little known before this great event, became the mother of the Saviour, and Joseph, the carpenter, became His earthly father. When God was looking for someone to be of service to Him, He saw whose hearts and lives were devoted to Him and could be used.

It was the shepherds on the hillside who received the tidings of great joy when the Saviour was born. They found the babe wrapped in swaddling clothes, not in fine linen. It was a quiet star that guided the wise men to the town of Bethlehem and shone above the place where Jesus was. It took the little town of Nazareth to fulfill the prophecy of our Saviour, who was called a Nazarene.

When Jesus began His ministry, He chose a few fishermen as His disciples. The humble home of Lazarus, Mary, and Martha granted him rest and refreshment. It was only a boat that served as a pulpit one day as Jesus was preaching. The five loaves and two fishes of a little boy were all that was needed to feed a multitude. Common water turned to wine at Jesus' word. The mud beside the path became useful to Jesus when He needed miracle-working plaster to restore sight to the blind man.

Today God can take your succinct words of kindness and your seemingly inconsequential deeds done in love and make them great for His kingdom's sake. God does not need our ability to do His work, only our willingness to be of service to Him. He can take the common, small things of life and use them to bring honor and glory to Himself.

One talent have I to take to the sky,
While others are blessed with ten of the best.
Why should I complain, my duty refrain?
No never, no never, not I!

—Author Unknown

June 17

The Lord thy God in the midst of thee is mighty; he will save, he will rejoice
over thee with joy; he will rest in his love, he will joy over thee with singing.
—Zephaniah 3:17

When trials or pressing duties come our way, we can remain calm and trust in the Lord. Why? Because the One who is in us is mighty. He will strengthen our hands to complete the task given to us. Claiming His promises, we will not become fearful or discouraged even though things do not go as we had planned. We can learn to trust that God, who knows all things, will send us exactly what we need to grow closer to Him. He will never leave us or forsake us, but He will bring us through victorious. Then as we rejoice in what God has done for us, we will know that God is also rejoicing with us.

> For every man shall bear his own burden.
>
> —Galatians 6:5

I was a typical teenager, always dreaming. Someday when I would be married and have a home of my own, I would use all my ideas to decorate, design, and arrange. The future looked promising. I could already see the lace tablecloth on my dining room table. I would have some huge rocks in my front lawn. Ferns everywhere . . . I had an imagination.

I stayed single and kept getting older. When I left home, I lived in an apartment by myself, and then later a friend and I bought a mobile home. I decided I could enjoy at least some of my dreams. I went to town and bought the tablecloth I liked. We planned where we wanted our flowers. We planted and watered and had our own little garden. I really liked weeping willow trees and was elated to find one at a local greenhouse.

And so I kept following my dreams and pursuing my goals. In the same way, you don't have to wait until that husband of yours comes along to start creating a beautiful environment or to pursue a goal. Invite your friends and have that candlelight pizza supper you dream of having. Take time now to do the projects you've always thought of doing someday.

God has given you ideas, and He wants you to develop your talents. If you do not see Him closing a door, take the opportunity to walk through the door and experience something new. If you enjoy a special kind of lighting in your home, arrange it now. Make your home a cozy place. You love to climb mountains and go on nature walks? Take a friend and go.

Your development as a woman is important to God. Ask Him to help you stay balanced as you pursue your dreams, so that you do not become a selfish person. But do keep your dreams alive; they help you stay young! You will be surprised at what lies just around the corner. The burden of waiting for your dreams to come true can disappear if you work on making parts of your dream happen today instead of dwelling on the burden. ✳

Behold, we count them happy which endure. Ye have heard of the patience of Job, and have seen the end of the Lord; that the Lord is very pitiful, and of tender mercy.
—James 5:11

A hard, dry clump of fibers. It looks like a piece of dirt that might as well be crushed with the foot and forgotten. But wait a minute—it is something more than that. It is a chrysalis from which will emerge a beautiful butterfly. It is not lovely now, but this is one of the stages it must go through on its way to becoming a creature of splendor. However, it will take some time. If it would be crushed, God's perfect plan would be spoiled. So it must not be disdained but respected and protected with great care.

The chrysalis is also a thing of value because of what it teaches. It teaches me that sometimes the Lord wants me to *be* rather than to *do*. Only when I am still can He get my attention. This does not mean that I should spend my life in inactivity. Just as God knows when the time is right for the caterpillar to enter the chrysalis stage, so He knows when the time is right for me to enter such a stage. I may go through low times of sickness or injury. Sometimes everything may seem to go wrong. Even spiritually, I may seem to be at a standstill and not hear any answers. But in those times, instead of allowing myself to be crushed and pulled apart, I need to trust God to work out His plan. A thing of splendor will emerge.

Consider people who went through dormant stages in their lives, and notice the results of the dormancy. Joseph's imprisonment in a foreign land resulted in his family being saved from famine. When Moses was shepherding in the lonely wilderness, God was preparing him to shepherd the flock of God to the Promised Land. Paul's time in Arabia was a time to contemplate and commune with God in preparation for his world-changing ministry. Our Saviour suffered a time of dormancy as well—and His crucifixion was not the final word. He rose again and proved that He is victor over death.

Take courage when you are going through something that you need to endure. God's heart is compassionate toward you, and He will enable you to rest in Him during your time of darkness.

Say not, I will do so to him as he hath done to me:
I will render to the man according to his work.

—Proverbs 24:29

Do you ever find it a challenge to forgive someone? Maybe the person said something that cut you to the heart, or she may have thoughtlessly taken advantage of you. Maybe it was even done out of spite.

Forgiveness is the sweetest balm for wounds. It is a healing oil both to the forgiven and the forgiver. It is a higher law than the Old Testament standard of justice, which was "an eye for an eye and a tooth for a tooth." Forgiveness is noble and divine; it means pardon without penalty. It outweighs judgment, yet it never sacrifices truth and right.

Put yourself in the shoes of the servant in Matthew 18. He owed lots of money but was forgiven. After that he went out and harshly demanded a small amount of money from someone who owed him. Obviously, his course of action was unjust. The lesson is clear: if Jesus has forgiven us so much, why should we have a problem forgiving others?

Yet forgiveness is not easy. True forgiveness is impossible without love. Asking God for His power is essential if we want to forgive.

Allowing resentment to fester is easy, but when we do that, we harm no one as much as ourselves. When wew hold a grudge toward someone else, we display a lack of gratitude to God for His forgiveness toward us, and God will not look on that lightly.

Can we love, bless, and pray for those who mistreat us? Is it possible to attain to this standard of Jesus? Yes, by the grace of God we can forgive others, because God has forgiven us—and His power is available to us.

June 21

The harvest is past, the summer is ended, and we are not saved.
—Jeremiah 8:20

Summertime—a time of peace, relaxation, and contentment. Summertime means growth for your plants. The intervals of sunshine and rain keep the grass lush and green. Trees benefit from the thunderstorms and wind as they set their roots deeper into the ground. Leaves provide shade from the heat. Summertime is a time of consistency. The spring blossoms lasted only a short time, but soon the more lasting flowers take their place in bloom. Summer . . . a time you can comfortably do what you planned to do without interference from cold, snow, and sleet.

Is it summertime in your heart? Enjoy the showers of blessings God sends your way (Ezekiel 34:26-27). Rejoice for the gladness in your heart (Psalm 4:7). Rest in the peace the Lord has given you (Psalm 4:8). Give God the glory if your life is bringing forth fruit (Matthew 7:17).

And then "remember Lot's wife." God delivered her and her family from death in Sodom, but she failed to continue in His commands. Her life was saved, but only temporarily. We, too, can easily become complacent while we enjoy summertime in our lives. "And no marvel; for Satan himself is transformed into an angel of light" (2 Corinthians 11:14). Guard your soul lest "summer is ended and [you] are not saved." ✳

....

....

....

....

I do set my bow in the cloud, and it shall be for a
token of a covenant between me and the earth.

—Genesis 9:13

God created the rainbow about 1,650 years after the Creation. This new feature was a token of God's covenant with man for all generations throughout time, reaching even us today. God said that He will look upon the rainbow and remember His everlasting covenant.

As we observe a rainbow and stand in awe at its beauty, do we consider His promise and what it means to us? Do we think of the fact that God is also looking upon it?

A rainbow is a free display from God and beautifully typifies His promise to us. I have never seen an upside-down rainbow or one with square corners or mixed-up colors. The consistency of the rainbow shows that we can count on God's promises. They are unchanging.

When do we see rainbows? God sends them in times of storm, when there are dark clouds and rain, when the sun peeks through. Similarly, it is in times of difficulty that God's promises softly steal over the soul, shining like a rainbow in the midst of the storm.

I stand in awe as I observe a rainbow, its soft colors blending and adorning the sky. It seems to calm my soul and bring me to a place of reverence before God. It is here to send me a message of hope and joy before it fades and is gone.

Are you passing through a time of testing? Find your own rainbow—a promise from God in His Word. Take courage; He cares for you!

....

....

....

....

June 23

For the Lord God is a sun and shield: the Lord will give grace and glory:
no good thing will he withhold from them that walk uprightly.

—Psalm 84:11

A thunderstorm with its blinding flashes of lightning and loud crashes of thunder can cause fear. Our minds did not fashion it, and we cannot control it. During the storm we do not see its benefits; we can only seek shelter and wait, hoping the storm will not cause much damage. Finally it dies away, the sun bursts through the clouds, and our eyes behold a splendor more glorious than before. Now bright and green, the grass is turned into a carpet of glistening jewels. The air is fresh and invigorating. Bird songs, silenced by the storm, seem to be clearer and more beautiful than before. The farmer rejoices because the thunderstorm has released nitrogen into the air and the rain has conveyed it to his crops, giving them a much-needed boost.

A thunderstorm is not the only kind of storm that looks beneficial in hindsight. Sometimes I experience a storm of circumstance that God uses to cleanse and refresh me. I can sense it coming but can do nothing to stop it. Troubles and uncertainties crash louder than thunder. The agony of my soul is as sharp as the flashing lightning. I can only seek shelter and wait until the onslaught has ceased. Finally I can see the benefits of the storm. Its threats and booms caused me to seek shelter in the grace of God. He is a perfect shelter, and the storm helps me to see that I must depend wholly on Him. Just as being partly exposed in a thunderstorm is dangerous, I take a great risk in life if I do not gather all of myself under the grace of God. He wants to carry me through my entire life. The storm has shaken loose the thoughts of self-sufficiency. God's promises become sparkling jewels, and songs of praise become meaningful. Such splendor I see!

Ask, and it shall be given you; seek, and ye shall find; knock, and it shall
be opened unto you: For everyone that asketh receiveth; and he that
seeketh findeth; and to him that knocketh it shall be opened.

—Matthew 7:7-8

A traveler decided to visit the Big Sur area south of San Francisco along the Pacific Coast. The area was a photographer's delight. To prepare for his travels, he studied magazine articles, researched at the library, and contacted the area Chamber of Commerce—all for more information about the place he wanted to tour. In his search he found a paragraph describing an eleven-mile drive on the bluffs above the ocean. The drive was described as an incredible side trip.

After his arrival in California, he could find no additional information about this eleven-mile drive. He did find the road, however, and decided to travel it. The sights along the way were even better than he had expected. Best of all, near the end of the drive he came to a view he had not realized he would ever have the opportunity to capture with his camera. He had seen a picture of Bixby Bridge before, but he thought it was only possible to view it from an aerial position. He was delighted as he positioned his camera.

When I thought of this account, I began comparing it to the hidden treasures in the Word of God. God is incomprehensible to the natural mind, but through the Spirit we can understand the deep things of God. The challenge was there for me. Had the traveler not taken time and effort to search out the little he knew, he would have missed the chance of a lifetime to photograph Bixby Bridge from that point. He would have missed seeing the ocean from the heights. He would not have seen the redwoods and the ferns in the peaceful canyons.

I had to ask myself if I make the effort to study and search out Scriptures I know little about. Do I want to know more? Do I take time to commune with God? I know that God works through my mind. If I always rush from one thing to another in my busy schedule, how can God reveal truths that I need to know?

Taking the time to pray, to think about God's Word, and to evaluate what is happening in your heart will allow you to reach new depths of relationship with God. Your mind will be reinforced with truth, and you may see new angles of truth that you never realized before. But remember that God will not force this relationship on you. He wants you to ask, seek, and knock. Think about what you might miss if you do not have a hunger and thirst for more righteousness, and let that thought inspire you to seek. ✻

The night cometh, when no man can work.

—John 9:4

Somehow the day has slipped away, and I did not accomplish much. As the afternoon shadows lengthen into evening, I realize that I need to make this day count while I still can. Gone is the opportunity to work with early-morning vigor. With a sinking feeling, I realize that some tasks will not get done at all or not in the way I desired.

This reminds me that life's day is slipping away. If I do not make use of its opportunities now, I will see my day lengthen into an eternity with regrets. What opportunities do I have? I have opportunities for relationship and for service, things that will help other people want to know God more. I have daily opportunities to move at the Spirit's bidding. Sometimes I realize with a sinking feeling that the opportunity was here, but I was looking out for myself or chasing after some fleeting fancy. I will never get a wasted day back, but I do have today. And even this moment holds golden opportunities.

June 26

She openeth her mouth with wisdom; and in her tongue is the law of kindness.
—Proverbs 31:26

What draws us to a friend? Is it her looks, her height, her money, or her talents? The Bible says, "The desire of a man is his kindness" (Proverbs 19:22). We want to see kindness—the true expression of love—in our friends.

Dorcas's life has challenged me. The Bible says she abounded in good deeds and acts of charity, and she was known for her seamstress skills. Her life and death were a well-known testimony for God. After she was gone, she was sadly missed because of her thoughtfulness to the poor and lonely.

We know very little of Phebe, whose name means "radiant." Her short description in the Bible reads, "She hath been a succourer of many" (Romans 16:2). As a servant of the church, she looked out for others. She was not some great heroine, but she lived her life to the glory of God and in service to others.

We should not be out to make a name for ourselves or to gain personal merit or favor. Love in our hearts should motivate our deeds. We have ample opportunities to show kindness to others in simple things that we do not even think about, such as a tender look, a smile, or an encouraging word. It is a privilege to aid others and relieve their needs. Let us faithfully give assistance where we can, remembering that "inasmuch as ye have done it unto one of the least of these my brethren, ye have done it unto me" (Matthew 25:40).

....

....

....

....

They that sow in tears shall reap in joy. He that goeth forth and weepeth, bearing precious seed, shall doubtless come again with rejoicing, bringing his sheaves with him.

—Psalm 126:5-6

Meditations of One Leaving the Mission Field

My two and a half years in a children's home in Honduras have proven to be a real blessing to me. It has been a challenge to teach and train the little children in the nurture and admonition of the Lord, answer their questions (sometimes difficult ones), and give them the love and security that their blood parents should give them. We need wisdom to understand the deep feelings of rejection they experience from their own mothers.

Patience is a much-needed virtue here. So often when we go to town for something, we hear, "Tomorrow we will have it," or, "Tomorrow it will be ready." But we go the next day, and again they say, "Tomorrow." These experiences, combined with the patience needed to work with children, certainly should have made me a more longsuffering person!

A new worker, Martha, has come to care for the children I have had in my care—Daniel, nearly three years old, Dorcas, nearly two years old, and one-year-old Alan. I carried Alan out of the hospital the day after he was born and have cared for him ever since. Leaving these children after caring for them so long tears at my heart.

A sideline responsibility for me has been to take care of the small clothing store. It has been interesting to sort through clothes, mend them, and sew suspenders to keep in stock. It is special to see the joy Hondurans receive when they go home with a warm blanket or a much-needed dress. One six-year-old school boy was so happy when his teacher bought him a pair of suspenders. He put them on as he was leaving. Giving of my time to bless others has blessed me tremendously.

I hope that those back home think often of the missionaries they know. I pray that they will take time to encourage their missionary friends not only when they live away from home, but also during the adjustments of moving back. I know I will need much encouragement to make the transition.

June 28

But when his disciples saw it, they had indignation,
saying, To what purpose is this waste?
—Matthew 26:8

Mary came to Jesus and poured her expensive ointment on His head while He was eating. What indignation the disciples felt! Such a waste! They felt the money could have been used to feed the poor.

Did Jesus think it was a waste? No, He knew she was the only one who would anoint Him for His burial. Later other women came to the tomb to anoint Jesus' body, but they were too late . . . too late to "waste" themselves on Jesus.

When a china plate is broken, we sweep up the pieces and throw them away; the plate is worthless. But we are different—we become useful to God only after self is broken.

Surrendering our lives to the Lord is not always an easy choice. It could mean feeling rejection from our loved ones or giving up what the world calls a successful job to serve the Lord.

Our culture does not consider higher education the norm as mainstream culture does. This is because we value practical skills that can often be learned at home or from apprenticing with skilled craftsmen. The world may look on and say, "What a waste! Your youth have talent that could be further developed by more training." But Jesus does not consider it a waste for youth to learn skills that will in later years profit their families. Parents can give their teenagers a wealth of knowledge about the art of homemaking and reaching out to others with care and compassion.

The world may tell you your life is a waste. They may not understand why you spend so much time in church services and visiting other communities. They may not understand how you can willingly share your money to help pay others' hospital bills. But you only need to ask yourself, "Does Jesus consider what I am doing a waste?" If you do not serve Jesus now, you may soon be too late to "waste" yourself on Him. ✸

198

> Whose adorning let it not be that outward adorning . . .
> But let it be the hidden man of the heart.
> —1 Peter 3:3-4

Have you ever been tempted to do something to attract someone's attention or to gain approval? We need to be aware of our motives when we make decisions about our appearance. How we dress, comb our hair, and conduct ourselves all play an important part in our testimony to others. The temptation to gain approval by how we look is often present among women—possibly more so when we are young, but it is still felt as we get older. The opposite attitude is a meek and quiet spirit that does not seek to gain attention.

If you feel you lack a meek and quiet spirit, you may wonder how to cultivate that sort of attitude. One way is to spend time with older women who have gained this gift through experience and possibly difficult trials. Cultivate friendship with these precious souls who have much wisdom to impart. Their advice carries great value.

We can be neat and attractive without being gaudy and popular. When a woman chooses to wear a simple, modest dress, she allows her countenance to shine more clearly. The face and its expressions speak louder when we do not try to draw attention to our body and clothes. The inner you then shines!

Our bodies are not our own—we are bought with a price. Therefore we ought to glorify God in our bodies.

June 30

It is of the Lord's mercies that we are not consumed, because his compassions fail not. They are new every morning: great is thy faithfulness.

—Lamentations 3:22-23

Are you wanting something new and exciting for your life? We have probably all experienced times when the routine of our duties has become monotonous. Even then, let us never forget, with the dawn of each new day God again extends His love to us. Something new for every day of our lives is the mercy and compassion of our loving Father. We may fail, but God's faithfulness never fails. Our health may fail, our life's dreams may shatter, or other trials may cloud our pathway; but with God's love and mercy shining upon us, we have something bright to help us along even in the hard times.

My family went through an extremely difficult time when an accident claimed the lives of a sister-in-law and a niece, leaving a small nephew hurting and motherless. Early one morning soon after the funeral, two of my sisters and I were at our place of work. We were moving on with life, but we did not feel particularly joyous.

Mrs. Hall, our first customer, arrived. She came bouncing through the door, glancing from one of us to another before popping the question, "Well, what's new?"

My sister responded, "The mercies of God are new every morning." This reminder brought us out of our gloomy reverie, and afterward our conversation centered on pleasant things. We later thanked God for the opportunity we had to show this neighbor that the circumstances of life do not have to bog us down continually in gloomy despair.

May the love of God shine in your life today—it is something to be enthusiastic about. 🌀

....

....

....

> And he took of the stones of that place, and put them
> for his pillows, and lay down in that place to sleep.
> —Genesis 28:11

Stones for pillows? Hard stones with rough surfaces and sharp edges? Other people at home in their beds probably had softer, more comfortable pillows; but Jacob used what was available, and he slept in spite of the discomfort.

Stones for pillows? How can I rest on stones of disappointment, sorrow, loneliness, and affliction—stones whose sharp edges bring discomfort into my life? Sometimes when the night of strife and weariness descends upon me and I desire rest, I find nothing except these stones. Can I rest on these stones? I can, but only if I have a spiritual vision. I can rest on the stones of sorrow and disappointment, knowing that a sovereign God allows them as a means of refining. I can rest on the stone of loneliness because it helps me to reach out to God and others. I can rest on the stone of affliction because it helps me to feel the sufficiency of God's grace. I can rest on the stone of adversity because through it I learn the value of prayer.

Sharp edges and rough surfaces become smoother when I learn to use what God makes available to me. Jacob was assured of the presence of God as he rested on these stones. It was so real to him that he anointed his pillow-stone in worship to God. If I rest on the stones in my life instead of wishing for something more comfortable and soft, I will have a daily worship experience.

....

....

....

....

....

July 2

Esther carefully pulled the weeds from the soft soil around the carrots. Although working in the garden often gave her a tired back, it was also rewarding and relaxing.

This morning Esther had come out to the garden for that purpose. She felt she needed to rest beside the still waters. Although her hands were busy, her heart was with God. She thought about what a privilege it was to have the God of Jacob for a refuge and help.

Esther lived with her father, whose mind was failing. Because of this weakness, he had become very dependent on her. Esther often prayed for strength and wisdom to communicate with her father wisely and lovingly.

In the past months, Esther had once again seen the hand of God in her life. Although her human nature questioned just what God was doing, she knew He was guiding her step by step.

It all began when a widower asked for her friendship. Esther had mixed feelings and knew she could not make that decision alone. She cried with the psalmist, "Lead me, O Lord, in thy righteousness . . . make thy way straight before my face" (Psalm 5:8). She wanted nothing but the Lord's will for her life. Now that the desire for companionship had risen strongly within her, she submitted the desire to God whenever she thought about it. Night and day she had pleaded with God to show her the way.

"Sit still, my daughter, until thou know how the matter will fall," the Spirit had prompted her.

Deep within her, she longed to share her life with a good man, yet she felt the rising conviction that perhaps the Lord was saying no. The crucial moment had come when Esther shared her request with her father. He had tried to be understanding and willing to accept the potential changes in his life, but the future looked bleak and impossible to him without his daughter's help.

Esther had wept and poured out her heart to God, her greatest source of comfort, yielding and surrendering her life to His choice for her. She realized that God answers prayer through His Word and Spirit, through men of God, and through circumstances. As her fingers moved through the soil now, she believed that God was letting her know His will. All she needed to do was to accept His choice.

She did. Even though it meant giving up a potential relationship, Esther's heart was at peace as she remembered the words from Psalm 18:30—"As for God, his way is perfect." It had been a time of trial for her, but she knew that walking through this valley of shadow had brought her to higher ground in her walk with God. She arose to her feet determined to follow her Lord wholeheartedly.

July 3

The Lord thy God in the midst of thee is mighty; he will save, he will rejoice over thee with joy; he will rest in his love, he will joy over thee with singing.
—Zephaniah 3:17

God rejoices in the love He receives from you. He in turn expresses His joy in singing. He rejoices when you love Him with all your heart, soul, mind, and strength. God is jealous; He desires and deserves your total devotion.

God rejoices to wash away your sins that were red as crimson. He makes them as white as snow. He rejoices so much to hear you speaking with other saints that He has a book of remembrance written of what you speak about. He rejoices to open the windows of heaven and pour out blessings upon you, so much that you cannot receive them all.

Do you hear God singing over you? When you take time to be in His presence and think about His gifts to you, you will marvel as you hear the song unfold.

Proverbs 31:10-31

The Virtuous Single Woman

10. A virgin with virtuous character, who can find? She is worth far more than rubies.
11. Her parents have full confidence in her. She is a valuable asset to them.
12. She is a blessing to them all the days of her life.
13. She seeks a fulfilling job and works willingly with her hands.
14. She is as busy as merchants' ships, always seeking new ways to work more efficiently.
15. She gets up while it is still dark. She helps her mother provide food for the family and assists others with their duties.
16. She uses good judgment in investing her money. She carefully tends to her possessions.
17. She works vigorously; her arms are strong for her tasks.
18. She finds fulfillment in knowing that her work is well done. Her lamp burns late at night.
19. She is content as a woman, fulfilling God's plan with dignity.
20. Her sensitive spirit sees when others are hurting. She reaches out to them and gives them words of encouragement.
21. When problems arise, she has no fears, because she has an open relationship with her heavenly Father. She knows He will provide all her needs.
22. She wears neat and modest dresses; her beauty radiates from within.
23. Her companions are well respected. They, like her, are of noble character.
24. She makes favorable impressions and supplies her friends with valuable advice.

25. She is clothed with strength and dignity, free from anxiety and worry.

26. She speaks with wisdom and is a wise and loving counselor.

27. She is concerned for the welfare of others and does not eat the bread of idleness.

28. She will be called blessed. Joy radiates from her to others.

29. Many women do great things, but a noble character surpasses them all.

30. Charm is deceptive and beauty is fleeting, but a woman who fears the Lord will be praised.

31. In every aspect of life she will be highly esteemed. Her crown of splendor awaits her at the pearly gates.

....

....

....

....

....

....

....

....

....

....

....

....

....

....

July 5

Take therefore no thought for the morrow: for the
morrow shall take thought for the things of itself.
—Matthew 6:34

One time I was sharing with a friend my concern about a situation I was facing. I was afraid that real problems would develop from that situation. She merely smiled and said, "Just take one day at a time." What good advice! I quickly discovered that I could cope with the situation—today. What happened with the problems I felt could develop in the future? The Lord took care of the situation and the potential problems, and proved there was no need for me to worry.

All the challenges and responsibilities of life are much easier to handle one day at a time. After all, today is God's gift to us. He has not yet given us tomorrow, and if He does, He will see to it that it will be a good gift. So, let's thank the Lord for today and trust Him for tomorrow.

And the Lord appeared unto Abram, and said, Unto thy seed will I give this land.
—Genesis 12:7

Life has many perplexities. Unpleasant and dizzying surprises happen. Plans and hopes sometimes do not work out, no matter what effort we expend to bring them about. A calling from God is felt, but it seems nothing can be done to speed up the process of entering into that calling, and mundane life goes on.

Abraham experienced some of these things. God told Abraham that He would give the land of Canaan to his posterity—but Abraham had no children. On top of that, Canaan was inhabited by pagans. How would it come about that his seed would one day possess it?

Once he reached the land of Canaan, Abraham had no permanent dwelling place. He kept moving around. But he built an altar and worshipped the Lord.

He had to part from his nephew Lot and take second best because Lot selfishly chose the best for himself even after Abraham had cared for him as his own son. Again, after this unpleasant experience, God promised to give the land to his seed—but Abraham still had no children. What was his response to these situations? He built an altar and worshipped the Lord.

What enabled Abraham to worship God in spite of perplexities? Nothing but his faith. Every time God appeared to him with the promise concerning his descendants, he had no more visible evidence that the promise would be fulfilled than he did the time before. Yet he kept worshipping and God kept speaking to him. It was this connection that kept him faithful. Because he had the assurance that God's favor was upon him, he did not give up hope when his situation did not change. He went on believing in such a way that he could still worship in spite of not knowing how, when, or where God would fulfill His promise. ❧

> But godliness with contentment is great gain. For we brought
> nothing into this world, and it is certain we can carry nothing
> out. And having food and raiment let us be therewith content.
>
> —1 Timothy 6:6-8

Imagine David, the shepherd boy, sitting on a rock in the green pastures. His sheep are feeding on the grass nearby. Satisfaction envelops him as he gazes across the valley to the distant mountains. The cheerfulness in his heart bursts out in praise to his Creator through a song. With peace of mind he realizes that God has each detail of his life planned.

David was an example of contentment. He did his best wherever he went. His position changed from shepherd boy to armourbearer, and later he was anointed king over God's people. Whatever his position, he seemed content to fill it.

A contented person will not be upset when God changes his position. The opposite is also true. A discontented person finds many reasons to think he needs more, no matter how much he already has.

The Apostle Paul had learned that riches, poverty, fullness, or hunger did not determine his happiness. He had learned the secret of contentment. He was satisfied with whatever came his way.

You may face a change in your responsibilities, or you may struggle to feel content with your wages. You may have other circumstances that do not seem ideal at the moment, but in whatever situation you find yourself, remember Hebrews 13:5—"Be content with such things as ye have: for he hath said, I will never leave thee, nor forsake thee."

....

....

....

....

July 8

Give, and it shall be given you; good measure, pressed down, and shaken together, and running over, shall men give into your bosom. For with the same measure that ye mete withal it shall be measured to you again.
—Luke 6:38

Gifts of food and money. Transportation. Housecleaning. Visits. The list would get too long if I would mention all the kind deeds others have done for me. No list of words can adequately express my appreciation for these gifts of love. No words are rich enough to describe the beauty I see as these acts are performed. But I am not able to repay; I stand a pauper. What shall I do? What does God want me to do? Does He expect me to wear myself out trying to express my appreciation or trying to carefully keep a record so that I can return something for all the acts of charity? Or is it my pious duty to apologize profusely about my weakness and inability?

God's will for me is both simpler and harder than any of that. He wants me to live in His grace. I am thankful that He keeps a record and that it is always up to date, not missing the smallest deed as I could easily do. We may simply show appreciation and then leave the matter with Him. He does not need my help when He pours blessings on the doer.

If I would always be self-sufficient and independent, I might deprive someone of the blessing God wants to give her for her kindness. I would be blind and unfeeling to the touch of God through others. I could not learn from them. So why should I apologize for the way God made me?

I go forth trusting and praising Him for His wisdom in making me needy, His blessing in giving me friends, and His faithfulness in rewarding where I cannot.

> For I reckon that the sufferings of this present time are not worthy
> to be compared with the glory which shall be revealed in us.
> —Romans 8:18

This verse is so true, yet how hard it is to willingly suffer for Jesus' sake. When we get our eyes off Jesus, our troubles begin. Are we willing to bear the cross of Jesus? The cross is where my will and God's will meet. We must humbly bow our heads and say "Amen" to His will, whatever the cost may be. This submission brings courage to our souls, and we can move forward with renewed vigor and strength, looking to Jesus to keep filling us with Himself. Satan's discouragement is real, but we do not need to sink beneath that discouragement, for God is also real. He longs to be our constant companion and friend.

The Christian life is a continual battle. There is always new territory to conquer. We may have surrendered our all to the Lord, but certain areas of our lives seem to require a daily surrender. In total obedience to God's Word and in the strength of the Spirit, let us keep pressing on. Each victory will help us another to win.

When we are complete in Jesus, we have fullness of joy. We can then experience a peace that passes all understanding. When living in Jesus and doing His will, we find all our needs abundantly supplied. The world may consider our lives dull, but they do not know the true joy and lasting peace we experience as we find our completeness in Jesus. When we have faith that our future glory will outweigh our present struggles, we can accept the questions of life without needing to know the answers. Pray for a deeper faith in His completeness today.

....

....

....

....

Yet in his disease he sought not to the Lord, but to the physicians.
—2 Chronicles 16:12

As my friend was cleaning Mrs. Palmer's bookshelf, she came across a large volume entitled *When Everything Goes Wrong*. Curiously she opened the book, intending to scan through its contents. But instead of a book with helpful advice, it was a cleverly disguised box containing a bottle of wine and two goblets. The advertisement in the box guaranteed that this was quality wine from a long-established company. My friend put the box back on the shelf. It was not the Christian answer to "when everything goes wrong." But it left her with a question.

What do you do when everything seems to go wrong? Where do you turn when your world seems to cave in? What do you do when you have no answers to life's questions?

In verse 8 of 2 Chronicles 16, the seer reminded Asa of a time when he had encountered a host of men with many chariots and horses. Because he had relied on the Lord, he had won the battle.

Later in his reign, he no longer sought God when things went wrong. The disease in his feet became very serious, yet humans were his only source of consultation.

Man can never take God's place in your life. Any answer the world has for you when everything goes wrong will surely fail. Finding power within yourself or drowning your sorrows in addictions or entertainment will only produce negative results.

As God gives you trustworthy family and friends, share your frustrations with them and be encouraged. Keep in mind, however, that you will receive what you need most when you are down on your knees with God. Tell Him all about your situation, and then trust that He will help you.

God's quality of help is far superior to anything man will ever come up with. He has been in control before any long-established company.

Call unto me, and I will answer thee, and shew thee
great and mighty things, which thou knowest not.

—Jeremiah 33:3

Have you ever felt lonely? Have you felt you must speak to someone, but you were afraid everyone was too busy or would not understand? You are invited to call on God.

You might normally pray out of habit or because you are asked to pray, but have you ever allowed yourself to be thrilled with God's invitation to come and talk to Him, the Power that made all? He knows that you were not made to carry the heavy burdens you sometimes try to bear. He knows that you have no defense against the enemy and are likely to be defeated. So He invites you to bring all your burdens and battles to Him.

He is never too busy. Listening is part of His business, and He always understands. Sometimes you may be ashamed to tell others about the battles in your mind, but God sees all the arrows that the wicked one shoots at you, so there is no need to feel ashamed to tell Him. Just as sure as His invitation, so sure is His answer. Jesus Himself was tempted in all points like as we are, and He was not reluctant to call on His Father for help.

It is a blessed feeling to have turmoil and agony of spirit replaced by the peace of God.

I will both lay me down in peace, and sleep:
for thou, Lord, only makest me dwell in safety.
—Psalm 4:8

This verse speaks of complete trust in an almighty, sovereign God. We could worry about many things, and we have a natural tendency to do so. When I moved to the southern states, I was sure I was moving to a land of poisonous snakes and spiders. Sometimes we worry about unexpected and unfortunate events, such as the accident that happened to my brother, in which all the fingers were severed from his right hand.

Possibilities of what could happen are many, but why worry? Faith in God will see us through. In the two years I have lived in the South, I haven't seen even one poisonous snake or spider. As for my brother, he worked through the trauma of his accident and adjusted well, now leading a normal life. What a blessing to rest assured that absolutely nothing will transpire in our lives outside of God's knowledge and overruling power.

When I was an upper-grade teacher, I taught a series of safety classes one term. The aim was to become safety conscious and be aware of possible hazards that we might face. But we did not focus only on preventing anything that could happen to us. I emphasized that after we have done our part in taking proper precautions, the rest is in the hands of God.

How thankful I am that I have One in whom I can with all confidence entrust my very life. I can always claim my Father's divine presence and protection as I remain in His will.

"The angel of the Lord encampeth round about them that fear him, and delivereth them" (Psalm 34:7).

....

....

July 13

Sing, O barren, thou that didst not bear; break forth into singing, and cry
aloud, thou that didst not travail with child: for more are the children of
the desolate than the children of the married wife, saith the Lord.

—Isaiah 54:1

Because I love children dearly but have not had any of my own, I find this
verse comforting. Sometimes I struggle to accept my state as a single woman,
but then I read this verse and I can rejoice again! I can have children too, and
the Lord says I can have many more than married people can. Usually school
has not progressed far into a new term until I am talking about "my" children.
I have students, siblings, nieces and nephews, other children in the church and
community, and youth group girls who need love. In a sense it is different, but as
a mother is needed by her children, so I feel needed by those around me.

Let's rise to the challenge, friends. There is no time to waste in thinking about
ourselves. There is much work to do and the laborers are few. Many people long for
comfort and encouragement. They need help and advice in trying situations. As we
rely on God and live with a song on our lips, He can enable us to help others!

215

Why seek ye the living among the dead?
—Luke 24:5

Just why would we expect to find someone who is alive among the dead? Who could enjoy living in a graveyard? We read of a man who had his dwelling among the tombs, but he had an unclean spirit and a depraved mind. The Romans had a fear of the dead and did not like to enter the catacombs where the persecuted Christians gathered for worship services. So we conclude that it is not normal for the living to be among the dead.

For the Christian, it is not normal or possible to live in victory among the dead things of the world. I cannot expect to go home from church encouraged and inspired if my attention has drifted from the Word being preached. Neither can I expect the blessings that come through fellowship if I selfishly slink back and put forth no effort to meet others. I cannot expect victory over my bad attitude toward someone if I constantly look for and bring up the faults in her life. I will not hunger and thirst for the Word if I do not spend enough time in it to whet my appetite. Victory over wrong desires will elude me if I don't surrender my desires to Christ. I will not gain victory if I do not spend enough time in prayer.

As long as I desire victory but am unwilling to deny myself, I am seeking for the living among the dead. I will not find it there. I will find victory only in a life that has resurrected with Christ.

> ... that there be no complaining in our streets. Happy is that people, that is in such a case: yea, happy is that people, whose God is the Lord.
>
> —Psalm 144:14-15

Are you one of the happy people or are you a person who complains? God's Word has much to say about the common sin of ungratefulness.

The children of Israel complained when they were thirsty and there was no water. They murmured against Moses when the water was bitter and undrinkable. They complained because they grew tired of manna to eat. There were those God punished with death because of this.

I have to ponder how I would have responded. More important, I need to think about how I respond to my present unpleasant situations. As I consider how God so bountifully blesses and cares for me, I know why ingratitude displeases Him.

In Matthew 20 we see employees murmuring against their employer. They thought they were unfairly paid. Do we sometimes think that life is unfair? If we see someone with more of something than we have, can we rejoice or are we covetous? Maybe we think the past was better, and we forget to count the blessings of today.

The queen of Sheba's testimony of King Solomon's kingdom was, "Happy are thy men, happy are these thy servants, which stand continually before thee" (1 Kings 10:8). Is this the testimony of those who observe our walk of life? Can they see our faith in God and a calm, quiet happiness? The queen of Sheba also said to Solomon, "Blessed be the Lord thy God, which delighted in thee" (1 Kings 10:9). We must express contentment and gratitude so people can say the same of us and our God.

July 16

Wherefore I put thee in remembrance that thou stir up the gift of God . . .
—2 Timothy 1:6

God has given to each of us certain characteristics, abilities, and talents. We may not always be aware of all our talents. The important thing is that we use our abilities to the glory of God and in service to Him.

We may be tempted to envy someone else's talents. "I wish I could organize events like Ellen . . . If only I could think of attractive dishes to bring to carry-ins like Amanda does." But we must be content with how God made us; He wants us to fill the little spot He gave to us. How ungrateful it would be for us to say to God, "Why have you made me this way?"

God made each of us and gave us our individual talents. Therefore we have no reason to feel we are better than another person.

Talents are a blessing, but we need to relate rightly to them, lest we end up in either of two ditches! We could feel like the individual who was given a single talent and went and hid it. He may have felt he did not have anything worth much anyway, so he didn't put forth effort to gain and serve where he could. Those in the opposite ditch feel quite important, maybe even indispensable. From this point of view we will be inclined to look down on others who may not be as talented as we are. We need to realize that we all have gifts that are distributed by God. We are responsible to God for what He entrusts to us. We may have latent gifts that need to be stirred up and used for someone's benefit, to the glory of God.

Your spiritual gifts can and should be used in practical ways to serve others. Whether God gave you the talent of sewing, writing, art, music, or anything else, you can edify the body of Christ with that gift. 🖙

I beseech thee for my son Onesimus, whom I have begotten in my bonds.
—**Philemon 10**

To Titus, mine own son after the common faith . . . —**Titus 1:4**

Unto Timothy, my own son in the faith . . . —**1 Timothy 1:2**

Paul was unmarried, yet he claimed three men as his sons because of their mutual faith. Jesus had no children, but He influenced more people than anyone else ever did or ever will. His presence left such an unmistakable mark that even hardened judges noticed His character in His followers. These disciples, in turn, influenced others to be more like Christ. Down through the ages, this influence has been passed on until it has reached me.

Patience and cheerfulness in affliction. Interest in others. Unselfishness. Compassion. These virtues have developed in my life because of the powerful influence of others, even though I am not their child.

While parents have a tremendous influence on their children, character and faith are not passed on only through bloodlines. Single people have opportunities to influence many people. It does not take many words to make an impression. Just being in someone's presence can leave an influence, whether positive or negative. Whatever kind of influence you leave will be passed on. Even if you influence only one person a day, you are still making an impact on that person and on the world.

To leave an edifying and consistent influence, I must stay in the presence of Him whose character is holy and unchanging. I am a daughter of the King, and the more time I spend in His presence, the more I will be influenced by Him and act as a daughter of His should.

....

....

....

....

Then said Jesus unto his disciples, If any man will come after me,
let him deny himself, and take up his cross, and follow me.
—Matthew 16:24

Jesus set a perfect example for us in living a life of self-denial. He was rich but became poor so that we, through His poverty, could become rich (2 Corinthians 8:9). Because He loved us, He put our need ahead of His own. "Even Christ pleased not himself" (Romans 15:3).

Other Bible characters also illustrated the virtue of self-denial. Moses was willing to give up his position of fame, honor, and riches in Pharaoh's court for the sake of his people. He had eternal values in focus.

The widow who gave her last two mites to the Lord challenges us. It is easier to share with others out of abundance, but self-denial comes into focus when we give what costs us greatly.

Queen Esther was also willing to deny herself for her people—even to the extent of her life. She was more concerned for others than for herself.

Self-denial is the opposite of selfishness. It brings happiness, rest, and peace, while enthroning self brings pessimism, restlessness, and turmoil. To deny means to disown. Can we disown our selfish desires, disregard our begging self, and refuse to give in to our own whims?

If our self-life is dead, we will not nurse hurts when we are mistreated. If self is dead, evil will be overcome with good, no matter what is said or done to us. We will not rise up in retaliation or bitterness.

Self-denial includes more than giving up our wishes, rights, and pleasures for the sake of others. It also includes giving up our way, our dreams, and our goals in loving submission to God and His will for us.

Self-denial is choosing the narrow way that leads to unfathomable riches and glory.

Ye were ensamples to all that believe.
—1 Thessalonians 1:7

You and I occupy only a small, secluded part of the world. Does it matter what we do? If we stop and consider, we realize that all those with whom we have social relationships do affect our lives and we affect theirs. Maybe our influence doesn't reach very far, but that fact makes it no less important. We do not need to be in someone's presence for a long time to influence him or her. Some people I met only once have affected my life and character.

If you step into a home with small children to help for a week or two, you may become vividly conscious of your influence. You may be startled to hear and see your echoes as the little ones pick up words or manners of your own, whether positive or negative. Other times, however, we may not be aware of how we have influenced others.

As a teacher, I could not help but notice the many ways that my students unconsciously influenced my life. For example, I picked up one student's way of forming certain letters of the alphabet. If it was so easy for me to pick up their habits, I knew my habits were rubbing off on them as well.

Even Solomon, the wisest man, was subject to the influence of others. His wives adversely affected him by drawing him to false gods in his aging years.

What kind of influence am I? Am I drawing my friends toward Jesus? I want to serve the Lord fervently so that my influence may encourage those around me. God forbid that anyone should stumble and fall because of me.

July 20

Delight thyself also in the Lord; and he shall give thee the desires of thine heart.
—**Psalm 37:4**

I think of the various desires I have. When my weary body desires rest, I must do something to obtain that rest. I will not get it by continuing to toil. Instead, I must stop working and make rest a priority over work. When my hungry body desires food, I will not get full simply by wishing for something to eat. I must put forth the necessary efforts to make eating a priority over whatever else I am doing.

I desire fellowship and companionship. This desire can be satisfied in various ways—through friends, through marriage—but ultimately only through God Himself. What must I do to fulfill that basic desire for communion? I cannot get it by wallowing in self-pity and bitterness. Rather, I will have it if I delight myself in the Lord and allow Him to become the desire of my heart. If the Lord is my delight, He will be the guest at my table, the passenger in my car, the One who listens to my problems as well as the One who has the answers. But just as I cannot expect to have my bodily needs met by merely wishing them to be met, so I cannot expect to have my spiritual needs met without making the Lord my delight. If He is my focus, I will desire only what He desires. This is possible only as I allow His will to have priority over mine.

If the Lord is my delight, I will bring Him my needs in prayer. He understands the needs of my heart, and He will meet those needs.

> Be sober, be vigilant; because your adversary the devil, as a
> roaring lion, walketh about, seeking whom he may devour.
> —1 Peter 5:8

Some years ago a minister brought out the message of this verse in a way I have not forgotten. He described a nest of young pigeons high on a beam in the peak of the barn. Far below is the barn floor, where hungry cats prowl. In the nest there is safety, but just outside the nest lies impending danger. A careless little squab that is not aware of the danger may fall over the side, sealing his fate. He is sure to be devoured.

Our situation is much like that of the young squabs. We are safe when we stay in God's hands and in His will, but stepping outside of His will brings us to a place of danger. We also have an enemy that is watching our every move, eagerly waiting to devour us. Our souls are at stake; we dare not be foolish, careless, or indifferent.

Am I an example of the believers in this area? Can those younger than I safely follow me, or do I carelessly close my eyes to the dangers of not remaining close to my Lord? It is a sobering challenge. "Wherefore gird up the loins of your mind, be sober" (1 Peter 1:13).

July 22

Peace I leave with you, my peace I give unto you: not as the world giveth, give I unto you. Let not your heart be troubled, neither let it be afraid.
—John 14:27

Are you passing through a trial, grieving the loss of a loved one, or suffering with a chronic or terminal illness? Maybe you do not know where God wants you, and you struggle to discern His will. Do you feel discouraged, neglected, or unneeded? Do you wonder if God cares as you pass through the fire?

When their brother lay critically ill, Mary and Martha sent an urgent appeal to Jesus to come to them. But it seemed as if Jesus did not care; He did not come until it was "too late." Lazarus died and his body was laid to rest. The sisters knew that if Jesus had only come, He could have healed Lazarus. And even now, He was not there to comfort them during this time of grief and loss. Did Jesus not care?

We know that He did. He wept, comforted, and restored. Yet He had seen fit that His beloved friends should pass through this bitter trial and drink the cup of sorrow.

So, even though it may seem as if God has not heard, yet He says, "My peace I give to you in the midst of the storm. Though the waves leap and the wild water roars, do not be troubled; rest in me. I care and I am with you."

And after a while came unto him they that stood by, and said to Peter,
Surely thou also art one of them; for thy speech betrayeth thee.

—Matthew 26:73

The sun is setting. Twilight is deepening. From all directions animals venture out of their burrows, hollows, and crevices. Nighttime affords a measure of protection for these defenseless creatures who must find food. Man sleeps on, unaware of the life and death struggles that occur every night.

For the curious, though, dawn may reveal a partial story. Footprints on the muddy bank, the sandy beach, or the freshly fallen snow are like signatures in a hotel register, telling us who has come and gone. The marks are distinctive. The curved path of the single-footed clam will not indicate that a turtle with his dragging tail had been there.

Our actions also leave distinctive marks behind. The heart filled with love leaves a legacy of regarding the feelings of others. Joy lives on through songs sung and cheerful words spoken. A heart at rest with God will leave behind the signature of peace. Longsuffering means that patience is near. The gentle woman will leave footprints of kindness behind her. Goodness is readily noticeable through the good deeds done for others. A woman with faith will show the evidence of good works. The humility of the meek woman will be appreciated as she performs menial tasks. A temperate woman will show her moderation by remaining unruffled during trying times.

So, whether on the muddy bank, the sandy beach, the freshly fallen snow, at home or abroad, you tell on yourself. If you have been there, you will leave behind marks of identity that reveal your character. What you are is what is seen.

Casting all your care upon him; for he careth for you.
—1 Peter 5:7

Committing everything to the Lord when we've experienced the heartaches and disappointments of life may not seem easy at all. We may feel that the trials and sadness we encounter deter us from giving our worries and fears to Him. It takes a firm belief in the goodness of God to trust Him even when we question why He allows negative things to happen. Only when we choose to worship God in the midst of our questions can we turn our trials, troubles, and disappointments into smiles that brighten the way for others.

When the storms of life beat down on us, can we hear the words of Jesus, "Peace, be still"? Suffering in our Christian life prepares us for greater service. Joseph was an excellent example for us to follow. It took a strong faith to surrender his life to the Lord and accept his lot in life. Though he was in prison so long, away from his family and friends, he kept on serving faithfully and joyfully. The constant presence of God kept him strong.

Surrendering to Jesus and allowing Him to be Lord brings rest to our hearts. The future truly is in God's hands. He is able to help us to trust Him daily. Doubts and fears create confusion, but faith in God brings clarity. Our loving Saviour will guide us every step of the way when we are willing to let Him lead.

> Woe unto them that call evil good, and good evil; that put darkness for light, and light for darkness; that put bitter for sweet, and sweet for bitter!
> —Isaiah 5:20

The world's view of life is opposite from the Christian's. The Christian woman may be tempted to move toward the world's way of thinking, but she might not realize how detrimental that can be.

The world places much emphasis on worldly riches and will stoop to committing works of darkness to obtain them. The Christian places emphasis on spiritual riches and will suffer the loss of all things if necessary to obtain them.

The world uses forceful, hasty methods to fill their self-centered desires. The Christian waits before the Lord with a surrendered spirit and gives glory to Him.

The world thinks a life of ease will bring happiness. The Christian knows that a life of suffering and sacrifice for the cause of Christ will bring everlasting joy.

The world tells its young people to be somebody. Christians tell their young people to become nobodies and to let Christ be the Somebody in their lives.

The world needs noisy entertainment to soothe its spirit. The Christian is comforted through the fellowship of the Holy Spirit.

The world does not want to think about death, but the Christian knows that death is the gateway to a better life.

The world has no time for God. The Christian's source and power for living is God, so he makes time with God a priority.

The world is troubled by the signs of the times, but the Christian looks up, for redemption is near.

When the Christian woman stays focused on Christ, there is no room in her mind for the influences of the world.

July 26

The Lord is good unto them that wait for him, to the soul that seeketh him.
—Lamentations 3:25

Sometimes we must go through the valley of heartbreaks and disappointments to be more useful to God. When I experienced a broken courtship, I felt as if God was refining me in the fire. What spurred me on was knowing that I would be more like Jesus after I went through this trial.

Anyone who has ended a special friendship feels some level of hurt. Our response to the hurt is what we have to decide for ourselves. If we respond with God's love in our hearts, even though we are hurting deeply, God will give us grace to accept the present circumstances. He will also further reveal His will to us as we seek Him.

Waiting on the Lord is a necessary part of the process. As we wait, He will continue to pour His goodness upon us. He brings peace to the troubled soul and will heal our hurts and wounds, but He might not do it instantly.

Good things will come out of our valleys of heartbreak because God brings redemption to those who wait for Him. One of those good things might be the ability to minister to others who are coping with similar experiences. If we continue to cling to a belief in God's goodness and let His love flow through us, we can reflect upon the past and share positive encouragement with others who are hurting. As we seek His will for our lives, He will never cease to shower His goodness upon us.

And the night following the Lord stood by him, and said, Be of good cheer, Paul.

—Acts 23:11

Did Paul have reason to be of good cheer? Was it possible in his situation? The previous verses say that things were in such a state that the chief captain was afraid lest Paul should be pulled to pieces. And the following verse tells of the proposed hunger strike of certain Jews who determined to kill Paul. Yet God says, "Be of good cheer." In other words, "Be glad, rejoice, take courage."

When your road is rough and full of thorns, it may help to remember the examples of people who faced hard situations and yet continued to be joyful. Naaman's wife's maid found herself in a difficult situation, yet it seems she took life in stride. Paul and Silas sang while they were in prison. Are you able to sing in all of life's circumstances, or has your song been stilled?

Our Saviour, who walked on the earth before us, can give us a buoyant grace to help us stay afloat during the storms and stresses of life. We need this upward pressure to help us rise when we would naturally sink. Are you allowing Him to give you His grace in your situation?

If your joy has flickered and gone out in the disappointments of life, there is hope. The Saviour can renew the flame. "For thou art my lamp, O Lord: and the Lord will lighten my darkness" (2 Samuel 22:29).

....

....

....

....

....

July 28

And the eye cannot say unto the hand, I have no need of
thee: nor again the head to the feet, I have no need of you.
—1 Corinthians 12:21

My sister and I sold homemade rolls from our bakery. She was an expert at shaping the dough into rolls that turned out beautifully. She made dozens of them at a time, and it took her quite awhile. She didn't mind, though—she labored willingly because she wanted to please the customers. The only problem was that I was left with a good portion of the rest of the work.

One day I decided to take a turn at shaping the rolls. I thought it might not take as long for me as it had for her. I was right; I did get them done faster. But when we checked the rolls later, we knew why the tops were not as smooth and full as usual. I had not taken the time to make the product as attractive as I should have. When I realized that my sister had a special aptitude for shaping rolls, I gladly left her with the job.

Later as I pondered the situation, I realized that God had given me just what He wanted me to have. He also gave my sister talents. I have no right to try to take her place in life because I feel I can do something better or faster than she can. If I try to do that, I complicate both our lives and we feel defeated. As I accept the gifts of my family members and friends, I can encourage them in their talents. In that I will find true contentment and happiness, because I will see them be successful.

God wants me to be all that I can be—no more and no less.

....

....

....

....

1 Thessalonians 5:14-24

"Be patient toward all men." We must be patient with those who do not show love to us.

"See that none render evil for evil unto any man." We do not need to allow bitterness in our hearts. God can enable us to respond with His love.

"But ever follow that which is good, both among yourselves, and to all men. Rejoice evermore. Pray without ceasing." As soon as we are tempted to be bitter or unloving, we must be in prayer. We need Jesus to help us love others.

"In everything give thanks: for this is the will of God in Christ Jesus concerning you." Thank Jesus for every new day. Thank Him for grace to overcome the trials of today. Thank Him for everything.

"Quench not the Spirit." Let us live so close to God that we can hear His still, small voice.

"Hold fast that which is good. Abstain from all appearance of evil. And the very God of peace sanctify you wholly; and I pray God your whole spirit and soul and body be preserved blameless unto the coming of our Lord Jesus Christ." We cannot be blameless when we try with our own effort, but God is able to sanctify us and infuse us with His power to live like Him.

"Faithful is he that calleth you, who also will do it." How precious it is to know and experience the faithfulness of God. He will not allow us to be tempted above what we are able to bear. Rather, He will teach us through our temptations and turn us into gold as we fight temptation with His strength. He turns bad things into good—lessons of love in the midst of hate, peace in the midst of questions, joy in the midst of trials, and longsuffering and patience with difficult people and situations.

July 30

Take heed therefore that the light which is in thee be not darkness.
—Luke 11:35

Take a tour with me into a Pacific Coast lighthouse. We pause a number of times to catch our breath on our walk up the steep incline to the lighthouse. The view below us is altogether lovely, yet we realize why a lighthouse is needed at this specific spot. The rocky coastline would be a dangerous place for ships in a storm.

We are permitted to enter the building that was once occupied by the station master. Much has changed since the light is now operated by radio control from the city. We are told about the days when whale oil was burned to produce light. The station master had to be meticulous, keeping his building spotlessly clean. The smoke from the lamp tended to cloud the lens and keep the light from shining its brightest. The station master was constantly cleaning that lens. He could not risk letting his light become dim because of a buildup of grime. His utmost concern was the welfare of the seamen on the ocean.

Think of yourself as a station master. Are you concerned that your light shines to those struggling along in darkness? When a sinful habit is allowed in your life, the lens darkens and the light dims. If sin remains in your life, others may shipwreck because you failed. But when you refresh yourself in God's Word, your light shines brighter.

Another interesting feature of lighthouses is that they were not always built on the highest points of land. If a lighthouse was too high, it would shine above the normal fog level, which would be useless for ships. Being at just the right place at the right time is much more important to God than being at the top where everyone will easily notice you on a clear day. ✹

> Abide in me, and I in you. As the branch cannot bear fruit of itself,
> except it abide in the vine; no more can ye, except ye abide in me.
>
> —John 15:4

I was trying hard to understand the Lord's will for me and just what it was that He would have me do. Questions hit me daily, frustrating me. *Where do I fit into the church? What is my spiritual gift? What can I do to help?* I kept probing the mystery, but my search was not turning out answers.

Then quietly and sweetly, yet plainly and unmistakably, the Spirit brought a wonderful message to me. He did not say, "Go convert the heathen." Nor did He say, "Go visit the sick and needy." He simply said, "Abide in the Lord and He will show you what to do." I felt the mystery being unveiled, and I was filled with peace and stability. The Lord showed me that if I abide in Christ, I do not need to struggle to bear fruit. I will bear fruit naturally when I am connected with Him. He showed me that a spiritual gift is not something the receiver needs to be overly concerned about. A person does not have to run after a gift from God; she only needs to receive it. The Giver is the One who is responsible to distribute the gifts and to see to it that no one is without a God-given purpose.

There is no question whether or not my heavenly Father knows which gift is appropriate for which Christian. So, instead of seeking after a gift, I need to seek after Christ and abide in Him so that He can work through me and cause that gift to bear fruit. I do not bear fruit for myself. I bear it for Christ, to glorify Him; and for the church, to beautify it. 🍃

....

....

....

....

So is the kingdom of God, as if a man should cast seed into the ground; and should sleep, and rise night and day, and the seed should spring and grow up, he knoweth not how.

—Mark 4:26-27

The unusual sight caught my attention and held it. Out of the crook of an old maple tree rose a bright yellow sunflower. It drank in the rain and waved its cheery head in the summer breeze. I smiled as I watched the sunflower, wondering how it got there. I decided that a bird must have dropped a seed on the way from the bird feeder to the lofty branches of the tree—and it most likely did not realize what it had done.

It was only a seed dropped carelessly and in an unlikely place, but what an inspiration it created. It has done much more for me than the vegetable plants growing in neat rows in their usual places in the garden.

You can sow the Word in unlikely places too. Who knows how much a soul may benefit from a Gospel tract on the table in a restaurant? Your thankful attitude in spite of the constant rain—who knows what it will do for the store clerk who is always complaining? Your assisting hand as you help the aged grandmother cross the street will encourage both her and those who may be watching you. A prayer, a word, a deed—you may never know all the beautiful results that will blossom forth.

It was only a tiny seed dropped by an insignificant bird, but how I have enjoyed that sunflower!

The slothful man roasteth not that which he took in
hunting: but the substance of a diligent man is precious.
—Proverbs 12:27

Working hard to provide for ourselves and our families is a virtue. When we have achieved the fruits of our labors, it is virtuous neither to hoard nor waste them. While we would not say that every frugal woman is a daughter of God, we know that God's daughters make wise use of the things God has given them. Working hard, being thrifty, and using what we have seem to go together.

If you already have several sweaters in your closet, do you really need the new sweater you want? Should you sew yourself another dress when you have lots of scrap pieces that you could be sewing into children's clothes for a busy mother? It will not hurt you to wash dishes with the soap you received in your grocery shower even though it is not your favorite kind. Share your leftover muffins with your neighbor instead of letting them grow mold.

The slothful man does only what he enjoys doing. He takes pleasure only in killing the prey, and he does not want to bother with starting a fire or roasting the meat. It does not bother him to waste the meat.

One aspect of frugality is to keep what we have and not waste the fruit of our labors. But the other aspect of frugality is to get rid of things we don't need. We need to be balanced; saving your toilet paper rolls and empty glass bottles will have little value unless you have a definite use for them.

Today, ask God for wisdom on how to make the best use of your possessions.

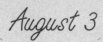

Let us hold fast the profession of our faith without wavering; (for he is faithful that promised).

—Hebrews 10:23

Shades of night were falling across the land. The yard light sensed that it was time to go on duty. It flickered on but seemed to waver. It kept flickering and quivering as though it could not decide if it wanted to pierce the darkness. When it finally did, I marveled at the difference between the beauty of bright, steady light and the uncertainty of flickering, wavering light.

Rejection, sorrow, indecision, and cares throw shades of darkness over the lives of many women. They long to feel acceptance, comfort, and encouragement. They long to feel an unwavering, strong support. The Lord may call me to be a light that pierces their darkness. But I will be like a wavering light if I cannot decide between things such as these:

* My expense or someone else's need
* Half-hearted obedience or a whole-hearted commitment
* Saving my reputation or stooping to raise the low
* Giving my time for others or spending it selfishly

If I constantly waver, it is a sign that I do not trust the God who has called me. It is a sign that I consider myself more important than others or even God. If the Lord sees me waver, He cannot use me—uncertainty cannot be trusted. But if He sees bright, steady light, He will make use of that light.

> Finally, brethren, whatsoever things are true, whatsoever things are honest, whatsoever things are just, whatsoever things are pure, whatsoever things are lovely, whatsoever things are of good report; if there be any virtue, and if there be any praise, think on these things.
>
> —Philippians 4:8

If these things pervade our thinking, we have enough to keep our minds occupied all day long. We do not have the desire or time to think evil, negative thoughts that defile us.

"What thinkest thou?" (Matthew 22:17). It is good to stop and ponder this question and evaluate your thoughts. Are your thoughts encouraging, upbuilding, and positive? Or are they shallow, negative, and discontent? You probably think all the time. Do you dwell upon God's faithfulness, considering the great things He has done for you? Do you consider the handiwork of God in nature and stand in reverence and awe before Him? Do you ponder the path of your feet to see if you are going the direction God wants you to go? Do you meditate and feed upon God's Word? Do you encourage yourself to think thoughts of faith? When you feel discouraged, does your mind turn to Jesus? Our minds should often turn to the One who created us and sustains us. When we are filled with Him, we will naturally consider one another.

Your thought patterns determine the kind of person you are. "For as he thinketh in his heart, so is he" (Proverbs 23:7). Are your thoughts continually gloomy and negative, or are they beautiful, loving, and godly?

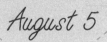

But speaking the truth in love, may grow up into
him in all things, which is the head, even Christ.
—**Ephesians 4:15**

Growth is the gradual process of development. As Christian women, we should grow in the grace and knowledge of God and in the fruit of the Spirit.

In plants, growth is promoted through nutrients, sunshine, and enough wind to produce sturdiness. Parallel factors promote spiritual growth in our lives. We gain nutrients through feeding on God's Word. Basking in God's love brings life-giving sunshine to our lives, and trials and chastening make us strong.

Our growth rate may be difficult to determine. We may not realize that we are growing, but when we look back later, we see signs of growth. God's Word is a sure measure by which to check our growth. Are we gaining victory when we are tested? Are we growing in maturity and becoming more like our Master?

The Bible refers to us as trees of God's planting. God is concerned about our growth much like a farmer is concerned about his crops and a mother about her baby. We need to ask ourselves which we resemble more, a stunted tree in the desert or a flourishing tree by the water.

"The righteous shall flourish like the palm tree: he shall grow like a cedar in Lebanon. Those that be planted in the house of the Lord shall flourish in the courts of our God" (Psalm 92:12-13).

August 6

I know that thou canst do every thing, and that
no thought can be withholden from thee.

—Job 42:2

Do you consider small, "normal" things as blessings from God meant just for you? If you have not done this, you can start now.

One opening morning glory on a quiet walk—just for you.
The full moon shining into the bedroom—just for you.
An encouraging phone call—just for you.
A chickadee's clear call—just for you.
A song chosen at a church service—just for you.
A child's innocent question—just for you.
The rainbow in the sky—just for you.
The minister's message—just for you.

You can observe your natural surroundings and find things "just for you." We feel God's nearness if we notice little things; they are His gifts to us, ways that He shows His love.

Before the sister who started this book passed away, she gave a hibiscus plant to one of her dear friends. In time it got a disease and quit blooming. A long time later, shortly after Verna's funeral, the plant sprouted a blossom. Only one blossom, yet it seemed personal and symbolic.

Yes, God sends small things into our lives to brighten the day. He reminds us in unusual ways that He cares about us. If you want to hear His voice and marvel at His power, stop and notice the little things today. ✳

August 7

Charity . . . seeketh not her own, is not easily provoked, thinketh no evil.
—1 Corinthians 13:4-5

The love of God in our hearts will reach out to all those with whom we interact day by day. Loving the person who always sees things our way is usually no problem. But we usually experience moments of tension with those whose faults we can see on a daily basis, such as a co-worker or a housemate. Why is this a problem? The longer we are together, the more we tend to notice our differences.

Unless the love of God is a real part of our lives, these differences can become irritating to us. Often the differences are just little things that tend to become bigger issues as they are repeated day after day. Some examples might be the unpredictable way your friend parks her car, the paperwork she leaves scattered around the room, or the cluttered sink that gives evidence of what she had for a snack. It could be a stack of clean dishes she left in the drainer or the disorganized way she hangs her clothes on the line. It could be some personal habit such as whistling, or even the ability to sing and talk the minute she arises in the morning.

How do we cope with these little things that have become a big sore to us? We need to consider what love would do. Remember that you might have habits that bother her as well. You may park your car perfectly, but maybe your slow, methodical way of cleaning bothers your friend. Her morning cheerfulness bothers you, but your morning quietness may irritate her just as much.

Everyone is different, so we need to accept the perfectionist as well as the scatterbrained. Talk to each other about your differences. You need not mention everything that bothers you, expecting her to change all her ways to please you. But you can point out to her that the grass is dying and ask if she could park her car on the driveway. If she points out something that you can change to make her happy, do it cheerfully. Ask God for grace to overlook the things that do not matter, like the wash that always dries no matter if similar types of clothing hang close together or not. Quietly and cheerfully clean up the kitchen and dry the dishes that bother you. Ask God to help you see the good qualities of the other person instead of the imperfections. "Wherefore receive ye one another, as Christ also received us to the glory of God" (Romans 15:7).

Remember, love thinks no evil. 🌀

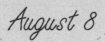

August 8

An excellent spirit was in him.
—Daniel 6:3

Daniel challenges us because of the way he served God while away from home. He exhibited the all-important quality of faithfulness, and even the rulers could not find fault with him. We, too, need to be consistent and faithful Christians no matter where we serve. Because of God's grace and His continual work in our lives, we can become more like Daniel—a blameless person.

Jesus is the perfect example of being blameless. We can become more like Him by simply surrendering ourselves to Him and trusting Him even in circumstances that we cannot understand. Daniel probably did not understand at first why God allowed him to be thrown into the den of lions. When we let go and let God have His way, life is filled with blessings, for we truly are in His will. His sustaining grace keeps us faithful every day.

When we draw near to Jesus in faith, we can lean on His gentle arms, rest quietly, and trust in Him. We can feel the warmth of His love. We sense our need of God when storms and temptations come. It is then that we draw nearer to Him, which deepens our relationship with Him and enables us to praise Him for the trials of life.

Just as the Lord did not allow Daniel to be tested beyond what he could take, neither will He allow us to be tried with more than we can bear.

A good man out of the good treasure of the heart bringeth forth good things: and an evil man out of the evil treasure bringeth forth evil things.

—Matthew 12:35

The strands of embroidery thread that I find throughout my house and on my clothing tell people that my needlework consists of embroidering—not knitting, crocheting, quilting, or weaving. The numerous strands also show that sometimes I fail to put away all the thread. The evidence is indisputable.

My attitudes and feelings are also evidence of something. When I am filled with worry, I show that I am not trusting God to lead me and keep His promises. Rather, I show that I am trusting my own reasoning more than the sovereignty of God. When I find myself struggling and fighting within, I give evidence that my self-will is not completely crucified.

I would not think of trying to convince someone that I do crocheting when the embroidery thread is so obvious around my house. Yet sometimes I try to convince myself that I believe in God's love, while the evidence proves that I am not resting in Him. Sometimes I tell myself that I am justified in my bitter inward struggles, yet my self-will is obvious.

Just as my house looks more orderly when I put the thread away and put the stray strands in the wastebasket, so my life will display the beauty of Jesus when I dethrone self and let Him reign.

For I say, through the grace given unto me, to every man that is among you, not to think of himself more highly than he ought to think; but to think soberly.
—Romans 12:3

Pride is a dreadful enemy for the Christian, coming slyly and taking many forms. We need to be on guard continually lest it gain a foothold in our lives.

How does God look at pride? He hates it and calls it sin. He cannot get close to the proud heart, because it is an abomination to Him.

What are the results of allowing pride in your life? Your heart will be hardened and deceived. Contention instead of peace will rule in your life. Pride brings a person to shame and ultimately to destruction.

How can we detect pride? We can easily see it in other people, but we may not see it in our own lives. In fact, when we judge others as being proud, we are often showing evidence of the same sin in our own lives. Eliab accused his younger brother David of being proud, but reading the account gives us the impression that Eliab was the one with that fault instead.

You may want to test yourself to see if you can detect pride in your life. Do you want to become someone important? Do you have a strong desire for recognition, wishing that your work would be more visible and appreciated? Do you despise others in your heart? Do you evaluate yourself as strong and others weak? Do you compare your works with other women and pat yourself on the back for the good job you do?

Instead of pride, "Let another man praise thee" (Proverbs 27:2). Instead of superiority, "Let each esteem other better than themselves" (Philippians 2:3). Instead of conceit, remember that "God is in heaven, and thou upon earth" (Ecclesiastes 5:2).

Bear ye one another's burdens, and so fulfil the law of Christ.

—Galatians 6:2

Dear Friend,

Today I am not feeling well. As I lie here on my bed and gaze across the fields to the school where I know you are, I think of the past. Allow me to reflect on those times and what your friendship meant to me.

During my years of teaching school, people often asked me, "How was your day today?" And then I could share with friends or my students' parents about the special moments of that day. During those times I could seek counsel, share frustrations, and gain new courage. I suppose as a teacher I felt that my life was important to the community. You know how it is: children look up to you, and parents and the school board show appreciation for your efforts.

I was single and lived a fulfilled life with meaningful work and friends like you. But sometimes I longed to share my life with a man of God's choice. (What girl does not dream of that sometime during her life?) Yet, more than anything else, I wanted God's will.

During my eighth year of teaching, God brought a good man into my life. It was the beginning of many changes I faced. While joy filled me, I also faced apprehension of my future at times.

Throughout our courtship, I still loved you and all my single friends. But where did I belong? I was neither married nor single. Thank you for being patient with me while I was trying to adjust to these changes. I needed your prayers, thoughts, and opinions—your continued friendship. Your support meant so much. I did not mean to change as much as I did, but it was a necessity in my new role.

Now I am married. I love my husband more than anyone else on earth; God meant it to be that way. However, I do not feel that a husband is to be his wife's only friend. You were important to me before I married, and I cannot erase your friendship.

At school the walls used to vibrate with children's energy, but at home the walls are silent, now that my husband is gone for the day. No faces light up with understanding as I teach them to read. No one needs my assistance during art time. I miss those times; teaching was my life. While I am not jealous of you or dissatisfied in my current role, I do want you to know how much I still need you. In fact, I probably need you now more than I ever did before. I crave those times of sharing with you.

Now in my sixth month of pregnancy I am laid up in bed. Thank you for the flowers you brought and the cards you sent at just the right times!

I am not the only one who needs you. All your other married friends do too. Often we married women are told how our single friends need us, and I do want to be here for you when you need me. But sometimes I wonder who needs who the most. I only know we need each other.

—*Your newly married friend*
❀

....

....

....

....

....

....

....

....

....

....

....

....

August 12

Hold up my goings in thy paths, that my footsteps slip not.
—Psalm 17:5

"Dear Jesus, keep me close to you so that my footsteps do not slip from the right path. I know you will draw close to me as I draw close to you. I have dreams in my heart about the future, but I open my heart to you. If there are any dreams you want to take out, I am willing for you to have your way. I want you to work out your plan. I give you every area of my life because I know that if I hold anything back, my feet will start slipping away from you. Keep me, Lord, through the desires, fears, and temptations that I face."

August 13

Neither yield ye your members as instruments of unrighteousness unto sin: but yield yourselves unto God, as those that are alive from the dead, and your members as instruments of righteousness unto God.
—Romans 6:13

Think of all the heroes of faith mentioned in the Bible. Why do their lives still speak to us thousands of years later? It is because of their submission—their willingness to yield to God's will. In contrast, looking at the lives of ungodly people mentioned in the Bible will reveal that their wickedness was due to their lack of submission. Today that is still the difference between the godly and the ungodly. Submitting to God brings joy, rest, satisfaction, and peace. Lack of submission brings bitterness, struggle, confusion, and turmoil.

Through nature, God teaches us this truth. There would be no harvest if the seed would not fall into the ground and die. There would be no light if the sun and the moon refused to follow their God-ordained order. The hen would have no chicks if she would not submit to sitting still on her eggs. Seeds die and lose the substance of what they were before, the heavenly bodies follow the same unchanging routine year after year, and the hen faithfully sits on her eggs for twenty-one days. Because of these things, there is life, light, and fruitfulness.

The world and the flesh do not understand how submission and dying yield such benefits. Instead, they tell us to "be somebody." Children think they would be happier if they could have their own way, but parents who are older and wiser know this is not true. They know their children will be better equipped for service if they learn submission. My heavenly Father, who knows my sphere of service, knows that I will be more fruitful if I die to self, follow His teachings, and submit to His plan for me. My natural inclinations do not understand these things, yet I will come to an understanding when I live in submission.

Pride goeth before destruction, and an haughty spirit before a fall.

—Proverbs 16:18

The life of Absalom, son of King David, vividly testifies to the truth of this verse. We can read of his confident ascent to the top of his pedestal, and then we witness his fast descent to shame.

Despite all his rare opportunities as a prince, he was not content, but lifted himself in pride. One evidence of this was his refusal to speak to his brother for two years. Finally, in his anger, he deceived his father, killed his brother, and fled to his grandfather.

After three years he was permitted to return home, but he was still not a submissive son. Through suave and persuasive speech, he gathered a following and went to Hebron to make himself king.

From there, he went downhill. His three sons were gone, so he built a monument to his name. As it turned out, he wasn't even buried there.

He lost the battle to take the kingdom from his father, and in his escape his head got caught in a tree. Apparently all his companions had deserted him and he was alone when Joab killed him in his defenseless state. He was not given a decent burial; rather, he was thrown into a hole and covered with stones.

How sad that a handsome young man with great potential had such an ending because of pride. How about you? Is pride in your life causing you to go in a direction other than what God intended for you? Do you feel over-qualified to do some small job you have been asked to do? Remember where pride took Absalom, and ask yourself if you want to end up the same way. 🌀

August 15

So when they had dined, Jesus saith to Simon Peter,
Simon, son of Jonas, lovest thou me more than these?

—John 21:15

Jesus questioned Peter three times in succession with these simple words. He asks us the same question: "Do you love me above all others?" He wants our undivided devotion. He loved us so much that He gave Himself to die for us, and He desires our love in return.

Think of these words from Song of Solomon 8:6 as a plea from God to you:

"Set me as a seal upon thine heart." God wants you to hold Him close in your heart. He wants a prominent place in your interests and thoughts.

"As a seal upon thine arm." This is as a readily visible reminder that you belong to Christ.

"For love is strong as death." Love is binding. If we truly love someone, we will love that person through joys and sorrows. We will be willing to give up anything for the one we love, even if it means giving our lives.

"Jealousy is cruel as the grave." God is a jealous God and will not share our love, worship, and adoration with another.

"Many waters cannot quench love" (Song of Solomon 8:7). Though water is used to quench fires, nothing can quench, dampen, or drown true love, which lives on into eternity.

Is your love and devotion to God this fervent? How often would Jesus need to ask you, "Lovest thou me?" Have you gone back to "fishing" as Peter had? Consider what you are fishing for in life. Does Jesus need to question your love?

....

....

....

Blessed be the God and Father of our Lord Jesus Christ, who hath
blessed us with all spiritual blessings in heavenly places in Christ.

—Ephesians 1:3

Among my pleasant childhood memories are some unforgettable places: a lazy creek, a store with unbelievable treasures, and my aunts' house where I was made to feel special. The passing of years as well as of people have changed these places. Charms of childhood give way to realities of adulthood. Sometimes I feel a twinge of sadness as I realize that these places will never be the same.

But I know of another place more wonderful than a memory. I do not need to watch it change with the years. I do not need to feel guilty of dwelling on the past when I think about it, because it is a present reality.

It is my heavenly place, my position in Christ. Much as I enjoyed my happy childhood places, I could not always be in them. Perhaps I was too little to go, or it was not my turn to go. And I always had to leave. In this other place, I can always stay there no matter how "little" I am. It is always my turn, and I never have to leave.

I see this place with my spiritual eyes instead of my natural eyes. My favorite childhood places had peculiar sights, sounds, and smells that I recognized when I was there. Likewise, my place in Christ has distinct attributes that help me recognize when I am there. One of them is the communion of the Holy Spirit. He reveals things to me and provides answers to my questions. Another feature of my heavenly place is enjoying the things of God. When I am there, I enjoy hearing and talking about spiritual things. There I do not complain, because I am abiding in His wonderful presence.

If I stay in my spiritual heavenly place, God will someday take me to a visible heavenly place. My heavenly place in the present will be transferred to a heavenly place in eternity.

And this is the confidence that we have in him, that, if
we ask any thing according to his will, he heareth us.

—1 John 5:14

Elijah was not a Christian with special powers; he was a human being just like us. When he prayed earnestly that it would not rain, it didn't rain for three years and six months. Then he prayed again and it rained! Numerous other times God answered Elijah's prayers. Through his prayers, the widow's son was brought to life. Through his prayers, fire fell from heaven and consumed his offering on Mount Carmel.

Did you ever earnestly pray for something only to feel that your prayers were going no higher than the ceiling? Does God seem deaf to you at times? It may seem as though God does not hear our petitions when He does not answer them. Nevertheless, we know He hears, cares, and has our best interests at heart.

We notice the simplicity of Elijah's prayer on Mount Carmel in comparison to the prayers of Baal's prophets. Notice also that Elijah did not ask something for his own honor but rather for the cause and glory of God. He asked for something that only God could do, and everyone knew it. When God answered by fire, the people fell on their faces and said, "The Lord, He is God." They did not worship Elijah.

Immediately following this, Elijah prayed for rain and God hearkened to this petition as well. In the next chapter, however, Elijah's life was threatened and he fled into the wilderness alone. He was discouraged and requested that he might die, but this time God did not grant his request. God still had work for Elijah to do, so He provided nourishment to strengthen Elijah and encourage him.

Sometimes God may not grant our requests either, but we must remember that we cannot see all His purposes. No matter how discouraged you may feel, God will always come through for you and meet your needs as well. ☯

> Be not deceived; God is not mocked: for whatsoever
> a man soweth, that shall he also reap.
> —Galatians 6:7

The task was tedious, and it took me longer than I thought it would. I had tried to make fine, even stitches when I embroidered the flowers, and I finally completed the task. But then I made a shocking discovery—I had used a wrong thread color. It would not look right once the rest of the design was embroidered. I had to pick it all out! Had I looked at the directions more carefully, I would have spared myself all that extra work. The directions were correct, and I could not have gone wrong by following them.

God's wisdom is always trustworthy and can be followed without fear of remorse. His Word gives us valuable directions, which, if followed, will not result in bitter reaping. Many angry arguments would never exist if the words "A soft answer turneth away wrath" would be heeded. Many individuals would be spared deep humiliation if they would take to heart the words "Pride goeth before destruction." There would be less remorse over the past if "Thou shalt love thy neighbor as thyself" would always be practiced. There would be fewer unfulfilled hopes and plans if people would wait on the Lord instead of rushing ahead. There would be fulfillment rather than disillusionment and frustration if the command to "Seek ye first the kingdom of God and his righteousness" would be heeded.

God's Word is a safe guide. I have nothing to lose by following it. There will be no bitter reaping, no undoing, but rather a harvest of joy and gladness.

And the Lord said unto him, What is that in thine hand? And he said, A rod.
—Exodus 4:2

God asked Moses a simple question when Moses was trying to convince Him that he was not able to lead the Israelites out of Egypt. The answer to this question was, "A rod." It was a simple yet necessary tool that Moses was familiar with in his task of herding the sheep. God asked Moses to cast his rod on the ground and it became a serpent. When God told him to pick it up by the tail, it became a rod again. When God commissioned it for His service, this simple tool became the rod of God. It was used many times in proving the power of God.

The rod was used to show God's power when Moses called forth the plagues, divided the water of the Red Sea, and later fought the battle with the Amalekites. Moses' rod did not have magical powers, but when yielded to God, God used it to do great things.

Now, ponder this question for yourself. "What is that in your hand?" Is it just a simple tool? Are you *just* a babysitter, a cleaning person, a nurse, a seamstress, a teacher, a cook? Are you *just* someone who does various tasks with no title to your name? Are you willing and happy to use what is in your hand today, even though it may be *just* a simple tool? Are you willing to serve where you are? God can use you if you are willing to commit yourself to His service. Use the gifts and abilities He has given you. He can do amazing things with the tools He has placed in your hands.

God does not expect you to serve in matters that you do not have gifts or resources for. God blesses according to how you serve, not what type of work you do. Seek to improve your service where you are, using those things that are in your hands today. 🌀

But I say unto you, Love your enemies, bless them that curse you, do good to them that hate you, and pray for them which despitefully use you, and persecute you.

—Matthew 5:44

In the Old Testament era, Israel fulfilled the law by loving their neighbors, who were fellow Israelites. But Jesus says that no matter how someone may treat you, you are responsible to love them in return. If they seek your hurt, you are still to love them. To love means more than just not resisting them or not paying them back with evil; it also includes having no bitter feelings. It goes beyond treating them coolly; it means having a heart of genuine love for them. Having compassion for your enemies and seeking their welfare is not humanly possible! It requires a divine filling of God's love.

If Christ had not given us this higher law, our standard would be no different from that of the carnal man. There is nothing noble or holy about doing good to someone if you expect that they will repay you. Even the worst sinner tends to return kindness to someone who has shown him a favor. We attain to no higher level than him, unless we can relate to those who mistreat us with the supernatural smile of heavenly love.

Jesus, our role model, prayed that God would forgive His persecutors. Ask God to fill you with His Spirit today, enabling you to pray for anybody you have trouble relating to. It will be an important step in becoming more like Jesus. ●

....

....

....

....

....

Every branch in me that beareth not fruit he taketh away: and every
branch that beareth fruit, he purgeth it, that it may bring forth more fruit.
—John 15:2

Resting on the couch one day, I reached for a book from the bookcase nearby. Suddenly I saw that I had missed some dust during the weekly cleaning. From my current position, I had a view into the bookcase from a different angle, and it was obvious that I had overlooked that one corner that I thought to be dust-free.

Another time I was scrubbing the floor. When I moved an object to clean beneath it, I saw evidence that moving it was not part of the usual cleaning procedure. Had I not moved it, I would have thought the floor was spotlessly clean.

I realized that in my spiritual life as well, I sometimes encounter surprisingly revealing situations. They are the kind that make me wish I could escape to a place where I would not have to face reality. It seems as though life would be easier if everyone had a perfectly agreeable personality. But if they did, my intolerance of others would not be revealed. It seems it would be nice to have someone with a kindred spirit on hand to talk with at all times, but if I did, I would not realize how discontent I am. It seems if I had close relatives in my church so that I had a niche where I fit in, I could cope better. But then I might not learn to deal with my self-pity.

The same principle applies to the dusty bookcase and the dirty floor. Surface impressions do not satisfy a virtuous housekeeper. She will see to it that there is in-depth cleaning done periodically. She also knows that if she does not move objects and clean behind and underneath them, at some point her half-hearted cleaning will be revealed.

Neither do surface impressions satisfy God, who cares deeply about His children. He provides opportunities for me to see what is deep within my heart. When uncomfortable situations arise, what is in my heart comes to the surface. When I recognize my self-centeredness, I can deal with it. If it would remain hidden, I would be so full of self that there would be no room for God's enabling power to work in me. I would become a stumblingblock instead of a useful servant for God's kingdom.

God purges me, getting rid of any hindrances to growth, and then He makes me fruitful. I am thankful for His cleansing power.

> For as the heavens are higher than the earth, so are my ways higher than your ways, and my thoughts than your thoughts.
> —Isaiah 55:9

Lena sighed as she propped her tired foot on the chair. It was time to get it elevated again. A few days ago she had sprained her ankle, and now she was not able to go to work. Not only was her foot tired right now, her mind was also tired—weary of thinking about why misfortunes like this had to happen.

She opened a book to help pass the time and came across a poem. The poem stated that for every sorrow that comes our way, the Lord also sends a joy. It also mentioned that when the Lord's one hand takes something away, the other always gives. Then Romans 8:28 came to her mind, and she decided to start thinking of the bountiful blessings God had granted her. True, she could not go to work, but she could enjoy being at home, relaxing, and getting a little sewing done. *God's thoughts certainly are different than our thoughts,* Lena mused. She was grateful that He had turned her thoughts in His direction.

Cast thy bread upon the waters: for thou shalt find it after many days.
—Ecclesiastes 11:1

During a time of grieving, I visited a church where I knew several people. After the service, an acquaintance greeted me.

"I have been wanting to talk to you," she said. "You have always had an encouraging word for us when we chanced to meet." I knew she was referring to the conversations we'd had about her handicapped daughter. Until then, I had not realized how she appreciated my interest.

She asked how I was coping, and she listened attentively to my feelings. Her loving manner was healing for me.

We sometimes tend to be overly cautious of speaking to people about their burdens, such as a recent grief or a child with special needs. We feel awkward or fear that we might say the wrong thing. Yet a caring heart can go a long way. I have learned that if I take the opportunity to show interest in a child's development, the parents are usually eager to discuss his or her progress or chance of development.

Had neither of us dared to reach out to each other, we would both have been deprived of the privilege of a listening ear. Sympathy could not have been given or received. God can show us how to discern the difference between prying and listening, and to know how to convey a caring spirit to a burdened person.

....

....

....

....

....

In this account, we find David fleeing before his son, Absalom, who has stolen the kingship. David's heart is torn by grief; he is weeping as he flees.

As if that were not enough, Shimei comes out, curses, throws stones, and casts dust at David to deepen the wound. He falsely accuses David, calls him a man of Belial, and declares that God is repaying him for his wickedness. His words sound spiritual, as though he has a message from God to curse David.

Humiliated and shorn of respect, yet not embittered, David walks on along the opposite hillside. One of his loyal servants requests that he might go over and silence Shimei in death, but David refuses to give him leave. He says, in essence, "Let him curse, for the Lord has told him to curse me. Leave him alone; my own son has risen against me, so it is natural for this man to do the same. It is all a part of God's plan. God is overruling."

What an attitude! He did not have retaliation in mind nor did he say, "I can only take so much! Why all this evil? Why are all men risen against me? Where is God, anyway?"

David's response challenges me to recognize God's controlling hand in life's bitter tests. I can know assuredly that nothing will come my way without God knowing it and overruling in it. Out of the evil that others do to me, God will bring about His divine purposes. He will never forget about me, and I can trust Him. 🌑

....

....

....

....

August 25

In all these things we are more than conquerors through him that loved us.
—Romans 8:37

Stories of mighty conquests appear on the pages of history. Conquerors fought long and hard to gain victories. For a short while they ruled over their empires, only to be overcome by another conqueror.

The wonderful news is that I have more to gain than all those conquerors did. I have the privilege of claiming a kingdom that will never end. No other conqueror will be able to overcome it, and I can be safe in it as long as I claim the victory.

That kingdom is the kingdom of God within my heart. Like the conquerors of old, I must have a method of obtaining and maintaining this kingdom, but that method stands in stark contrast to theirs.

Empires in history were won by weapons and cruelty. Fierce fighting overcame the enemy. But I will win the kingdom of God only if I quietly relinquish my hold on one enemy: self. I must let it go because it only gets in the way and hinders me from gaining new territory. When self is dethroned, no conqueror can overcome God's kingdom in my heart, because the almighty Conqueror sits on the throne. My enemies fall before Him. With His help, I can take new ground in addition to what I gained earlier.

Tradition says that Alexander the Great sat down and wept when there was nothing more to conquer. I do not have that fear, for as long as I live on earth, I will have more to conquer and further glories to experience. These glories will go on even in eternity. My Conqueror is everlasting, and He will take the treasures of His storehouse of glory and share them with me.

....

....

> Now all these things happened unto them for ensamples: and they are
> written for our admonition, upon whom the ends of the world are come.
>
> —1 Corinthians 10:11

Many years ago there lived a woman about whom we are told very little. We do not know whether she was generous, hospitable, and gentle, or if she was of a churlish nature. We have no record of her name. She is simply referred to as a certain man's wife, and we also know she was a mother.

Because of a small act of disobedience, she died an unusual death that has been recorded as a lesson for us. We seldom speak of her, but Jesus referred to her when He said, "Remember Lot's wife" (Luke 17:32).

What did Jesus have in mind when He tells us to remember her? What did she do that was wrong? It may seem like a little thing: God had told her not to look back, but she did. She was disobedient to God's command.

Why did she turn around to look at the city she had just left? Maybe she was loath to leave her home and her married children. She may have been curious, wondering if Sodom would actually be destroyed. Whatever the reason, she disobeyed and looked back.

From Lot's wife, we can learn that we need to be willing to deny self and give up earthly pleasures if God calls us to. It is detrimental to look back with longing hearts at things we've given up. Our possessions must not be too dear to us. Lot's wife left them but apparently never gave them up.

To warn us against seeking self-preservation, Jesus told us to remember Lot's wife. He goes on to say, "Whosoever shall seek to save his life shall lose it; and whosoever shall lose his life shall preserve it" (Luke 17:33). Seeking His will instead of seeking to protect our own lives will ensure that we are preserved for eternity. 🌀

…but I give myself unto prayer.

—**Psalm 109:4**

Which set of circumstances builds the most vibrant, steadfast Christians?

* Fiery stakes, torture chambers, deprivations, afflictions, trials.
* Easy money, luxurious vacations, abundant possessions, comfortable life.

According to history and observation, it is the first set, the one that seems least likely.

We need to turn down the offer of ease and possessions. Why? Because the offer is not without price. The price is our hearts—hearts that will eventually be lured away by things around us if we do not give ourselves to reading the Scriptures and praying daily.

In America, Christians do not experience much persecution. But the devil has not slackened his efforts; he is only using a different approach, one in keeping with his character—sly, cunning, and tricky.

When life seems hard and full of perplexities, Christians turn to God for guidance and strength. When life is easy, a feeling of self-sufficiency creeps in and the need for God is not felt as strongly. Unless Christians are alert and dedicated, they do not realize the price they are paying for a life of ease. They will pay with hearts that are lured into the world and its system.

So if God keeps on sending trials into your life, give yourself to prayer and thank Him for those trials. That is what keeps you feeling your need of Him. It keeps your eyes on Him and keeps you from paying the price for a life of ease.

But by love serve one another. For all the law is fulfilled in one word, even
in this; Thou shalt love thy neighbor as thyself. But if ye bite and devour
one another, take heed that ye be not consumed one of another.

—Galatians 5:13-15

When people are going through times of distress, our sympathy or lack of it
shows how close we are to the heart of God. Job's three friends exhibited
a lack of sympathy; Job found them to be miserable comforters. They evaluated
his situation and passed judgment without first having walked a mile in his shoes.
Job's heart cry was that those who are afflicted should be shown pity by their
friends (Job 6:14). Are we able to weep with those who weep?

When we are caught in the midst of trying circumstances, it is challenging
to remain calm and patient toward others. We may be going through personal
distress at the same time that our church is facing relational difficulties. Are we
then able to retain our integrity and remain calm, or do we become frustrated
and start accusing others?

I once witnessed a scene of utter confusion where biting, devouring, and con-
suming one another was actually taking place. An ant nest had been disturbed
when a beam was removed. The big black ants became frenzied and began racing
around, snapping viciously at each other and literally ripping each other apart. It
was a sobering demonstration. They were all in the same critical situation, yet they
took it out on each other. What could have resulted if they had calmly worked
together to find and build a new home during their difficult time? Read 1 Peter
3:8 and Ephesians 4:32.

August 29

They have addicted themselves to the ministry of the saints.

—1 Corinthians 16:15

At eighty-three years old, Becky is a faithful single sister in the church. Through the church, God has led her into various localities in her later years. She has had adjustments. Though she does not have much to call her own, she possesses a strong faith in God that surpasses any earthly treasures she could own. So when Becky told me her life story, I listened.

Her father died when she was three years old. Her mother faced many hardships in caring for her family, especially when a baby joined the family six months after their father died. But when this baby was eight months old, their home was blessed with a new father. Even after another child was added to the family, their father treated the rest of the children just like his own. They rarely thought of him as their stepfather until they became older. When questioned whether he was her stepfather, Becky had to think before answering.

Her brothers and sisters all got married. When her stepfather died, her mother took up sewing. But Becky was not gifted in sewing, teaching, or other work that could have brought a steady income. She did not seem to have a call to special service; rather, she worked for her brothers and helped wherever she was needed. When her mother needed her, Becky stayed with her until she passed away.

When her nephew sold the farm where she had been living, she moved into a trailer near their home. Several years later, their congregation started an outreach. Becky's nephew and family were asked to move to help establish the new church. Rebellion arose in her heart at yet another change in her life. Finally, however, she realized that she was rebelling against God, so she gave herself up and accepted His will. God blessed the move, and she enjoyed every day in her new congregation.

Nine years later, the church had grown and felt the need to begin another outreach. Becky dreaded the partings that this would create in her church, not realizing that she would be one of those who would move. When her nephew and family were chosen to move, she just accepted it and went along. She testifies that although there were adjustments, she still enjoys her new location.

Becky has never become a famous person, accumulated wealth, or had children of her own, yet she brightens her corner wherever God places her. She cares about others and always seems to have a word of encouragement for everyone she meets. Becky seems "addicted to the ministry of the saints" and is happy in her role.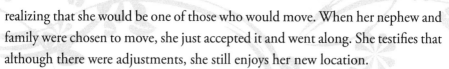

According to your faith be it unto you.
—Matthew 9:29

How often do I limit God's blessings for me through the smallness of my faith? The widow who came to Elisha for help was in dire need. Her bills were past due and she did not have money to pay them. The creditor was coming to seize her only assets.

"What do you have in your house?" the prophet asked, pointing her to her own resources, scanty and seemingly insufficient though they were. When she was commanded to borrow vessels from the neighbors, she did so. As far as her faith ventured, so far was it rewarded. She sold the oil and paid her debts.

How many containers would I have borrowed? How great would my faith have been? Do I sometimes limit God because of my lack of faith? According to our simple trust in God to supply our needs, so will we be rewarded.

....
....
....
....
....
....
....
....

I delight to do thy will, O my God: yea, thy law is within my heart.

—Psalm 40:8

God appeared to Abraham one night with an unusual command: "Take now thy son, thine only son Isaac, whom thou lovest, and get thee into the land of Moriah; and offer him there for a burnt offering" (Genesis 22:2).

Can you imagine Abraham's struggle as he spent a sleepless night surrendering the treasure of his old age? The very next morning, Abraham rose early to prepare for the journey. Hebrews 11:19 says that Abraham had faith "that God was able to raise him (Isaac) up, even from the dead." What faith in God! And so father and son journeyed together to the hills in unquestioning obedience to God's command. The two climbed Mt. Moriah together. There Abraham gathered the stones, laid the wood in order, and bound his son as a lamb for sacrifice and laid him on the wood. At God's command, Abraham gave up his dearest treasure—his son of promise, the crown of his old age and his hope for descendants. What a surrender of will, desires, and future to God!

God enables us to do this too. When His Spirit says, "Sacrifice your desires to me," we must obey without question as Abraham did. We must let our wills be bound and laid on a spiritual altar. We must kneel by the altar in true surrender and sacrifice it all to God. In surrender and acceptance we find peace.

God has a plan for your life, but you cannot see it all now. He only asks you to lay down your will so He can work. Place your hand into His today, surrender your all to Him, and rise to walk with God. He who holds the future will plan the future for you.

September 1

For whosoever shall keep the whole law, and
yet offend in one point, he is guilty of all.
—James 2:10

The man's words were impressive. It seemed he only had to open his mouth and a flow of Scriptural knowledge and instruction poured forth. The woman's convictions and dedication to principles of separation were something to emulate. This man and woman were convinced that they knew God's will.

But however sincere these people may have been, they seemed to lack victory in some areas of their lives. Discerning that caused me to check my own life for inconsistencies. God is glorified more by my walk than by my talk.

Sewing a garment extra securely in some places and more loosely in other places will not make a sturdy garment. The loosely sewn places will soon open and let in cold, rain, and snow. So it is in my life. If I study about and discuss only those areas in which I am strong, I will have problems too. Weak areas in my spiritual life, if not taken care of, will open my soul to many dangers.

The Christian should be strong both in Bible principles and in their applications. Jesus told the Pharisees, who were strong in certain areas and weak in others, "These ought ye to have done, and not to leave the other undone" (Matthew 23:23).

Serving God with our whole hearts will enable us to live consistent lives. If God sends us conviction, admonition, and rebuke, it could be that He desires to see more consistency in our lives.

—Proverbs 31
(paraphrased for single women who work for Christian employers)

Who can find a virtuous woman? Her price is far above rubies.

The heart of her employer safely trusts in her; he knows that she will not waste his money. She will do him good and not evil all the days of her employment.

She seeks to learn all she can about her job and works willingly to the best of her ability. She is a blessing to her employer, bringing new ideas and developing new skills to benefit the business.

She does not complain about needing to work overtime to accomplish her part of the task so that others can do their work on schedule.

She is capable of carrying out responsibilities and making decisions in the best interests of the business.

She learns from manuals and other work-related material, continually open to improving how she does her job.

She is loyal to her employer and speaks well of the business when she is not at work.

She is not above doing mundane tasks that are not a part of her main responsibility. She is sensitive to the needs of her co-workers, always willing to help those who have more work than they can finish and always ready to inform newcomers about company policies and procedures.

She is not afraid of deadlines, for she has done her best to carefully complete each step of her work on time.

Applying knowledge and insight, she is characterized by efficiency and skill.

If her employer needs time away from his business to care for church responsibilities, she can fulfill her responsibilities in his absence.

Strength and honor are blessings the Lord gives her for faithful service, and she shall rejoice in time to come with the rewards of knowing her work was well done.

Others may seek her help and counsel, for she opens her mouth with wisdom;

and in her tongue is the law of kindness.

She has a good understanding of the work in her department and seeks creative ways to profit the business when her own workload is light.

Her fellow employees rise up and call her blessed; her supervisor also, and he praises her. A woman who fears the Lord will be praised.

Give her of the fruit of her labors, and let her own works praise her in the presence of others. 🌑

> . . . and shall leave me alone: and yet I am not alone, because the Father is with me.
>
> —John 16:32

Loneliness is something all women face, whether single or married. In this verse Jesus felt alone too. People railed against Him and wanted to kill Him. As if that weren't enough, Jesus also knew that one day soon even His closest friends would forsake Him. Through all of this He said, "I am not alone, because the Father is with me." Do you hear the note of victory? God had not forsaken His Son. He was there to listen, to care, and to understand Jesus' innermost being. He will do the same for you as you avail yourself of His presence. To know that you are not alone brings much joy, freedom, and peace.

Loneliness can stem from self-pity and self-centeredness. It may come from not trusting God for all the details of life. Follow the example of Jesus when He felt alone.

How precious to know that He cares about us and our needs. He longs to send fulfillment to our hearts. Sometimes I have wondered how the Lord will lead me, but then I marvel because His grace is sufficient day by day. If we continue to daily lean on the sufficiency of God's grace, we can be assured that someday we will be with Jesus face to face, never to be lonely anymore!

And that which fell among thorns are they, which, when they have heard,
go forth, and are choked with cares and riches and pleasures of this life.
—Luke 8:14

Do not apologize or feel inferior if you do not have as much going on in your life as others do. Do not feel cheated or left out if your life is not a whir of activity. Do not be dismayed when others can afford costly recreational activities or possessions.

Activity, position, and riches do not make us acceptable with God. Rather, as Jesus said, they can keep us from God. If you are not encumbered with many earthly cares, count it as a blessing from God. If you find yourself in a time of solitude right now, view it not as a burden or a handicap, but rather as an opportunity to fellowship and commune with God. The prophets of old who lived in seclusion, poverty, and loneliness received thundering messages and rapturous visions from God.

Listen to the words of the Apostle John, who was banished to the cruelties and isolation of the Isle of Patmos:

> I . . . heard behind me a great voice, as of a trumpet.
> I looked, and, behold, a door was opened in heaven.
> And I beheld, and I heard the voice of many angels.
> And I saw a great white throne.
> And I saw a new heaven and a new earth.[1]

Jesus Himself, when He needed strength and refreshment, sought solitude to communicate with His Father. We need to follow His example.

God may not choose to reveal Himself or His will to you in the same way He did to the prophets. Seek Him not for rapturous visions and thunderous messages, but seek Him because He is God—and you will find fullness of joy in His presence.

---

1   Revelation 1:10, 4:1, 5:11, 20:11, 21:1

Ye have sown much, and bring in little; ye eat, but ye have not enough; ye drink, but ye are not filled with drink; ye clothe you, but there is none warm; and he that earneth wages earneth wages to put it into a bag with holes.

—Haggai 1:6

A gardener sows seeds, envisioning baskets full of fruit at harvest time. To sow much and bring in little is failure. To be served a delicious meal but eat only a little is not satisfying. To be given a warm glass of water on a hot summer day is disgusting. To dress yourself with a sweater and feel no warmer than before is disappointing. When you work hard to earn money but your expenses are greater than your profits, you feel defeated.

This was Judah's condition at this time. The people attempted to live in luxury while neglecting God's house. Because God's house did not have first place in their hearts, God could not bless them.

Today we quote Matthew 6:33—"But seek ye first the kingdom of God, and his righteousness; and all these things shall be added unto you." No one else can decide what this verse means for you. You may be faced with a choice between two important things to do. You alone must decide what God is asking of you. Sometimes God uses circumstances or other people to show His will. Be open to counsel, and above all, seek God. Then it will be easier to keep your priorities right. Trust God to work out the details when you are sure that you are doing His will. ✸

Knowing this, that our old man is crucified with him, that the body of
sin might be destroyed, that henceforth we should not serve sin.
—Romans 6:6

Because carnality cannot inherit the kingdom of God, God provides a cross for each of His children. The cross is not an unattractive, cumbersome object of antiquity, nor is it an ornament of vain display or an object to be worshipped. We worship the Designer of the cross when we accept what it can do for us. It is an object of rest; without it there is no contact with Jesus.

That area of your life about which the Spirit keeps reminding you? Crucify it. You will not have rest until you do. The desires God asks you to crucify are things that will not benefit you. No one ever goes wrong by following God's will. Satan would have us believe that through surrender we lose all; instead, we gain everything.

The power to live a victorious life cannot be found in the old nature. Do not try to improve your flesh; rather, let it die.

For who hath despised the day of small things?

—Zechariah 4:10

Opportunities for the Single Lady

Laboring in God's vineyard,
In the place He's called us to:
This, my single sisters,
Is God's plan for me and you.

Our heavenly Father honors
The cup in His name given;
The tender word that's spoken
That points the way to heaven.

A friend may find new courage
When you just hold her hand,
Listen to her troubles,
And say, "I understand."

When little children's garments
Your willing hands have sewed,
The busy mother thanks you
For a lifting of her load.

Perhaps it was a letter
Or a phone call to a friend,
You never know the courage
And the comfort that you lend.

It could have been a visit
To someone sick in bed;

Perhaps it was a story
That to a child you read.

Yes, we need to labor
To supply our daily needs,
But let's have broader visions
Of kind and loving deeds.

Opportunities unnumbered
Lie at our very door;
I've only listed several,
You can think of many more.

Don't waste your time in brooding
That you have no family;
God has blessings for the married
As well as for you and me.

Our heavenly Father honors
The little things we do;
So we, who are His children,
Should find them joyous too.

Let's lift our eyes, dear sisters,
The fields are truly white;
Let's find, in loving service
For Jesus, our delight.

September 8

If the Son therefore shall make you free, ye shall be free indeed.
—John 8:36

Martha was a happy, contented single woman in her mid-thirties. The Lord was the source of her deep joy. She rested in His will and trusted in His guidance. Martha knew that God had chosen her to be single for a special purpose, and confidently she rejoiced daily that "The Lord will perfect that which concerneth me" (Psalm 138:8).

Ever since childhood, Martha had been surrendering her will to God. "Thy will be done in earth, as it is in heaven," she had prayed countless times. Yet when she realized that God might have chosen her to serve Him as a single person, she had not felt surrendered at all. It was then that she began to learn what surrender actually meant.

Martha had possessed a deep desire to share her life with a man of God's choice. Now God seemed to be saying, "No." This provoked a battle within her, but she found comfort, strength, and courage in prayer and in God's Word. With the passing of time, Martha came to surrender her own desires, hopes, plans, and self-will. She had learned that breaking the yoke of the oppressor was not done by fighting but by surrendering. Peace settled into her soul. This was a joyous, new beginning in Martha's life.

She also learned that surrendering to Christ was not a one-time event, but a day-by-day experience that became more and more meaningful.

One day many years later, Martha shared some of her past struggles with Susan, an older friend. Susan kindly advised her that her reasoning should be positive. Instead of asking, "Why me, Lord?" she should be asking, "Why not me?"

Martha accepted the advice gratefully. Even though by now she fully embraced the truth that God had the right to control the lives of His children, she found it encouraging to think, *Why not me?*

Martha rejoiced exceedingly in the peace of mind that honest surrender had wrought in her life. The Lord satisfied her soul's longing with His goodness. And most of all, she found that there was no greater love than God's love for her, a redeemed child of God. 🄱

I can do all things through Christ which strengtheneth me.

—Philippians 4:13

When I was working in a children's home in Honduras, one of the most stressful things I encountered was disciplining the children. It was difficult to know how to punish each misdeed in a redemptive way. One time when I was at my wits' end, I had to spank two six-year-old boys. After the punishment, I dismissed them from my room and sat down at my desk, feeling drained.

I picked up a card that someone had given me. It encouraged me not to desire an easier load, but courage to bear the one I had. Secondly, it encouraged me not to desire only the things I wanted in life, but to desire patience to accept frustrations as they come. And last of all, it encouraged me not to ask God for perfection in everything I do, but rather to desire wisdom so that I do not repeat my mistakes. How blessed I felt that there is an answer to every need. My strength was renewed to go on.

For what the law could not do, in that it was weak through the flesh, God sending his own Son in the likeness of sinful flesh, and for sin, condemned sin in the flesh.

—Romans 8:3

Is it possible to live for God in a world of sin?
Is it possible to obey all His commandments?
Is it possible to be victorious through rejection and alienation?
Is it possible to be nonresistant through accusations?
Is it possible to resist temptation in a weakened state?
Is it possible to perform a deed of love during intense suffering?
Is it possible to live a life of voluntary self-denial?

The flesh says it is too difficult to take a stand and obey all the commandments of God. It says it is impossible to stand alone and be mistreated. The flesh is weak and only wants to think of self. Surrender looks like foolishness and bondage.

Must we conclude, then, that the answers to our questions are negative? Think of Jesus. He was here with a human body and lived for God in a world of sin, resisted temptation in a weakened state, and lived a voluntary life of self-denial. When we look into His life for answers to our questions, we see that every one of these things is possible. It is only possible for us when we have the same power that He did. If we think in terms of what is natural or logical, it is not possible. Jesus laid down His rights, reasoned with a heavenly mind instead of a humanistic mind, and willingly surrendered to His Father. Because of this, He was comforted when He was rejected and forsaken. He felt grace and assurance when He was weak and falsely accused. His life proves that His power is greater than the flesh.

....

....

....

O my God, I trust in thee: let me not be ashamed, let not
mine enemies triumph over me.

—**Psalm 25:2**

David's prayer to God was, "Help me never give in to the things that tempt me, so that I need not feel remorse and regret. Don't let these things rule my life."

We have scores of enemies, foes that would injure and seek our hurt. Our enemies include pride, self-centeredness, gossip, envy, discontent, self-pity, discouragement, disrespect, and worry. We need to overcome these enemies that seek mastery over our daily lives. God does not want His people to be cowards or to be defeated.

As we consider warfare, we think of two opposing forces fighting each other. Usually one side wins and the other is overcome or surrenders and allows itself to be ruled by the winning side.

We need to stand solidly on truth. We dare not give up in defeat. God is willing and ready to help us. The psalmist cried out, "Deliver me, O Lord, from mine enemies: I flee unto thee to hide me" (Psalm 143:9). Since we are helpless to fight the enemies in our own strength, we must flee to God for protection and assistance. After that, we can go forth confidently in the strength of the Lord as David did when he met Goliath.

In this life, we will never escape the presence of the enemy. But like David, who found nourishment and divine strength to revive him and move forward in life's battle, we too can find strength in our Provider and Sustainer.

September 12

Happy is the man that findeth wisdom, and the man that getteth understanding. For the merchandise of it is better than the merchandise of silver, and the gain thereof than fine gold.
—Proverbs 3:13-14

Wisdom is a gift from God. Solomon and Daniel were both blessed with it, but the accounts of their lives are vastly different. It is easy to see why one life leaves a note of discouragement and the other a note of inspiration.

Solomon's life seems to begin on a mountaintop and end in a valley of tragedy. The opening scene in Daniel's life is in a valley. That valley not only rose to a peak, but it kept peaking throughout his life.

Solomon at one time used his wisdom in ways that glorified God, but toward the end of his life he fell away from God because of his riches and his many heathen wives. His widespread fame, which his wisdom had gotten for him, did not keep him accountable for his poor decisions.

Daniel was consumed with a desire to serve his God. He was more concerned that his wisdom be used to exalt God than to gather riches. Over and over when he was praised for his wisdom, he directed heathen minds to God. He was not out seeking anything for himself, and his wisdom showed itself only when he was called upon.

God still blesses individuals with wisdom. That wisdom is a blessing to the individual and to others only as it is dedicated to God and used to exalt Him. Wisdom pushed forward and set forth in an arrogant way is not true wisdom. It is a form of control, and it is not appreciated or sought out. Wisdom is wise enough to know that it needs the help of others. When Daniel was called upon to reveal Nebuchadnezzar's dream, he made the matter known to his three friends so they could pray with him.

Wisdom is not bold. It is humble.
Wisdom does not rush. It waits.
Wisdom is not pretentious. It is quiet.

Ye have not, because ye ask not.

—James 4:2

"Dad, I can't find my mittens," seven-year-old Jerry sighed.

Jerry's father threw more hay to the cows before he asked, "Where did you have them last?"

"I don't remember." Jerry's frustration was obvious.

Father and son searched the milk house and barn for the mittens, but they could not find them. Then Jerry's dad suggested, "We should pray about finding the mittens."

Jerry turned his dark eyes up to his father. "But, Dad, I want to find them myself."

We do not think of telling God we do not need Him. However, if our thoughts were prayers, would we be saying, "God, just let me go. I'll figure out this problem myself"?

We get up in the morning and remember the problems we faced yesterday. We pray our morning prayers, but we do not want to bother God with the details. We can handle the little things.

We would not actually say that. But think of how God feels when we face perplexing situations but do not ask for His help. God delights in providing for your needs, but how much of His work is hindered by your failure to ask for His help? The way ahead of you might not be clear and you might not know what to do. Have you asked Him about it, or do you want to find the mittens yourself? ✳

September 14

When I was a child, I spake as a child, I understood as a child, I thought
as a child: but when I became a man, I put away childish things.
—1 Corinthians 13:11

Each of us is on a journey toward maturity. Here are some signposts along
the road that will help us determine our progress. They show what a mature
person looks like.

A mature person is motivated by long-term goals rather than immediate advantages and pleasures. Be willing to endure and persevere amid colorful distractions
and present enticements. Remember examples from the Bible: Moses rejected his
earthly honor and fame for eternal benefits, and Noah spent many years building
the ark and preaching without response.

Maturity is the ability to accept life with its hard knocks, disappointments, and
changes without becoming easily hurt or discouraged. Can you accept these things
gracefully and retain your integrity as Job did? Or do you, like King Ahab, turn
your face to the wall and pout when things do not fall into place as you would
like them to? Joseph displayed a beautiful attitude toward his brothers in spite
of their mistreatment of him. He freely forgave them and held no grudges. Jesus
meekly bore reproach and stands as the perfect example of how to love enemies.

Another mark of maturity is the ability to humbly accept the way God made
you with your own limitations, talents, looks, and abilities. Accepting oneself
includes overcoming feelings of inferiority or worthlessness. God has created you
for a specific purpose and He wants you to fill your special place. This proper
perspective of yourself will also help you not to become selfish. It will cause you
to think of others. A small child tends to grab the biggest, brightest, and best for
himself without thinking of others, but maturity looks out for the other person.

A mature person will accept others with their varying degrees of maturity, seeing the
good in them and appreciating them for who they are. You will exhibit maturity when
you can see people as God sees them, be at peace with your own limitations, accept
disappointments without becoming bitter, and keep your focus on long-term goals.

In quietness and in confidence shall be your strength.

—Isaiah 30:15

Several years ago I was surprised to discover that during the seven years Solomon built the house of God, no iron tool was used or heard at the building site. The temple was built in reverence and quietness, without the usual construction sounds of saws and hammers. It reminded the people that God is to be revered, and quietness is a part of reverence.

A quiet spirit is a spirit at rest. Even when we need to speak out or when we are surrounded by noise, our inner spirit can reflect a certain quietness and peace. When we feel distraught or wounded, we can find healing by becoming quiet and communing with Jesus. If we have been slighted or misunderstood, our strength lies in quietness. We can live in humility, knowing that we do not need to right all that is wrong. Rather, we can simply give the threads to Jesus and let Him untangle the maze.

Sometimes we have too much to say. Like Job, we should at times lay a hand upon our mouths. True strength is shown, not by forceful language, but by quiet understanding and thoughtfulness.

....

....

....

....

....

....

....

September 16

For God is not unrighteous to forget your work and labour of love, which ye have shewed toward his name, in that ye have ministered to the saints, and do minister.
—Hebrews 6:10

Often in his letters Paul takes time to mention specific people who were special to him in some way. He could have merely said, "My group of friends," or "My brothers and sisters in the Lord," but he made the effort to name them. Were they all great preachers or prophets or miracle workers? Hardly. They were Christians who often worked behind the scenes. Some of these names appear in the Bible only once, and little is known about them. But notice what Paul says about his friends: "Onesiphorus . . . oft refreshed me, and was not ashamed of my chain" (2 Timothy 1:16). "I am glad of the coming of Stephanas and Fortunatus and Achaicus . . . for they have refreshed my spirit" (1 Corinthians 16:17-18). "Phebe our sister, which is a servant of the church" (Romans 16:1). They may have done only small things, but their love for Paul had a strengthening effect.

Such quiet dedication is worthy of my aspiration! Sometimes I do things behind the scenes, such as helping a busy mother prepare for company, praying and fasting in preparation for revival meetings, and destroying fresh spider webs at church on a Sunday morning. I should not be disturbed if the mother forgets to tell her company about my help, if I am not recognized for helping to bring about a revival, or if nobody finds out why the church house is immaculate on Sunday mornings. If the Lord wants these things to be made known, He may do so in His own time and way. If I cannot work behind the scenes, I need to examine myself to see if I get more satisfaction from being recognized and applauded than I do from serving the Lord. Love often works behind the scenes.

September 17

Are not five sparrows sold for two farthings, and not one of them is forgotten before God? . . . Fear not therefore: ye are of more value than many sparrows.

—Luke 12:6-7

It was one of those times when I had been out of work and wondering where I could find a new job. All efforts I had made to find another one seemed futile. I had been praying about it, but I found myself getting impatient instead of waiting on God.

The ring of the telephone interrupted my troubled thoughts. I forgot about the worries as I chatted with my friend. She told me how burdened she was for her sister who was battling cancer and would soon die in the nursing home. "But you know," she concluded, "Hattie is always so happy in her sickness, and the other day before I left her she said, 'God cares for the tiny sparrow, so I know He cares for me here in this bed too.'"

I felt ashamed and rebuked for my discouraged thoughts when I considered how Hattie trusted God in her situation. Even though I didn't have a job, I was healthy and finally had time to do some sewing projects. Instead of enjoying my time off, though, I had worried. I decided to put my trust in God, and He gave me peace and met my needs.

....

....

....

....

....

September 18

Thou shalt call, and I will answer thee: thou wilt have a
desire to the work of thine hands.

—Job 14:15

"Dear Lord, tonight I was at the song service. A lot of other people were there, but I was lonely. Carol, Janet, and Rebekah have each other. Bless their friendship, Lord, and guide them in their life choices. They are young and have many unknown steps ahead of them. Bless all the dating couples who were there. They looked happy; help their love to grow deeper. Be with the young-married couples and those with small children. May they create homes in which strong Christian families can thrive. Bless the grandparents in our church. Help them to be good examples to their offspring every day. And then, Lord, there were some who could not be there tonight. Be with the parents of the new baby, and be with Anna, who is having health problems. Give them strength for every day.

"Lord, I love to sing. I was especially inspired by the new song. I was happy to be there, but just a bit lonely. I am not feeling sorry for myself, but I have no one on earth with whom to share this feeling of loneliness. I knew you would understand. Thank you for all the blessings you send my way. In Jesus' name, Amen."

....

....

....

....

....

....

September 19

Let your conversation be without covetousness; and be content with such things as ye have: for he hath said, I will never leave thee, nor forsake thee.

—Hebrews 13:5

So often discontentment is associated with being single. Sometimes we imagine that a single person can never have a fulfilled and satisfied life. That is not true, but why are we tempted to think such thoughts?

God gave humans a natural desire for companionship, so to wish for the married life is only normal. But the challenge is to not constantly wish for something more or different. We must put our all on the altar daily when we have a struggle to accept our lot in life. We can rest in Him, knowing that Jesus Christ is our constant companion. We can trust Him because His Word says, "And behold, I am with thee, and will keep thee in all places whither thou goest . . . for I will not leave thee" (Genesis 28:15).

Companionship can also be found among other singles, especially those who have the same faith and interests in life. As the years go by, we can say with the psalmist, "I have been young, and now I am old; yet I have not seen the righteous forsaken, nor his seed begging bread" (Psalm 37:25).

"Dear Lord, help me to be content to fill a lowly corner here on earth. Even though I seem insignificant, yet I know I am special to you. Help me to give heed to the needs of others so that my life can be abundant and full. Cause me to remember that I am never alone because you are always with me, ready to give me love, hope, and encouragement. Thank you. In Jesus' name, Amen."

And he came and found them asleep again: for their eyes were heavy.

—Matthew 26:43

Then Simon Peter having a sword drew it, and smote the high priest's servant, and cut off his right ear.

—John 18:10

Then began he to curse and to swear, saying, I know not the man. And immediately the cock crew.

—Matthew 26:74

Simon Peter had walked with Jesus for three years, talking with Him and listening to Him. Yet here in the garden he displayed a character very unlike the Man he followed. Jesus had taught nonresistance in word and deed. Now that there was an opportunity to follow those teachings, Peter failed.

Perhaps Peter did not catch Jesus' urgency when He said, "Tarry ye here and watch with me." Perhaps he did not realize that watching with Jesus could spare him much sorrow. Whatever the reason, he did not watch—and he made some drastic mistakes.

What difference would staying awake have made in his behavior? Staying awake and praying as Jesus had told him to do would have given him strength to stand firm. He would have seen His Saviour in agony, and a fierce loyalty would have arisen in his heart. He would have heard Jesus say, "Nevertheless not as I will, but as thou wilt," stamping an unforgettable picture of complete surrender on his mind. Experiencing these things could have enabled him to remain nonviolent like Jesus instead of taking matters into his own hands.

Watching with Jesus—what does it mean? It means staying awake spiritually. It sometimes means staying awake physically to pray for someone or offer physical help. It means studying the Word to gain a clearer picture of who God is. It means spending time in prayer to gain the victory. Where there is watchfulness, there will be surrender instead of violence and turmoil.

September 21

Have not I commanded thee? Be strong and of a good courage; be not afraid, neither be thou dismayed: for the Lord thy God is with thee whithersoever thou goest.

—Joshua 1:9

Have we not all waded through the slough of discouragement where we were drained of courage and threatened with despondency?

Numerous factors cause discouragement. They may be temporary, such as a large task or a passing illness. Other circumstances may last longer, such as an ongoing relationship struggle that seems to get nowhere and only raises more mountains before you. You may not know where to turn for help. You may even succumb to "second-hand discouragement"—being with someone else who is feeling discouraged. Maybe someone around you is not doing her share of the work, as Martha felt when she became frustrated with Mary. Elijah became discouraged and wished to die when he felt so alone in the wicked world.

Disappointments are a part of life. Discouraging times come, things do not always go smoothly, we get sick, and we have burdens to carry. How can we overcome? Where shall we turn for help?

We must take courage, accept the trials, and pray for God's help. We need to confide in Him and remember the reward at the end of life. Heaven will be worth all the pain we need to go through to get there. Lift up the hands that hang down and make a conscious effort to rise above the circumstances. Encourage others and share your struggles with a friend. Remember that God is present. If He is with you, who or what can be against you?

....

....

....

....

There is a friend that sticketh closer than a brother.
—Proverbs 18:24

Since I am not married, I can read this verse as "there is a friend that is closer than a husband." I believe the enemy is seeking to discourage single women by trying to make them feel that without a husband life cannot be happy, fulfilling, or satisfying. But our Saviour is the best friend anyone could ever want!

People fail us and disappoint us, but our Saviour far exceeds our highest expectations of a friend. He never fails; He never disappoints. When our younger sisters and close friends marry, we struggle at times. But if we allow ourselves to feel that God is unfair, that we are missing out on something we need, or that we have some flaw that prevents us from being married, we will become discouraged and defeated.

God has created us and knows perfectly well what we need to conform us to the image of His Son. Let us be content knowing that He knows best. "But my God shall supply all your need according to his riches in glory by Christ Jesus" (Philippians 4:19). I praise Him because I have found the perfect friend! Like Him there is no other.

....

....

....

....

....

....

Pride goeth before destruction, and an haughty spirit before a fall.

—Proverbs 16:18

This verse states one of God's irrevocable laws. God set many such laws in motion, and no one can stop or bypass them.

The law of sowing and reaping is true in the natural sense. If you plant peas, you reap peas, not beets or corn. If you sow seeds of pride, you will reap a bitter harvest.

Because of the law of gravity, what goes up comes down. If we jump, we expect to return to the earth again rather than float around in space. The higher we jump, the farther and faster we fall. So it is with pride; when we allow it in our lives, we can expect God to abase us and bring us to shame.

Pride involves wanting to be great and wanting to be noticed. Haughtiness has the connotation of being scornful of others. You might want to elevate yourself, but the Bible says the outcome will be just the opposite—you will be put down. You may have observed that when someone is trying to impress others by boasting or doing things for attention, it works directly opposite of that. Showing off lowers a person in the eyes of onlookers, and bragging is repulsive.

"For whosoever exalteth himself shall be abased; and he that humbleth himself shall be exalted" (Luke 14:11).

So she gleaned in the field until even.
—Ruth 2:17

Among the golden sheaves we find the humble gleaner, Ruth, her back bent, her keen eyes searching for the heads of grain missed by the reapers. The blazing midday sun does not halt her quest to provide daily food for herself and her mother-in-law. The meager gleanings left by the reapers do not discourage her; she continues searching until evening. Slowly but surely, the sack slung over her shoulder becomes heavy with the precious grain as back and forth over the field she goes, in and out among the sheaves. Her diligence produced much fruit: in the evening when she thrashed her gleanings, she had about eight gallons of grain to take home to Naomi.

God needs more people like Ruth in His harvest field, more persistent gleaners to search among the sheaves and along the fence rows for the lost grains. Even if the return for the labor is scarce, each "grain" is precious in His sight. With purposeful persistence in labor, we can have a sack of lost grains for the Master. God may call others to gather in the full sheaves, while we may be left to gather the gleanings amid the stubble and along the edges of the field, but God counts us all as His royal gleaners. Faithfulness is more important to God than efficiency or quantity—He only asks us to "to glean in the field until even."

"He that goeth forth and weepeth, bearing precious seed, shall doubtless come again with rejoicing, bringing his sheaves with him" (Psalm 126:6).

....

....

....

....

Therefore let us not sleep, as do others; but let us watch and be sober.

—1 Thessalonians 5:6

When a member of the family does not get home until late in the evening, I sit up and wait for him. I hardly notice the growing darkness because I am watching intently for the lights of a certain vehicle. When I see lights heading my direction, but then the vehicle turns off before reaching our lane, I know it isn't the vehicle I am looking for.

I am also watching for Christ's return. The thought of His coming must occupy my mind to keep me from falling into a spiritual sleep. If His coming is foremost in my mind, the increasing darkness of the world will not alarm me. I will look past it as I look for His glorious appearance.

False prophets will arise. The vanity of their words can be identified by comparing them with the Word of God. If my eyes are on Christ and His Word, nothing else will qualify.

In summary, if Christ's coming is uppermost in my mind, I will watch with vigilance. I will not become overly disturbed at the forecasts of gloom but will maintain a vision of His coming, when He will have the final victory over these conditions. I will stay close to the One who is truth so that falsehood is easily recognizable. I will lift up my head, for my redemption draweth nigh!

And God shall wipe away all tears from their eyes; and there shall be no more death, neither sorrow, nor crying, neither shall there be any more pain: for the former things are passed away.

—Revelation 21:4

If we are faithful, someday we will stand in the dazzling splendor of a new world. God will freely provide all we need without us having to sweat, toil, skimp, or save. We will have no outside evil influence, nor any inner temptation to sin. There will be no possibility of falling away from what is right. We will never be hot, cold, hungry, or lonely. We will not need to work or sleep. There will be no wars, famines, accidents, or earthquakes. We will not feel worried or burdened about anything. We will not face stressful uncertainties, weighty responsibilities, or crushing disappointments. Discouragement will be a thing of the past, as will misunderstandings, problematic relationships, and all discomfort and pain. We will not need to fear anything. Failure will be impossible. God will clothe us in white, and our garments will never be soiled.

In heaven, we will always praise and adore our Saviour, never growing weary of doing so. We will no longer pray in faith, because we will see Jesus and live with Him. We will no longer need chastisement; we will rest forever. We will not need to strive to grow more like Him, for we will be like Him. Faith, hope, and expectation will be blessings of the past. They will be exchanged for reality with no fear that our pleasures will end. Forever we will be with the One who loves us with a perfect love and who makes us supremely happy. We will know fullness of joy and bliss such as we had never known before. Heaven will surely be worth it all!

....

....

....

....

> Their strength is to sit still.
> —Isaiah 30:7

Sit still? I protest against the idea. I tell the Lord that I need to know the answer now; I can't just sit still, because I have so many other things to do. But He calls to me again and reminds me there is no other way to hear His voice and feel calm. The people in Isaiah's day did not want to wait; they wanted to flee. But they also lost a blessing. Luke says, "In your patience possess ye your souls" (21:19). God teaches us when we are quiet before Him. He says, "Be still, and know that I am God" (Psalm 46:10). That is when we become calm and find new strength. "They that wait upon the Lord shall renew their strength" (Isaiah 40:31).

Another time we should sit still is when we face a great trial or adversity. We need not panic or despair; rather, we need to become quiet to hear God's voice and His promises, and the fruit of patience can come forth. "Knowing this, that the trying of your faith worketh patience. But let patience have her perfect work, that ye may be perfect and entire, wanting nothing" (James 1:3-4). Who of us does not desire perfection? This is the way to attain it. Allow God to do His work through each of life's experiences. Find the strength that comes from sitting still. ☙

....

....

....

....

....

....

Lest Satan should get an advantage of us: for we are not ignorant of his devices.
—2 Corinthians 2:11

I was sitting quietly, not suspecting a thing, when suddenly something slid over my shoulder and across the front of my dress. I shuddered in silent horror. A wasp? I was having problems with wasps getting into the house, so my first thought was to blame that creature as my silent invader. But no, after it stopped sliding and landed in my lap, I saw it was only a harmless bobby pin that had slid out of my hair.

After I smiled in relief, I thought about how the devil sometimes terrorizes people by leading them to believe what is not true. People might believe themselves guilty of sinning when they are severely tempted in an area. Others may feel that they have done something wrong because a vague feeling nags at them, yet they cannot pinpoint a certain wrongdoing. Some people seem to hear voices in their minds, telling them things such as "You don't fit in" or "You are a nobody." The devil knows which of his tactics will terrorize a woman to think she is a sinner, a misfit, or a nobody—when she really is not. The devil cannot harm the child of God who abides in His will, but he still makes a silent effort to bring doubt, confusion, and potential ruin to her life.

Once I realized that it was only a bobby pin that had landed on my lap, it no longer scared me; I saw it for what it was. If I am familiar with God and His Word, there is no need to become panic-stricken by troubled feelings. If I take a close look at them, I will see that fear is speaking, and not God. I can then place my trust in Him instead of living in fear.

> And they that be wise shall shine as the brightness of the firmament; and they that turn many to righteousness as the stars for ever and ever.
>
> —Daniel 12:3

What is more inspiring on a clear night than to step outside and admire the twinkling sky? After God had made the sun with heat and light to rule the day and the silvery moon to be lord of the night, "he made the stars also" (Genesis 1:16). Even though God did not create the stars first, you can be sure that He created them with purpose, intelligence, and careful design. He does nothing half-heartedly.

Like the stars, we may seem fairly insignificant from a distance, but we can still shine His light to those around us. The True Light shining through us illuminates the darkness of sin's night and lends a shining ray to point the way to God. Without the True Light, "which lighteth every man that cometh into the world" (John 1:9), we are nothing. We can generate no light at all. Jesus generates the light that shines through us and reflects His love.

Jesus often referred to His children as lights: "Ye are the light of the world" (Matthew 5:14). "Let your light so shine before men, that they may see your good works, and glorify your Father which is in heaven" (Matthew 5:16). Paul mentioned it as well: "In the midst of a crooked and perverse nation, among whom ye shine as lights in the world" (Philippians 2:15).

Cloud cover can obscure the light of the stars. Cloudiness in our spiritual lives can result from allowing something to mar or block our relationship with Christ. If we would shine brightly, we need to consider our relationship with Him daily. We will then inspire those around us.

Now it came to pass, as they went, that he entered into a certain village: and a certain woman named Martha received him into her house. And she had a sister called Mary, which also sat at Jesus' feet, and heard his word.
—Luke 10:38-39

D id you ever envy Mary, Martha, and Lazarus? They had the privilege of having Jesus as their guest! It seems their home held a special attraction to Him, and their hearts must have leaped with joy as He came walking up the path. Here He found a retreat from the pressures of the day. Here He could relax and be comfortable. At times He needed a place where He could rest His weary body or a quiet place where He could meditate and pray. He knew He was always welcome at the home of His friends.

Would you not be thrilled if Jesus knocked on your door and wanted to come in? You would go to great lengths to provide what He needed. You would be so overwhelmed at His presence that your schedule for the day would cease to have any importance.

The good news is that Jesus often comes to your door. He may not come in a shining, heavenly robe, but with tired, dusty feet as he did to that home in Bethany. Do you offer Him relief? He may come begging for a listening heart. Do you listen? He may come bearing a heavy load. Do you help to make it lighter? "Inasmuch as ye have done it unto one of the least of these my brethren, ye have done it unto me" (Matthew 25:40).

Behold thy mother!

—John 19:27

My bond with my mother began before I was born. Growth and childbirth strengthened that bond. My childhood memories center on activities that included Mom. Throughout my school years and teenage struggles, where else did I go but to my mom? Then, after I left home, it was wonderful to know that Mom thought about me and kept praying for me.

Memories are precious, but missing in them are the adult feelings that come to us only after we become mothers and see things from that standpoint.

Our son is only five months old, but his pain and hurts become my own. My heart yearns to see the child on my lap become a respectful, God-fearing person. Then I think of my mother. Did she have that longing for me? Did she also pray often for her baby? Did she dream of the time when I would return the love she so unselfishly lavished on me?

Some have lost their mothers at birth, during childhood, or in their teen years. Memories may become faint, but whoever loses a mother feels a keen sense of loss. Many of us still have our mothers. They have prayed for us for many years. Do we thank God for their priceless love? Do we treat them with respect? Do they know we love them?

If my mother had hopes and dreams for each of her eight children as I have for my son, then certainly she deserves all the appreciation I can give her for her love and support.

In His dying hours, Jesus left a message that we do well to take to heart today: "Behold thy mother!" ✸

I am the vine, ye are the branches. He that abideth in me, and I in him, the same bringeth forth much fruit: for without me ye can do nothing.
—John 15:5

A greenhouse is a refreshing place to visit. In the fall, thousands of mums of all colors line the greenhouse floor and the field outside. Their rich colors and full blossoms tell the story of a wonderful growing environment.

Then toward the end of the year, poinsettias line the shelves. Vein by vein and bract by bract, each one pushes out in brilliant reds, whites, and pinks.

In the spring, tiny blades grow day after day. Trays and trays of vegetable plants, flowers, hanging baskets, and houseplants replace the winter look.

With the proper soil mixture to grow in and the right amount of moisture, each plant thrives. The watchful eyes of those in charge quickly notice too many dead leaves or tiny spider mites. When a problem is detected, the plants are sprayed. Sometimes they need to be moved to a different location, or the temperature needs to be adjusted. Each plant needs just the right amount of sunlight or darkness to burst into its fullest beauty. If a plant was started from healthy stock, rooted properly, transplanted at the right time, kept disease-free, and watered properly, one can expect healthy, beautiful blossoms. Lacking any of these things could mean death to an individual plant or the whole crop.

If we nurture our souls as we nurture plants, we too will bloom in beauty and bring forth fruit. But it takes effort. We must notice the tiny spots of sin or deeds of unkindness in our lives. We must ask God to help us get rid of these things before they destroy us or hurt those around us.

We need to feed our souls with God's Word and water them with prayer, else we will become unproductive. We need the mind of Christ so that our lives are illuminated to know the will of God.

A healthy plant grows, matures, and yields an abundance of fruit. Long after the plant dies, we still enjoy the returns of that plant. Likewise, God's purpose for us is to bring forth much fruit. As we abide in the vine, Jesus Christ, we can bear fruit for His glory. Then, long after we are gone, the fruit of our lives can still touch others.

And he leaping up stood, and walked, and entered with them into the temple, walking, and leaping, and praising God. And all the people saw him walking and praising God.

—Acts 3:8-9

id this man overdo it with his thanksgiving? He had something to be thankful for, and he was not ashamed to let others know about it. In his gratefulness, he probably even forgot that there were onlookers.

Can those around us tell by our lives that we appreciate what Christ has done for us? Do we express our thanks to God? Or are we like the nine lepers who, although glad to be healed, forgot to say, "Thank you"?

Do we dwell upon God's benefits to us, or do we think negatively? Do we lift our hearts in praise, or are we prone to discontentment? Our circumstances do not determine whether we rejoice or not. As the saying goes, "If Christians do not rejoice, it is because they do not live up to their privileges." May it be our common experience to give thanks in everything.

See now that I, even I, am he, and there is no god with me: I kill, and I make alive; I wound, and I heal: neither is there any that can deliver out of my hand.

—Deuteronomy 32:39

Our God of love does not give and take away at random. What He does, He does with purpose, and He provides a balance for our lives.

As I reflect upon the past, my heart goes out to each of my acquaintances who has experienced a broken courtship, a painful severing from the one she was learning to love.

Memories of special times together become very painful after a broken relationship. If you have experienced something like this, it is of utmost importance to look to Jesus for comfort and healing. During this critical time in your life, when all kinds of discouraging thoughts try to overwhelm your mind, Satan wants you to believe that your purpose in life has ended. But that is not true at all. As you reach out to others, you will find many opportunities to be useful. You will find many who are also hurting and need a word of encouragement from you. By sharing, you will both be encouraged.

Set a goal for your life. Keep your mind occupied and see what you can do to bring joy to others. In so doing, you will bless others and experience joy yourself.

....

....

....

....

....

Then were there brought unto him little children, that he should put his hands on them, and pray: and the disciples rebuked them. But Jesus said, Suffer little children, and forbid them not, to come unto me: for of such is the kingdom of heaven.

—Matthew 19:13-14

Interruptions can seem like such a waste of time. It is unsettling to have a well-planned project or schedule go awry. The disciples, too, thought they should stick to a schedule. Why bother with trifles like pesky children? But Jesus did not share their feelings. His values were different; He was here to perform the will of the Father and to follow *His* schedule.

If I am independent and think I have a right to plan and follow my own schedule, I need to look at the life of Christ. Even though He knew His time on earth was limited, He calmly did what was necessary at the moment. Sometimes it was the thing He had set out to do; other times it was giving attention to an interruption.

When I ask the Lord to direct me throughout the day, I should not be surprised or complain if seeming hindrances arise and my well-laid plans are rearranged or annihilated. I need to remain calm and remember whose day it is and who is planning the day. God must think the interruptions are more important than the work I had planned to do.

By sending trying circumstances, God is forming my character. When an irritating substance lodges inside certain types of oyster shells, the oyster does not cast it out but encloses it with a beautiful protective covering. This is what forms the lustrous, much-sought-after pearl.

I want to allow God to use those "irritating substances" to form an ornament of great price within my spirit.

....

....

....

Be kindly affectioned one to another with brotherly love;
in honour preferring one another.
—Romans 12:10

When you are given a position of authority, you most likely desire to succeed. To accomplish this goal, you need the respect and cooperation of those who work under you.

How can you gain the respect of those you are responsible for? It is important to regard the feelings of those affected by your decisions. Be consistent and fair, and others will appreciate you. Compliment those who have done their best, even when you see need for improvement. A critical person is difficult to honor. If you respect those you are working with, most likely you will not encounter much disrespect from them.

What if you make a mistake? Do you fear that others will lose their respect for you? If you apologize for your failure, you will discover that respect is not lost by just one misstep. A humble person is not hard to respect.

At times you may wonder why someone does not respect you. Do not blame others if you have somehow failed. Bear responsibility for it instead, and work to earn respect. Build up good relationships and cultivate love in your life. You can easily lose respect if you show favoritism to certain people, catering to their desires to gain their favor.

Finally, if you want others to respect your position, it is imperative that you highly esteem those in authority over you. Above all, reverence God. You will better be able to respect others if you recognize God's authority over you. ✺

Now no chastening for the present seemeth to be joyous, but grievous: nevertheless afterward it yieldeth the peaceable fruit of righteousness unto them which are exercised thereby.

—Hebrews 12:11

If you have ever gone through a time of grieving, you know what a tremendous hurdle it can be. Some of us have lost a relative or a close friend in death, or we know the grief of discontinuing a special friendship.

When you are grieving, you may struggle with questions: *How can I ever go on with life as before? How can I live another day with all these memories that were dear to me but are no longer a highlight in my life?* God is full of love and compassion toward us. He will not leave us while our bleeding hearts are numb with grief; He will continue to go with us each step of the way if we draw close to Him. Time is a wonderful healer. As each new day dawns, our memories are one day further away than they were yesterday. Each day, God in His mercy continues to heal you. Slowly, life begins to flow back. The shock ceases to be so jarring. Other things begin to take place in your surroundings. Time is kind and brings relief for the heartaches that gave us such pain.

Even though we will always carry memories of a precious relationship or experience, it is still possible for them to lose their sharpness. Take courage, sister. God allows time to fade these memories as year after year passes. A time will come when we can cheerfully and happily go on with our life's calling.

Then he which had received the one talent came and said, Lord, I knew thee that thou art an hard man, reaping where thou hast not sown, and gathering where thou hast not strawed: and I was afraid, and went and hid thy talent in the earth: lo, there thou hast that is thine.

—Matthew 25:24-25

Although the Lord gives each of us a set of talents, aptitudes, or responsibilities, we sometimes hesitate to develop them and use them to their full potential. You may feel the Lord calling you to some task you would rather not do, or you may be burying your talent because you fear failure. Or perhaps you view others as more talented than yourself and are tempted to slink back, not using your own valuable gift from the Lord. Notice that the servant said, "I . . . hid <u>thy</u> talent." The talent is the Lord's, and you are His steward.

The servant did not use wisely what his lord had entrusted to him. He was afraid things would not turn out well if he tried, so his talent lay dormant and profited no one. Of all the excuses he stacked up, not one saved him from being called an unprofitable servant.

You are also the Lord's servant, and He wants to use you to benefit His kingdom. When He returns, it will not matter if you were multi-talented or one-talented. What will matter is whether you stepped out in faith and used your talent.

If you hesitate because you think your talent is not a "spiritual" talent, remember that all you do for the sake of Christ is a spiritual work. It doesn't matter if the activity is baking cookies, washing dishes, or witnessing to someone—it can all be done for His glory. God cares about our physical lives, and the services we perform with our bodies are important to Him. "And whatsoever ye do in word or deed, do all in the name of the Lord Jesus, giving thanks to God and the Father by him" (Colossians 3:17).

He healeth the broken in heart, and bindeth up their wounds.

—Psalm 147:3

Have you given up something that was hard to part with? If you have, it may seem your heart was cut into pieces. You may feel as though life will never be happy again.

I had the privilege of caring for children who were awaiting permanent homes. My most difficult thing was to give them up as they left me one by one. I dearly loved these children. I fed them, cleaned them, and disciplined them. I sat up with them during the night. I saw their first smiles and their first steps. They were a real part of me. But then came the day when I handed them over to someone else. I tried to prepare myself and them. I had learned to know each new mother well, and I usually handed the child over willingly (at least outwardly). It was a joy to see the happy expressions on the new parents' faces as they realized this child was theirs to love and care for.

But then they were gone, and I felt emptiness like a wound deep inside me. Tears helped a little, but Psalm 147:3 was the promise I clung to. Time was also a healer. I have learned to thank God for each little life that has touched mine. Each one has taught me so much! I continue to thank God for each child who finds security in a Christian home. Those who have not found security in a Christian home I commit into God's care by praying for them. I also thank God for healing my wounds.

If what you have to give up causes a wound, take courage. Look at it as God's perfect will, and trust God to heal your hurts. He will, because He cares for you.

October 10

O Lord, how great are thy works! and thy thoughts are very deep. A brutish man knoweth not; neither doth a fool understand this.

—Psalm 92:5, 6

The monarch butterflies' northeast-to-southwest migration puzzles even the scientists who study them. Monarchs flutter over the sand in Cape Cod, Massachusetts, before beginning their overland flight in August. They fly across the Mississippi River, over the plains, and through Texas before they reach their destination: Mexico. Near the middle of October observers see long, trailing clouds of butterflies come floating across Mexico to settle in oyamel fir trees in the central part of the country.

How can these butterflies, new to this area, recognize the same trees that their ancestors came to for many years before them? These butterflies do not live long enough to make the journey twice. What attracts them to this small area? How do they hold to their course during the 2,500-mile trip?

Another marvel that has taken place for hundreds of years is the rough-winged swallow migration to the ruins of an old mission sixty miles south of Los Angeles. Most of them arrive by March 19 every year, having flown thousands of miles to get there. The people of the town celebrate the return of the swallows every year on that date. After spending the summer nesting in the walls of the stone church ruins, they leave again on October 23. How do these birds know when it is March 19 or October 23?

Yet another mystery of nature concerns sea turtles. The sea turtle lives in the water except to lay her eggs. When the eggs hatch, the two-inch turtles work their way up through the sand and quickly head for the ocean. But no one knows where the young feed. They go out into the deep water and are not seen again until they weigh ten pounds or more. One would think fishermen or sailors might chance to see these growing turtles, but they never do. Some small sea turtles are preyed upon before they reach their secret growing place, but the rest of them are never seen again until they are nearly full-grown.

The mysteries of wildlife make us more aware that God's thoughts are deeper than our own. We stand in awe at His power. "O Lord, how great are thy works!"

308

And when she had so said, she went her way, and called Mary her
sister secretly, saying, The Master is come, and calleth for thee.
—John 11:28

"The Master is calling for thee." How soothing and precious these words must have sounded to Mary's broken heart. The Master, who meant more to her than anyone else, had cared enough to come to her in her sorrow. Not only had He made a special effort to come, but He also had a special message to share, away from prying eyes and ears. No wonder she arose quickly and came to Him. She poured out her heart to Him. And yes, He indeed had a special message, one that showed how much He cared about her needs and the means He had to help her.

Do you, like Mary, have a special need? Your Master is calling for you as well. He cares about you and has a special message for you if you will go to Him and tell Him about your needs. You may have gone to Him many times before, and perhaps you think He is weary of your constant requests or cannot help you with your problem. Jesus had met Mary's needs before, and He was willing—yes, eager—to help her again.

Today He is not waiting for you in Bethany of Judea. Bethany for you may be your own home as you meet Him in prayer or meditate on His Word. It may be the church as you worship there. He will meet you with a message wherever you come to Him.

October 12

And upon this came his disciples, and marvelled that he talked with the woman.
—John 4:27

If you study history, you know why the disciples were amazed that Jesus took time to talk with the Samaritan woman. Even the woman herself was surprised that a Jew would ask her for a drink. The Jews despised the Samaritan people, and some Jews even avoided traveling through Samaria. But Jesus, whose love reached out to people in all classes and categories, did not mind traveling through Samaria.

He took time to talk to this woman living in adultery. He told her about the living water—Himself. She received the Word, and her testimony helped many others believe. They even asked Jesus to stay for two more days.

We also need to tell others about this living water they can drink. We should never think others are too sinful or too morally good to tell them about Jesus' love for them.

My grandfather tells of his acquaintance with a Jew who came to the house from time to time looking for junk. Whenever he came around, they would talk for a while. Grandfather would often try to talk to him about Jesus, but the man never seemed interested. Realizing that something must be wrong, Grandfather prayed about it one evening after the man left. God's answer to his prayer was, "You do not have true love for him."

Grandfather confessed his pride to God and pleaded for true love and another chance to show love to the junk dealer. One day he came walking in the lane again. "God, help me love him," Grandfather prayed as he went out the door to meet the man. That day the man seemed more open than he ever was before, and for an hour they talked about God. What made the difference? The man felt Grandfather's love and concern for him.

Do we take time to talk to the women we clean for or the customers we have every week? Do we love them that much? Do we love our neighbors enough to talk to them about God? During our lives, we meet many people who will all meet God someday. Did we tell them about Him? Someday we will meet God too. Will we be ashamed that we have not told others more about Him?

He that hath the bride is the bridegroom: but the friend of the
bridegroom, which standeth and heareth him, rejoiceth greatly
because of the bridegroom's voice: this my joy therefore is fulfilled.

—John 3:29

John's disciples came to him rather perturbed. "John, the one you were with beyond the Jordan, the one you bear witness of, is baptizing and men are following Him." John's reply reveals a man at peace with himself and with God's plan. "Jesus is the Bridegroom. I am His friend. I will stay back, let Him take His bride, and rejoice with Him in His happiness. My own happiness is fulfilled that way."

There was no tinge of envy, no root of bitterness; in his heart there was only joy and delight at being able to witness the joy of the Bridegroom. He later said, "He must increase, but I must decrease."

Are you able to share in the joy of a bride and groom? Weddings can be an emotional time for us because the reality of change in relationships becomes final, but they are an important part of God's plan. We can pray that our eyes will see the beauty of the plan so that we can rejoice in it and allow our own agendas to fade.

Even when it seemed to others that Jesus was taking away John's ministry, John was sure that God's timing was right. If we are convinced about God's timing in our lives, we will find grace for the occasion.

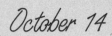

Peter seeing him saith to Jesus, Lord, and what shall this man do? Jesus
saith unto him . . . what is that to thee? follow thou me.
—John 21:21-22

Sometimes I think I know what other people need to build their characters. I
tend to feel that what the Lord uses to refine my life should be used in others'
lives too. Sometimes when I feel left out or lonely, I want the Lord to take others
through the same experience so that they know how it feels. I wonder why others
have certain privileges that are denied me.

Then I am reminded of the words, "What is that to thee? follow thou me."
It was none of Peter's business to know what Jesus wanted John to do, and it is
none of my business to know what He wants other Christians to do. They, too,
hear Jesus' words as they look around at others, possibly even me. Each of God's
children is unique and precious to Him, and He treats each one as an individual,
similar to how parents treat their children.

If I truly desire to be conformed to the image of Christ, I will fall before Him with
praise for each refining touch He adds to my life, whether He denies or gives me
something. If He would allow me to always do what others do and have what others
have, I would not learn to desire Him alone. I would be like a spoiled child who has
everything except a beautiful character. God knows how to bless me and help me to
grow, and my experiences will be God's unique arrangement for me.

....

....

....

....

....

October 15

My lovers and my friends stand aloof from my sore; and my kinsmen stand afar off.

—Psalm 38:11

Alone. Utterly alone. The ticking of the clock and an occasional crackle in the fire were my only companions. I was laid up and the family was gone for the evening. Lying there thinking about myself, my pain, and the hours ahead of me, I sank into despondency.

Even in a crowded hospital or in a busy airport with people milling all around you, you can feel all alone. Loneliness can be felt in any place where you lack meaningful connection with people.

Loneliness can take you where you do not want to be. It causes you to walk from window to window, looking out yet seeing nothing. Loneliness digs through the magazine rack but finds nothing interesting to read. Loneliness wishes the telephone would ring. It grows until you feel you can no longer bear it.

Brief periods of loneliness should not cause alarm, but to dwell on those thoughts and find a dismal solace in them leads to self-pity. We must get our minds off ourselves and onto God. We must think of others and do something for them or with them before wrong thought patterns lead us to despair.

Jesus knew loneliness. Though crowds thronged Him while He was helping them, who stood by and encouraged Him during His agony in the garden? No one. The crowds were gone, and the disciples slept. He faced His cross alone. But Jesus received strength from His connection with God. During His ministry He had spent time alone in prayer, and now as He faced death, that became His source of strength (Matthew 14:23).

Make prayer your source of strength whenever you begin to feel alone.

In the beginning was the Word, and the Word was with God, and the Word was God.
—John 1:1

That which was from the beginning, which we have heard, which we have seen with our eyes, which we have looked upon, and our hands have handled, of the Word of life.
—1 John 1:1

It is believed that John wrote his epistles to counteract false teachings the churches were facing. In spite of those who sought to undermine the Christian faith, he still had the same note of confident faith as he had earlier when he wrote the account of Christ's life. He was so convinced, he could not help but talk about the things he had seen and heard. He knew that Jesus was the Son of God who gives eternal life, and this was his message no matter what appeared on the horizon. Tertullian says John was dipped into hot oil before he was banished to the Isle of Patmos, but none of these hardships changed his mind. The passing of years and the changing of circumstances only solidified his belief.

My life also proclaims a message since I chose to believe that Jesus is the Son of God. The message is that He is Lord of my life. In the face of false teachers and deception, I need to remain convinced more than ever of the things that I have heard and seen. All my thoughts and motives will come under Christ's authority if I truly believe that He is the Son of God. With that settled, I can remain faithful no matter what is on the horizon today or in the future.

....

....

....

....

....

Let no man despise thy youth; but be thou an example of the believers, in word, in conversation, in charity, in spirit, in faith, in purity.

—1 Timothy 4:12

When my brother-in-law was getting ready for his wedding, he typed up the bulletin and included a few songs on it. He made a small mistake that went unnoticed until the bulletins had been printed—the word "Lord" had been typed "LOrd." The striking part of it was the number of weddings they attended later where the same mistake was seen. "I can always tell when someone uses our copy," my sister would say. "I see that capital letter where it does not belong."

The mistake was small—so small that others continued copying the error. How much more serious it is when we make wrong choices and then see someone following us!

Others will follow our example, not always realizing what they are doing. Can they follow us without fear of going wrong? When the children we influence become adults, do we want them to think the things we think, say the words we say, love the people we love, or go the places we go? Other do watch and follow us. We have control over our own actions, but we have no control over who follows us.

October 18

Man's goings are of the Lord; how can a man then understand his own way?
—Proverbs 20:24

Do all things without murmurings and disputings.
—Philippians 2:14

The view of my home from the top of the hill was different. Instead of looking horizontally at the house and the barn, I looked down on them. Instead of seeing only patches and spots, I saw the whole place. I had a distant, encompassing view rather than a close-up view. How refreshing it all was.

Another time I had the privilege of looking down on thousands of treetops. The sight was completely different from that of looking up through the branches and leaves of a tree. I was humbled and awestruck as I gazed at the swaying sea of green. It impressed me to realize that God sees each individual leaf among the millions of leaves below me. Then I thought of how He also sees me and cares for me.

The view from above is different. It takes in the whole plan, the complete layout. The view from below sees only patches and spots. The narrow view from below allows us only to look *at* things, while the wide view from above allows us to look *on* them.

You may wonder why the Lord has brought you to a certain place or put you in your circumstances. You may have struggles you cannot understand. God has a perfect layout, an overall plan into which you fit. He does not expect you to understand everything, because you do not have the view He does. But He expects you to trust His view and plan. He reveals enough of His plan in the Scriptures to give you a refreshing view even though you do not have the same lofty position that He does. Then someday, if you keep trusting, you too will see things from a heavenly point of view—and you will see that His plan was perfect. ◐

For thy Maker is thine husband; the Lord of hosts is his name.

—Isaiah 54:5

My Maker, My All

I was chafing 'neath my lot,
A single maid to be;
Yes, I nursed discouragement,
I know now, shame on me.

Your Maker is your husband,
The Lord God is His name—
Reading His Word, I found this verse;
It helped me bless His name.

When I stopped a bit to think,
I knew I had the best—
For what mortal, human man
Could ever bring me rest,

Sweet joy, and contentment too,
Like my Beloved One?
Who could care for me so well,
Besides God's perfect Son?

If I wish to stay above
Discouragement, my friends,
There is ought that I must do
Or pay the dividends.

Just like all relationships,
It is a two-way street,

I must always strive to be
Kind, gentle, pure, and sweet.

I know that He would have me
My all in Him confide,
And never a single thing
From my Beloved hide.

He, in turn, will ever be,
Far more than I could ask;
He always will be ready
To guide me through each task.

An intimate Companion
Who ever will be near,
A wonderful Provider—
Why should I ever fear?

He is my blessed Comfort
When storms around me roll;
Nothing can ever harm me
While He protects my soul.

Your Maker is your husband,
Oh, how it thrills my heart—
Helps me quickly turn away
Discouragement's sharp dart.

October 20

And in all matters of wisdom and understanding, that the king enquired of them, he found them ten times better than all the magicians and astrologers that were in all his realm.
—Daniel 1:20

What a test Daniel, Shadrach, Meshach, and Abednego faced! Yet they passed the test with unflinching faithfulness that influences us even today. When I meditate on the account of their lives, my faith is strengthened, knowing that God's people can have God's wisdom. Their wisdom and knowledge did not come from the kingdom of Babylon. They were ten times wiser than the Babylonian magicians and astrologers because their wisdom came from God. It was sufficient for whatever they were called to do—lead in the affairs of the kingdom, interpret dreams, or sit in the king's gate. The God whom they refused to deny even in this heathen city was their source of strength and confidence. The splendor and magnificence around them were dead things compared to the power and life their God supplied. That is why they were not moved when they looked at the great, dazzling image the king had set up. They could remain standing when others fell before it, and they could confidently explain their actions in front of a furious king.

Their fixed, unchanging obedience when tempted with the king's meat inspires and amazes me. Unusual circumstances were no excuse to transgress even a little bit. Had they transgressed, the results would have been tragic. Their "little transgression" would have cost their lives. Their source of wisdom would have been cut off, crippling Daniel when he was asked to interpret the king's dream. Then the king would have carried out his decree to kill all the wise men.

I sometimes think of myself as being in a strange land where, at times, I face dire circumstances and a furious king named Satan. If I make excuses to transgress a little bit, I will come under his service. His murderous decrees will be carried out on me. But if my heart is fixed on the God of Daniel, I will not be moved. I know He will give me wisdom. I know He will give me strength to resist deceptively dazzling temptations, enabling me to have a glowing testimony in the face of an angry king.

And God himself shall be with them, and be their God. And God shall wipe away all tears from their eyes; and there shall be no more death, neither sorrow, nor crying, neither shall there be any more pain: for the former things are passed away.

—Revelation 21:3-4

We often spend time dreaming of and planning for future events, but how much time do we spend thinking of our future home in heaven?

Comparing life here on earth to our future home in heaven makes us anticipate living there. On this earth we sorrow for the brother or sister who has gone astray. We experience pain in sickness. We often shed tears of sadness. Sometimes we must say goodbye to friends or loved ones who die. We wrestle with unanswered questions.

In heaven, all sadness will vanish. The joy of living in a place of complete love and belonging will never go away. We will be with the Answer to all our questions, living in His presence forever. In our mortal bodies, we cannot comprehend a place as glorious as heaven—but letting our minds dwell on the bliss that awaits us there motivates us to faithfully endure to the end.

If the whole body were an eye, where were the hearing?
If the whole were hearing, where were the smelling?

—1 Corinthians 12:17

Mr. Henderson did his job well. He was always at work on time. He spoke little and kept at his work. Whenever the crew repaired old buildings, Mr. Henderson was the one assigned to the foundation work—dirty, grimy work down in the ditches where nobody liked to be.

One of the workers approached the boss one day. "Mr. Henderson has worked for you for many years. Why is he still doing such dirty work? Why hasn't he been promoted to something more important than digging ditches?"

The boss, looking surprised, exclaimed, "Mr. Henderson, my foundation worker? I cannot afford to give the most important job on the site to a man less faithful!"

You may be asked to clean the church house or wash the dishes after the fellowship meal. You may be called on to do some typing for your ministers. Your acts of service might include taking care of children while some parents attend a school meeting. Those are small things, but what if no one did them? Many little things are not noticed when they are done, but when they are neglected, they are very noticeable.

Not everyone can be a carpenter on the rooftop or serve the bridal table at a wedding. Some need to dig the foundation or prepare the food where no one notices.

Be like Mr. Henderson—faithful in your corner!

And hereby we do know that we know him, if we keep his commandments.

—1 John 2:3

When the eunuch heard the truth, he asked for baptism. When Zacchaeus knew truth, he hopped out of the tree to do what Jesus wanted him to do. When Mary knew the Holy Spirit would overshadow her and she would bear a son, she said, "Be it unto me according to thy word" (Luke 1:38). We do not see these people waiting for years to do what they knew was right to do. God spoke the word and they obeyed quickly.

Perhaps we think it would be easier if Jesus came to our house today and told us exactly what to do. But Jesus promised us the Holy Spirit to guide us into all truth. Sometimes we see so many physical or monetary needs around us that we become confused. *What should I do now? What is most important today?* When I asked myself those questions, I decided to start praying in the morning, "Lord, what is your plan for me today?" When you ask for His direction and He shows you a need, don't ignore His promptings. Maybe you cannot write that letter within the hour, but you can put it on your to-do list and then put forth every effort to get it in the mail soon. You may be amazed at what you get done when you dismiss all excuses for not calling a friend or visiting a widow today. Being sensitive to the Holy Spirit's nudging brings untold blessings into our lives, just as obedience makes a happy child. ❋

October 24

And, behold, the man clothed with linen, which had the inkhorn by his side, reported the matter, saying, I have done as thou commanded me.
—Ezekiel 9:11

The man with the inkhorn had an unusual assignment. He was to go through the city of Jerusalem and place a mark on the forehead of all those who were grieved at the sins of Israel. Those without a mark would be killed by the five other men who had been with him.

God must have given the man with the inkhorn special wisdom, for he had a grave responsibility. If he did not put a mark on a man, that man was killed..

God has also given you a writer's inkhorn. He wants your tongue to be the pen of a ready writer (Psalm 45:1).

Have you fulfilled your duty to a wayward brother or sister in the church? You can pray for them and write or speak to them. Have you prayed for the youth in your church and encouraged them to faithfulness? Have you spoken to your unbelieving neighbor or written to your unsaved relative? They will be eternally doomed if they do not choose to follow Christ. Does your family know that you love them? You need to tell them so.

Whatever God asks you to write, be sure to write it. Then when you report the matter to God, you can have the same testimony as the man with the inkhorn: "I have done as thou commanded me." ✸

....

....

....

....

....

Who can find a virtuous woman? for her price is far above rubies.

—Proverbs 31:10

Any life dedicated to God becomes virtuous. God will work in that life, producing a heart that radiates compassion, warmth, understanding, and trustworthiness.

This heart will manifest itself in a life of diligence. A virtuous woman works willingly with her hands, be it a lowly or a lofty task. God will give her eyes to notice a need and the wisdom to know how to meet that need.

But God doesn't stop there. He gives the virtuous woman spiritual strength to withstand storms and turmoil. She will lift others in prayer and lighten their burdens. She will be able to share wise counsel and encouragement. God gives her the grace not to seek outward adornment or the favor of all people. She will not be consumed with the bondage of trying to please everyone.

God's work is miraculous and redemptive in the life dedicated to Him. He brings refinement and grace to that life, and makes it a blessing to many people.

Fear thou not; for I am with thee: be not dismayed; for I am thy God: I will strengthen thee; yea, I will help thee; yea, I will uphold thee with the right hand of my righteousness.... For I the Lord thy God will hold thy right hand, saying unto thee, Fear not; I will help thee.
—Isaiah 41:10, 13

The picture in these two verses has blessed me many times. When two friends walk side by side, the right hand of one is in the left hand of the other. If God had said He would walk beside me that way, the side away from Him might be exposed to danger.

But God says He will hold my right hand in His right hand. That puts me in front of Him like a baby whose father is standing behind, holding the baby's hands and helping him learn to walk. With the father in that position, nothing can reach or harm the child without the father's notice. What better picture could God give of His protection and care?

That picture became vivid to me one Monday morning. The unwelcome sound of sleet met my ears as I neared Shenandoah Mountain. Driving on slick roads is not my idea of a pleasant time! God had been helping me overcome my fear of hazardous road conditions, but I certainly didn't relish the thought of ice on the steep roads that wound over four mountains between my home and the school where I taught. But school was scheduled to begin in a few hours, so I continued.

I was relieved when Shenandoah Mountain lay behind me. Its hairpin curves were worse than those on the other mountains, and so far the road surface did not feel slick.

But as I started up the second mountain, I felt the tires slide. My heart sank. I knew of no houses close by where I could park my car and seek shelter, nor did I want to pull off to the side of the road and wait. Conditions would likely only get worse.

As I cautiously proceeded, the above verses came to my mind, and with them these comforting thoughts. *God is holding my hand in His—like a father who holds his child and lets him help steer in the driveway, but keeps his own hands firmly over the small ones on the steering wheel. God knows how to control the car even if I don't;*

I don't need to be afraid.

Before I reached the third mountain, I came up behind a truck that was spreading salt. What a welcome sight! I reached my school with no further trouble. Truly God had held my hand and had kept me from fear. How I praised Him!

October 27

Teach me thy way, O Lord, and lead me in a plain path.
—Psalm 27:11

"When I feel alone and forsaken, you are there to comfort, Lord. When I am lost or confused, you direct me. When I am tired and weary, you are my strength. For all these blessings, I thank you.

"I want to take your path, Lord. Make me willing to lay aside all weights. Show me the value of having a servant's heart.

"Bend my will, Lord, and mold it to yours. Teach me your way, even when it is rough and hard to climb. Grant me perseverance even when I do not see the fruit of my labors. Cause me to be content with the necessary things in life. Let my appetite for pleasure and ease diminish. I want to be a virtuous woman who lives for you only. Develop my spiritual life and help me to be pure; I want to be ready for your return.

"When I see others happily married, help me rejoice with them. If a friend weeps over a deep heartache, let me feel compassion. Give me a keenly sensitive heart to the needs around me, and I will strive to meet them by your grace. As you make my path clear before me, help me to walk in it joyfully. May your presence inspire me to be faithful."

> Yea, I have loved thee with an everlasting love.
>
> —Jeremiah 31:3

Why doesn't anyone want my company? I wish I had a husband to love me. If you have watched your friends date and marry while young men ignore you, you have probably had similar thoughts. Can we be happy facing life alone?

Being utterly alone is not conducive to happiness. But with God, we don't need to face life alone, even if we never marry. For me, the first key to joy is the assurance that God loves me. That sounds trite, but consider a minute—God, who spoke and created the mountains, oceans, stars, and the universe; God, who controls nature and men; God, whom the angels worship—this almighty God loves me personally. Jesus loved me enough to die for me, and He has promised that if I am faithful to Him, I will be part of His bride for all eternity. Since He loves me that much, it doesn't seem so important whether or not others love me.

Because God loves me, He wants to bless me and give me reasons for joyfulness. And because He made me, He knows best what will make me joyful. If He chooses for me to remain single, I am sure it is because He knows I will have more joy serving Him single than married.

I am happy, not only because I know God loves me, but also because I know He is in complete control of my life and circumstances. He not only knows what will make me happiest, He is also fully able to carry out His plan. If that plan includes dating and marriage, God will bring the right person into my life at the right time. I don't need to spend time and energy worrying about whether a special friend will show up or how to find him. I can leave that in God's hands and be happy now, filling the place He has given me today.

Another key to joy is service to others. God does not want me to isolate myself from others just because I do not have a husband and children. Rather, He has said I have more time to serve Him because I am single (1 Corinthians 7:34). And one way He wants me to serve Him is by using my opportunities to do good to those within and outside the brotherhood. Making others happy helps give my life meaning.

How can I be happy without dating? By resting in God's love for me, His control of my circumstances, and the place of service He has ordained for me. When I rest in these things, He gives me joy.

The Lord lift up his countenance upon thee, and give thee peace.

—Numbers 6:26

Elijah prayed and God sent rain, though it had not rained for over three years. He prayed that fire would burn up his altar, and it did. God worked through Elijah to show His power to others.

So why did he run when he received Jezebel's death threat? He even left his servant behind and went into the wilderness alone, sat under a juniper tree, and wished to die. The picture changed drastically from victory to defeat, from courage to depression, and from companionship to loneliness.

While there in the wilderness, he listened to the still, small voice of God again. God reminded him that the situation was not as bleak as he imagined.

When you face a difficult time in your life, keep your mind stayed on God, and He will keep you in perfect peace. Do not use your energy and efforts to run away from difficulties. Stay where you are, and pray until you hear God directing you in His still, small voice. When God's peace fills your life, you can face any stress that comes. ✳

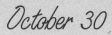

October 30

He shall offer it of his own voluntary will at the door of the tabernacle of the congregation before the Lord.
—Leviticus 1:3

The term *service* is widely used. It is used when speaking about those who commit themselves to help in another community for a year or two. They return and we say they are "home from service."

You might think of a teacher or a minister's wife as women of service. When you read articles or hear messages to single women, the term *service* is often mentioned. In one way or another we all have opportunities to serve another person or group of people.

The Israelites were commanded to offer rams without blemish, yet the offering was to be made of the owner's free will.

The church needs women who are willing to serve its people, women who sacrifice themselves for the cause of another, women who serve voluntarily. Those who sacrifice for another only out of obligation will never know the genuine joy of giving. Voluntarily doing God's will results in His blessing.

Serving others is a notable occupation. Often there is not much pay involved. Sometimes even the "thank you" seems forced. We can rest assured, however, that the reward we will receive at the end of life will be worth it all. ✸

> He was five years old when the tidings came of Saul and Jonathan
> out of Jezreel, and his nurse took him up, and fled.
> —2 Samuel 4:4

It must have been frightening for this little boy to hear that his father had been killed. Suddenly he was alone and in great danger. But someone cared for this child: his nurse. She took him and fled to safety so his life could be spared.

He lived, and many years later he received the land his father had owned. He also ate at the king's table every day.

If you are single, you may sometimes long for the love that a mother receives from her child. When you feel that longing, talk to Jesus about it. He will meet you in your desire and transform it to His will. His calling for you may include working with children in numerous ways—stay open to the creative possibilities God may reveal to you.

We are making a lasting impression on the children in our lives. Remember to look for the their potential; show that you care by taking an interest in their efforts and abilities. Take time for the little things they want to show you. We must help them thirst for God by acting like Jesus and honoring Him.

We can pray for those children as they grow into adulthood. The love and care we show to them in their young years will have far-reaching effects, helping them make decisions that will enable them to be with the King in eternity.

....

....

....

....

....

Again, the devil taketh him up into an exceeding high mountain, and sheweth him all the kingdoms of the world, and the glory of them.
—Matthew 4:8

And Jesus returned in the power of the Spirit.
—Luke 4:14

Jesus was tempted to become a sensation. He could have gained much attention had he used the opportunity to show His power. He could have made a name for Himself, but He kept His mission in mind instead. He had not come to gain shallow fanfare and applause. Had He yielded to the temptation, the sensation of His fame would soon have passed, and He would have lost His power. He was victorious because He kept His eyes on the reality that He came not to do His own will but the Father's. That is why we read the triumphant words, "And Jesus returned in the power of the Spirit."

The lesson for us is clear. When we are tempted to reach for recognition and draw attention to ourselves, we will do well to remember Jesus' example. The applause we might gain will be fleeting, and our lack of real power will be revealed. We will show that we are actually controlled by our flesh rather than by the Spirit of God.

Jesus possessed all power, but He was willing to wait for His Father's directions to manifest that power. He was willing to wait and did not choose temporal attractions. Therefore He gained honor, glory, devotion, and worship unlike anything the devil had to offer. Thousands of years have passed, but He still receives glory today and will continue to receive glory throughout the ceaseless ages of eternity.

....

....

....

....

....

And they came to him from every quarter.

—Mark 1:45

Just what made Jesus so attractive? His physical appearance? I do not believe so. During that time period, there was much unrest and fear. Somehow He won the hearts of the simple and commanded respect even of the doubtful and contentious. He had a straightforward, honest, and open character marked by humility. There was no falsehood, bigotry, or deception in His manner. Fear, callousness, and partiality held no part in Jesus' life. His compassionate heart reached out to the widow, the guilty, the hurting, the sick, and the hungry. Children were cradled on His lap. His magnetizing personality drew people, and His enemies feared that the world had gone after Him. He did not condone sin, yet He accepted the sinner. Occasionally, specific mention is made of women following Him because of the respect He showed to them.

Jesus is no longer here in person, and He has given us the responsibility to carry on His work. Do we draw people as He did? We can do this only by spending much time with the Father, as Jesus did. He has sent His Spirit to direct and teach us, transforming us and infilling us with His qualities. Are we allowing His Spirit to fill and transform us daily?

Then king Darius wrote unto all people . . . I make a decree, That in every dominion of my kingdom men tremble and fear before the God of Daniel: for he is the living God, and stedfast forever, and his kingdom that which shall not be destroyed, and his dominion shall be even unto the end.

—Daniel 6:25-26

Daniel's faithfulness to God and God's protection over him when he was thrown to the lions touched the heart of King Darius. Before this event, the king had not trusted in the God of heaven, but now he was convinced beyond a doubt that the one true God was in control of all things. He felt so strongly about it that he made a law that everyone under his jurisdiction had to worship God also.

We can only guess what might have happened if Daniel not remained faithful. He may have escaped the lions' den, but King Darius would not have come face to face with the power of God. King Darius would have continued to think that he himself had all power and was worthy of worship. His subjects would probably have continued as pagans without a knowledge of God.

Your faithfulness in trials will strengthen others. Someone may move from a cool relationship with God to one that is on fire. Another person may see that you possess the power she once did and realize that it is possible to retain that power. An unbeliever may observe your life, puzzled at how you can remain calm and cheerful. Be faithful! God may use your response to trial to reveal Himself to her.

In spite of great difficulties and an uncertain future, Daniel unflinchingly prayed three times a day. Herein lay his quiet strength. The blessed communion with his God was too valuable to lose, even if it meant being thrown into the lions' den. Who knows what heavenly comforters surrounded him there? An effectual prayer life preserved his body and soul and brought a nation to the knowledge of God.

....

....

....

I will instruct thee and teach thee in the way which
thou shalt go: I will guide thee with mine eye.
—Psalm 32:8

I see here a process of preparation and a promise of leadership for my path into the future. God says He will do it with His eye. Can I trust an eye to direct me? Because God's sight is not limited to my scope of vision, I can indeed trust His all-seeing eye to guide me.

In close relationships, an eye can speak volumes. When I have a close relationship with God, His eyes can guide me powerfully. Because my attention is on Him, I can catch His direction, His will, and His heartbeat. What is He focusing on? Sometimes He directs me to other helpers, perhaps some counsel, trial, or experience. A sermon or a book can inspire me further in my walk with Christ. I must stay focused on His line of vision, even if I do not understand it. If I don't keep my vision aligned with His, my sight will become clouded and I will lose the path. We carefully cherish and protect our natural eyes. Are we that diligent in preserving our spiritual eyesight?

I am amazed at the many references we have to the eyes of God. I am blessed to know that He sees everything and that He cannot fail. God is faithful, and He promises to guide us even unto death.

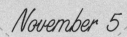

Praise ye the Lord. O give thanks unto the Lord; for he is good: for his mercy en-
dureth for ever. . . . They soon forgat his works; they waited not for his counsel.
—Psalm 106:1, 13

Surprising as it may sound, I was burdened with blessings. I had so much to be thankful for. My list of blessings was long, and my heart overflowed with thanksgiving—yet I felt an uneasiness that kept me from rejoicing to the fullest. I had a nagging fear that these blessings would not last long, and I had a vague feeling of guilt that I had too much.

I followed this train of thought for a while, but then behind those thoughts came another one—a truth from God. It was so simple and yet so profound that the guilt and uneasiness fled before its brilliance. It was this: *These are blessings from God; gifts that He means for me to enjoy.* How beautiful! The negative feelings vanished, replaced by peaceful gratitude coupled with responsibility.

God pours out His liberal blessings beyond what we deserve because He is a kind and merciful Father. But like any father, He expects appreciation for the things He gives. When we receive an answer to prayer, a pleasant surprise, or a blessing of any size, we must not forget to thank the Lord in the midst of our ecstasy. When we talk about our blessings, we should without hesitation acknowledge the Lord, whether we tell a Christian or a non-Christian. God is glorified through this.

Unthankfulness results in forgetting God. When this happens, people give glory to something other than God, and the results are degradation and corruption. Giving glory to God results in joy and fulfillment.

And from the daughter of Zion all her beauty is departed: her princes are become like harts that find no pasture, and they are gone without strength before the pursuer.

—Lamentations 1:6

Sometimes we find ourselves in places of lamentation like those referred to in this verse. A princess finds that her once-captivating beauty is slipping away from her. A strong male deer can no longer find pasture to feed upon, and he grows weaker and more desperate by the day.

You might identify with this. At times you may feel as though death, whether physical or emotional, pursues you, and you have no more strength to run away. Being reduced to something less than what you were can be a miserable state, but it remains a reality of life, whether temporary or permanent. You have served others. You have given to others. You have cared for others. Now, suddenly, your cup is empty, your beauty is gone, you cannot find any refreshing green pasture, and you have no more strength left. You are not sure of the next step, and you are tired of trying to figure it out.

You can cling to the truth that there is hope. Accept the short periods of depression, and then ask yourself, *Do I feel this way because I am not feeling well today? Do my feelings stem from a physical problem, or do they come from an emotional or spiritual problem?* Give yourself some time, and never make an important decision when you feel pursued or your strength is gone. Spend time in prayer, and then find someone to share your depression with so that you can begin to recover.

Read Isaiah 40:28-31. When God renews your strength, a drastic change will take place in your outlook. ✳

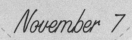

November 7

Thus saith the Lord, Set thine house in order; for thou shalt die, and not live.
—2 Kings 20:1

When I am expecting company, I set my house in order. I put away the things that I neglected to put away earlier. I run the vacuum cleaner over the carpet and sweep the kitchen floor. The dishes stacked in the dish drainer are put away. Even though they were covered with a dish towel, their presence on the countertop would have been visible.

Someday Jesus will call me away, whether by death or by His coming. Then nothing will be more important than having my spiritual house in order. I do not want to have things lying about when He comes—the neglected prayers, the ignored voice of the Spirit, the postponed spiritual disciplines. I do not want to have a build-up of impurity in my life, an accumulation of things stacked up that should have been put in their proper places a long time ago—the grievances, slights, and misunderstandings that have not been forgiven. I may have managed to cover them with a cloak of pretense, but to the Lord they are in plain sight.

The residue will not have a chance to form if little things are swept away at their first appearance. Regular spiritual maintenance will ensure that I am ready whenever He calls me to Himself.

> And I will fasten him as a nail in a sure place; and he
> shall be for a glorious throne to his father's house.
> —Isaiah 22:23

Sometimes a single person finds herself like a wanderer without a sure home. She has no family responsibilities to hold her to one locality. This can greatly bless those she serves because she can be so versatile. Many places of service are easier to fill because she is free of family responsibilities.

However, for the "wanderer" there are adjustments unknown to the person securely rooted in family life. The adjustments include the ongoing process of co-ordinating with other people, especially in the personal way of living arrangements. Singles who live together see each other's true selves, and it is with a risk that one person lives with another. If the single person lives with a family, she must accept the weaknesses and faults of that family; much giving is required. Some people may find this journey smooth, but others may feel "at sea" in a family not their own. Whatever the case, it takes time to build relationships, confidences, and trust.

At such a time as this, God says, "I will fasten him as a nail in a sure place." A nail indicates strength and usefulness. A sure place indicates security. What a promise! In the preceding verse, God promises opportunities that will not be taken away. Then in our verse for today, He promises continued blessing, "a glorious throne to his father's house."

To the single person without posterity, this is a blessed comfort. God will bless her future and make it secure. She has a place to fill: "And they shall hang upon him all the glory of his father's house" (v. 24). There is a future for the single person in the Lord's work. God's carpentry is trustworthy. When He fastens a person in a sure place, His work will never fall apart.

These are they which were not defiled with women; for they are virgins. These are they which follow the Lamb whithersoever he goeth. These were redeemed from among men, being the firstfruits unto God and to the Lamb.

—Revelation 14:4

Some people do not follow Jesus because of no certain place to lay their heads—no secure dwelling on this earth. The virgins follow because they see in Him a place to lay their heads—a security for their souls and a resource to meet all their needs.

Some people feel they have some earthly duty to perform before they can follow Jesus. The virgins follow the Lamb because He has redeemed them from the things of the earth, and He is now their joy. He enables those who follow Him to have proper priorities. He gives direction and strength to meet demands and duties.

Yet others make excuses because of family ties. The virgins, because they do the will of the Lamb, are His sisters and He is their brother. He will care for them and supply all their needs.

Those who "follow the Lamb whithersoever He goeth" will follow Him if He leads them into places of solitude to meditate and pray. They follow if He leads into quiet chambers where the shades are drawn, even if others are enjoying their labors in the bright sunshine. They follow if He leads into places and circumstances of low income, even if others are earning much more. If He leads from place to place, they follow Him even when others seem to have a more permanent abode. They will follow Him until He leads them into His eternal fold.

And there shall be a tabernacle for a shadow in the daytime from the heat, and for a place of refuge, and for a covert from storm and from rain.

—Isaiah 4:6

A hiker walking trails in Point Lobos State Reserve in Monterey, California, may feel the intensity of the sun's rays beating down on him. But the Cypress Grove Trail will eventually lead him to the shade of the cypress trees growing along the rugged coastline. Temperatures can be as much as fifteen degrees cooler under the shade of these scraggly trees. What a refuge from the heat, and how grateful the hiker is for relief! He can sit and drink from his water bottle, view the panoramic scenes of the ocean, and be refreshed before continuing his walk.

Sometimes on our path through life, the struggles become so intense that we can hardly enjoy the journey or see any beauty in life. Satan is trying to hinder our progress by sending doubt and worry our way. But God always provides a shelter from the storms of life. Entering His presence and resting in Him will refresh and strengthen us to go on.

Reading God's Word can lift our spirits even when we are weary. Prayer can release the pressure built up inside of us. Even a short prayer during a harried moment will bring us closer to God's peaceful presence. As we sit in God's shadow, His Spirit communes with our spirit and helps us on our journey to wholeness. ✸

Iron sharpeneth iron; so a man sharpeneth the countenance of his friend.
—Proverbs 27:17

The knife in my hand was dull and ineffective. Only by exerting much pressure could I get the job done. I furrowed my brows in frustration, but then remembered that I had a sharpener in the drawer. After the knife and sharpener made contact, the knife glided amazingly well. My work was soon completed with minimal effort.

I had to think of the difference a few words from a friend can make. When I share the burden that weighs me down and makes life so hard, it disappears quickly. I can smile again, and the confusing situation becomes clear. I am encouraged by my friend's touch, a wave of her hand, or a few words. These things say, "I am glad you are alive on earth at the same time I am," and I find new enthusiasm for living. My God who supplies for all my needs often supplies through the thoughtfulness of a friend.

Now if "a man sharpeneth the countenance of his friend," I see that the sharpening business is not a one-way affair. I cannot escape the responsibility to sharpen others as well. A person is not at the height of usefulness when he is sad, worried, lonely, or discouraged. When someone is struggling hard, her spiritual vitality is sapped. Here is where I must make purposeful contact, remembering what I appreciate when my countenance needs to be sharpened.

Pray and ask God to help you sharpen the countenance of your friend. He can give you personalized direction on what your friend needs at the moment, and you will help her to live to her fullest potential.

November 12

> For the joy of the Lord is your strength.
>
> —Nehemiah 8:10

Although it eludes exact definition, the characteristics of joy can be described. It is the pleasure experienced in the presence of God. It is a possession God has given you that no man can take away. Joy is a feeling you carry when you are reaping the good you have sown. It is the sunshine you spread from one person to another through cheerfulness. When you are exactly where God wants you to be, you feel the blissful happiness of joy.

Joy does not depend on things going the way you want them to. It is dependent on a heart set on God. Joy is being at peace with yourself even in awkward or uncomfortable situations when you would rather be somewhere else. When in the company of others, joy means feeling at home and breathing freely. Joy is contentment, fascination, and delight in being the person you are. A joyful woman is living a Spirit-filled life. ✸

November 13

When the poor and needy seek water, and there is none, and their tongue faileth for thirst, I the Lord will hear them, I the God of Israel will not forsake them.
—Isaiah 41:17

Are you hungry and needy and poor,
Thirsting for fellowship solid and sure?
Loneliness, tears, and rejection your lot,
Bitterness tempts in word and in thought?

No one comes to your door with a smile
And steps inside to chat awhile;
No one calls with a greeting gay
To invite you over to spend the day.

Do you feel a vague stirring in your mind,
Speaking of peace you're longing to find?
Even though it is hard, sit down and be still;
It is your life that God wants to fill.

Jesus gives light, and He's shining for you;
He can add to your life a heavenly hue;
He desires to show you that He is the best,
And no other like Him can really give rest.

How could He draw you to His fatherly heart,
If He would not often call you apart?
Sometimes He denies the things that you crave,
Knowing your spirit would be enslaved.

You often pray, "Lord, help me to grow;
Help me your holy likeness to show."
But He uses hard methods to answer your prayer
And to fit you for service His message to share.

So when His voice you recognize,
Submit and you'll receive a prize:
You'll be surrounded, filled with light—
And you will see His plan aright.

For there is not a word in my tongue, but, lo, O Lord, thou knowest it altogether.

—Psalm 139:4

May we think evil of others as long as they do not know it? Hear what the Scriptures say:

For the Lord searcheth all hearts, and understandeth all the imaginations of the thoughts (1 Chronicles 28:9).

For his eyes are upon the ways of man, and he seeth all his goings . . . therefore he knoweth their works (Job 34:21, 25).

For the Lord is a God of knowledge, and by him actions are weighed (1 Samuel 2:3).

For mine eyes are upon all their ways: they are not hid from my face, neither is their iniquity hid from mine eyes (Jeremiah 16:17).

Can any hide himself in secret places that I shall not see him? saith the Lord. Do not I fill heaven and earth? (Jeremiah 23:24).

For thine eyes are open upon all the ways of the sons of men (Jeremiah 32:19).

He revealeth the deep and secret things: he knoweth what is in the darkness, and the light dwelleth with him (Daniel 2:22).

For the Lord knoweth the way of the righteous (Psalm 1:6).

For all my ways are before thee (Psalm 119:168).

For the ways of man are before the eyes of the Lord, and he pondereth all his goings (Proverbs 5:21).

And Jesus knew their thoughts (Matthew 12:25).

The Lord knoweth them that are his (2 Timothy 2:19).

Do you want to think evil of others even if they do not know it?

And the seventy returned again with joy, saying, Lord,
even the devils are subject unto us through thy name.

—Luke 10:17

The Lord's way always works! Jesus sent out seventy workers, instructing them how to act and what to do and not to do. The mission of the seventy was successful, and they came back rejoicing.

Jesus instructed them not to take along extra baggage, which would impede their progress and bring extra cares. Extra baggage still does that. He asks us to step out in faith with the assurance that He will supply our needs. When we doubt and worry, we are carrying extra baggage that weighs us down.

Jesus told the men to be heralds of peace. To spread peace, one must radiate the peace of God. Following His instructions to be satisfied with whatever is provided plays a large part in establishing peace. The Lord's work is not accomplished by complaining.

Jesus also instructed the seventy to take time to heal the sick. If we do not find time to visit, help, and encourage those in the midst of trials, we are ignoring an essential part of the Lord's work.

The details of God's instructions to us individually may vary, but no matter what they are, following them will always bring the best results.

If any man will come after me, let him deny himself,
and take up his cross daily, and follow me.
—Luke 9:23

The Bible speaks of dying daily and taking up our own cross. What is this daily cross, this daily death?

My days are quite pleasant. I live alone and face little demand to accommodate others' wishes. Self-sacrifice is not as mandatory for me as it is for the mother whose children are growing out of their clothes, whose meal preparations seem endless, and whose toddlers are demanding. I have a comfortable job that gives me free evenings and weekends. My income is sufficient to allow for good food and comfortable home furnishings. My schedule allows pleasure reading, long telephone visits, and enough sleep.

But somehow, when I am savoring these bodily comforts, my carnal appetites stir. *Ahhh, wouldn't it be sweet to have . . .?* And lustful imagination is soon galloping down that slippery track, especially if I have been feeding on an unsanctified reading diet. Is it because I have so many comforts that I have trouble accepting what I do not have?

I have learned that if I trim self with a rigid discipline of body, I can better maintain discipline of thought. That is why I seldom buy candy, and why I don't allow myself to read a novel all evening. It factors into my choice to make my life busy reaching out to others. It is a good reason to fast regularly. I need a dose of self-denial or self-sacrifice every day—for my own survival. I die daily, and how rich the living!

For the which cause I also suffer these things: nevertheless I am not ashamed:
for I know whom I have believed, and am persuaded that he is able to keep
that which I have committed unto him against that day.
—2 Timothy 1:12

It was not a sin for the Israelites to recognize their needs while traveling through the wilderness. It was not sinful to face the reality of a hot, dry desert and the need for food and water. It was not wrong for the spies to report that there were walled cities and giants in the land of Canaan. Their sin lay in not trusting God with these matters as they arose. By failing to trust, they were saying that He was unable to meet their needs. Their spirit of mistrust caused them to see only hot deserts, giants, and walled cities. Without faith in God, the situation appeared hopeless.

Like the Israelites, it is not a sin for me to recognize that life is not easy and that I have both spiritual and physical needs. But as those needs arise, I must commit them to God. He is able to handle those needs in the right way. If I have committed them to Him, that means that I trust Him to meet my needs in whatever way He sees best—even if that way may seem to be a long, drawn-out process.

The Israelites wailed and lamented about the giants in the land of Canaan. What an obvious sign of defeat before the battle! With God they could have overcome. But they saw only the giants and not the richness of the land that could have been theirs. That is what the devil wants me to do when I face spiritual giants and walls. He wants me to feel so overwhelmed that I do not think about committing them to God. When I succumb to hopelessness, I miss out on what God has promised to give me.

Christians will face deserts, walls, and giants, but when a person turns to God in quiet trust and commitment, the result will be victory, joy, and rejoicing.

And she had compassion on him.

—Exodus 2:6

Pharaoh's daughter was going about her normal life, but she noticed the unusual. A little basket lay among the reeds. Her compassion was sparked when she saw baby Moses cry. It resulted in saving the baby's life and providing a home and education for him.

When you are adorned with the gem of compassion, you possess a rare beauty. The seed of compassion begins in your heart and is cultivated and enriched by caring for others.

When you nurture a concern for those around you, you begin to observe needs. If you close your eyes to the needs of others, you do not have the love of God in your heart.

Dorcas had compassion when she sewed garments for the widows. Phebe had compassion on many people, including the Apostle Paul, a leader of the churches. Esther had compassion on the Jewish nation, and the nation was saved from destruction.

Compassion in your heart will be seen in your actions.

Let us therefore come boldly unto the throne of grace, that we may obtain mercy, and find grace to help in time of need.

—Hebrews 4:16

Two Thrones

In palace grand on a glistening throne,
King Ahasuerus made his decree known;
He was haughty, heartless, and unkind,
So his evil plan was designed.

His law set forth was stern and grave,
For the free man as well as the slave;
That no man or woman, great or small,
Must appear before him ere he call.

Unless the caller met the king's whim
The golden scepter was withheld
from him.
Then woe—his petition was
requested in vain!
The king in his wrath commanded
him slain.

Another King reigns on a
glistening throne,
Who also has let his decree be known
That every person, great or small,
My come to Him freely and
on Him call.

And should one come with
a trembling request,
With earnest desire and
yearning possessed;
He may approach the throne
with no fear in his heart,
For the kindhearted King
will not tell him "depart."

The King is seated on a throne of grace,
A throne of rest—a wonderful place;
Here we find mercy and comfort
and strength;
He does not mind if we stay
here at length.

The King is loving and understands
our desire,
His scepter is within reach when
we wish to inquire,
Those who bring Him a petition or plea
Can rejoice, for He gives the victory!

How precious also are thy thoughts unto me, O God! how great
is the sum of them! If I should count them, they are more in
number than the sand: when I awake, I am still with thee.

—Psalm 139:17-18

God's thoughts are constantly on His sons and daughters. He plans every detail of the pathway you are traveling. He knows your weaknesses and failures, and yet He loves you. He understands when the hard times in your life become dark spots, blotting out the joy in your heart. He helps to bear those burdens, and He also rejoices with you when the sun is shining and your heart is light.

Picture the sand on the beaches of the world. You could never count every grain of sand. David says that even if you could count the sand, God's thoughts would be more in number. That realization is overwhelming; our finite minds cannot grasp God's thought patterns. He calls you to simply sit back and wonder at how great His thoughts are toward you! ✳

November 21

For thou wilt light my candle: the Lord my God will enlighten my darkness. For by thee I have run through a troop; and by my God have I leaped over a wall. As for God, his way is perfect: the word of the Lord is tried: he is a buckler to all those that trust in him.
—Psalm 18:28-30

I was sure I would never make it over the wall before me. How would I ever be able to drive those 350 miles to where a new home and job awaited me? With no one to talk to, I would get tired. I was afraid of falling asleep, of being caught in a time-wasting traffic jam, or of getting a flat tire. Driving alone was simply not something I enjoyed. I knew I would have to rely completely on God's grace. I turned to Psalm 18 and read the psalmist's experience. When he needed help, God was there to help him. A calmness replaced my fears as I pondered on the above verses, realizing God has never changed since then.

Are you facing some wall right now? It could be a talk you have been asked to give, but you feel incapable of speaking. It might be leaving home to adjust to another field of service, or meeting with a person who has been unkind to you recently. Trust God to help you. He will lighten the dark way before you. He will enable you to run through that troop and help you climb that wall. Even though the way looks impossible, remember that when God leads you, He will go with you. God's way is perfect; He will give you as much strength as you need to accomplish the task.

Tell God your fears, commit it all to His care, and bravely take that first step that will get you over the wall. 🕮

....

....

....

....

Woe unto them that join house to house, that lay field to field, till there
be no place, that they may be placed alone in the midst of the earth!

—Isaiah 5:8

Some people focus so much on making money that they build a wall around themselves. As they build houses and gain land, they prefer to be left alone and leave others alone. The longer a person focuses on things like this, the smaller his world becomes.

Be careful that you do not keep on adding field to field in your financial world while your concern for others lessens. It works opposite of what it might seem to. Although you might gain land, you may suddenly find yourself alone and friendless.

You may be working hard and earning money. During the week, you might stay so focused on your own work world that when Sunday comes along, you feel alone. Why? Because you have taken time only for yourself and your own things during the week. When you take time to nurture friendships, you will be rewarded many times. Then when you need encouragement, someone will be there to help you as well.

Taking time to establish relationships might mean you have less money in your savings account. It might cost you a telephone call or lots of stamps to mail all your letters. But think of your other choice: loneliness, no mail, no friends, and no one to call—only fields and houses until you are completely secluded in your own world.

November 23

And the Lord had respect unto Abel and to his offering:
but unto Cain and to his offering he had not respect.

—Genesis 4:4-5

Cain's pretense was not acceptable to God. It is true that since he was a tiller of the soil, he may not have had an animal to offer. But if his desire had been after God, he could easily have acquired an animal. His strength did not lie in caring for animals, but he could raise crops, which he could have traded with Abel for an animal to sacrifice.

Sometimes I feel God's disapproval on my life because I have not made the sacrifice He asked of me. If my desire is after God, I will earnestly seek to know what is disappointing Him. If He tells me that I am not spending enough time with Him, I may need to sacrifice my reading, my hobbies, or my work so that I can meet His requirements.

I may not have the ability someone else does, but I can use the abilities I do have. If I do not have the ability to teach school, I can use the health and strength the Lord gave me to clean up the classroom for the teacher or help her with her bulletin boards. I may not have management ability, but I can encourage and lift up the hands of those who are in such a position. I may not always have the ability to meet someone's need, but I can make the need known to someone who has the ability to help.

God's disapproval of Cain's life was not because of his inability but because of his lack of desire to obey God. Had he been willing to wholly follow the Lord, God would have provided a way in which he could have served Him acceptably. He will do the same for me!

"For if there be first a willing mind, it is accepted according to that a man hath, and not according to that he hath not" (2 Chronicles 8:12).

Now I Nebuchadnezzar praise and extol and honour the King of heaven, all whose works are truth, and his ways judgment: and those that walk in pride he is able to abase.

—Daniel 4:37

What caused King Nebuchadnezzar to come to this conclusion and utter this impressive testimony? God brought him to the end of himself through extraordinary means.

As he gazed with pride over the wealthy city, feeling pleased with himself and his accomplishments, he spoke proudly and took all the glory for himself. Suddenly a voice spoke to him from heaven saying that the kingdom was no longer his.

The king's memory and understanding left him immediately. He still looked like a man, but he began to act like a wild beast, going out to the field to eat grass. He became a pathetic sight, his hair and nails growing until they were unmanageable. All this shows us the vanity of human glory and greatness. When we are tempted to take glory to ourselves, let us pause for a moment, consider King Nebuchadnezzar, and realize how God feels about pride.

After seven years in this terrible condition, the king looked up toward heaven, humbled and penitent before God. His reason was restored, and his lords now sought him again.

What was his response when God again restored his proper mind to him? No longer did he proclaim his own greatness. His servants had probably often said, "Oh, King, live forever!" But Nebuchadnezzar now praised the only One who lives forever and whose kingdom lasts. He saw his own smallness. He did not feel bitter toward God for bringing him to shame. His testimony of this humbling experience was the simple but profound truth: "Those that walk in pride he is able to abase."

Those members of the body, which seem to be more feeble, are necessary.
—1 Corinthians 12:22

How the strips and the fingers flew! I was touring the Longaberger basket factory, and it was amazing to see what a skilled weaver could accomplish in a short time. Beautiful, sturdy baskets were stacked on piles throughout the factory. There were flat baskets, round baskets, big ones, and little ones. They shipped six semi-truckloads per day. Each basket showed skill in workmanship.

As we moved on through the various divisions of the factory, we came to the place where the baskets were given a coat of finish. Here a worker placed baskets on large hooks on a moving track that carried them through a compartment where they were sprayed. Because the worker's job appeared to be easy, I thought his job would better suit me than weaving baskets. As I thought about this, a seemingly insignificant task took on a new importance in my mind. The beautiful, impressive baskets woven by skilled weavers might be stacked to the ceiling, but they would not be useful unless that one worker made it possible for them to receive a coat of finish.

If you think your place in life is insignificant, think of the far-reaching consequences if you suddenly refused to do anything. The sermons you hear may be ever so inspiring and encouraging, but they might cease to be that way if you stopped praying. The church might lose its non-conformity to the world if you ceased to be a faithful example in this. Church attendance would dwindle if you stayed home because of small inconveniences. One after another, people might let their minds wander to things other than the preaching of the Word if they see that you are daydreaming. Hands might hang down and knees become feeble if you would not start that chain of smiles and words of encouragement.

The next time you are tempted to think your life does not make a difference, remember the insignificant but important worker in the basket factory.

November 26

But if any man love God, the same is known of him.
—1 Corinthians 8:3

What is love? It is the first commandment of God. It is pure adoration of our heavenly Father that engulfs the heart, soul, and mind.

Love is the second greatest commandment as well. Love serves a neighbor with affection, understanding, and sympathy. Love is sensitive to the needs of another. It shows benevolence toward everyone. Love is a feeling of goodwill to all, including our enemies. Love will prize the friendships shared with others. It will speak only the truth about others, but it will remember that even some truths may need to be left unspoken. Love will edify other Christians. In close relationships between two people, love is the substance that binds together and yet produces enough lubricant to keep things running smoothly. Can anything else do that?

When you witness love in action in a woman's life, you are seeing the fruit of the Spirit in her. ❁

Satan himself is transformed into an angel of light.
—2 Corinthians 11:14

Although the spider web was unwanted in my house, I gazed at it in fascination. Maybe it was the parallel lines or the spaces between those lines. Whatever it was, something about that unsightly web was almost lovely. Some strange reasoning inside me wanted to leave it there. But my training in the ways of housekeeping and cleanliness overruled, and the web was destroyed.

Sometimes things that are many times more dangerous than flimsy spider webs catch our attention because of their alluring design. As we gaze at what is forbidden, a persuasive reasoning inside us wants to partake of it and enjoy it. After a while, it does not seem as unsightly as it did at first.

Why do I feel drawn to read a certain book when I know I should not? Its appeal to the flesh may be hidden in a beautiful setting or an educational overtone. Why do I want to dwell on thoughts of self-pity? Maybe it is a way for my carnality to receive attention. Why am I satisfied with offering a quick prayer instead of having deep communion with God? It could be that material things have become more attractive and important to me than spiritual things.

At first the spider web raised that quick instinct in me to sweep it down. Had I immediately destroyed it, I would not have noticed its attractive design. Had I left it there, it would not have gone away by itself. The fascinating design would eventually have become a thing of disgrace. It would have left a tell-tale sign about my lack of diligence as a housekeeper. But I am glad it is gone, because the place where it used to be looks much better without it.

Likewise, I choose to keep my inner spiritual temple clean. It is the place where the Holy Spirit dwells, and He deserves a place free of dirty corners.

> Inasmuch as ye have done it unto one of the least
> of these my brethren, ye have done it unto me.
> —Matthew 25:40

If you live alone, you may find yourself with a long evening ahead of you. In the quietness of your little kitchen, you have put away the last of your supper dishes, and it is only 5:00. You may have some housework to do, but motivation seems gone. As you sit down to re-read a book, you wonder what your friends are doing. Envy creeps in as you think of mothers who say they have such busy schedules that the day is always over before the work is done.

Wake up! Is it helping at all to sit there feeling sorry for yourself? It is time you do more for others.

Go help that busy mother who hardly finds time to relax. Visit that widow or grandparent who also has long evenings. Visit or call that sister who has been sick and missed the last church service. Sew clothes for some mother who cannot keep up with her growing family. Write a letter to that sister who is on the mission field, or to one you know needs some encouragement.

Helping to ease someone's load is a sure way to make a long evening short. Remember that you have done a deed for Christ when you have done it for someone else.

The Book of Joel

We like to make connections, getting to know each other's relatives and "who's who." But you have likely met people with whom you didn't seem to have any connections. They did not know your parents' names or your grandparents' names. They'd never heard of the place where you live. After a time of fruitless attempts to make a connection, you began to feel rather unimportant and obscure.

The prophet Joel seems to be a person like this. We know his father's name was Pethuel, but we read nothing of his mother. We do not know from which tribe he came. We do not even know where he lived.

We do know one thing. Joel was a prophet, and God gave him an important message for the people. Joel preached his message, but after that it seems he lived his life in obscurity.

When the church votes in a Sunday school teacher, perhaps you are never chosen. You get no call from the mission board to go the foreign field. Though you love children, no one asks you to teach school. But the things you are doing are important. In a hundred years from now no one may know who you were, but neither do we know who the prophet Joel was. His acts and his message, however, live on still. ❀

And be ye kind one to another.

—Ephesians 4:32

We all are afraid of something. Darkness is one of my worst fears. I am no longer a child, but I still cannot shake my fear of darkness. My imagination runs wild in the dark. I am scared, and it does no good for someone to simply tell me, "God will watch over you. Do not be afraid; there is nothing out there." I need a tangible way to face my fears.

We can help each other overcome our fears. Someone in your life probably faces a real fear. Parents may fear they are not teaching their children all they should. Maybe your friend is afraid of how she will react at her sister's wedding. You might have a brother who fears a negative answer from a girl he would like to ask to be his special friend. A friend might be afraid of driving a standard shift car.

Ask God for wisdom to know how to help people overcome their fears. You can commend parents on the strong points you appreciate in their children; it might give them courage. Tell the one who fears her sister's wedding that it will not be easy—you were there once yourself—but nobody said that tears at a wedding are improper. Maybe the young man who fears his answer from a girl just needs your opinion of how girls think. Share that perspective even though you cannot know the outcome, and tell him you will pray for him. You can help someone in a practical way by taking the time to teach her how to drive a standard shift.

The person who helps me most with my fear of darkness is the one who, without any questions or explanations, says, "Wait for me. I'll go with you." With a person by my side, the fear of darkness is greatly reduced. A late night walk even becomes enjoyable in the company of another. Fears are real, but so is the comfort of God felt through a friend. ✸

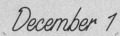

Be sober, be vigilant; because your adversary the devil, as a roaring
lion, walketh about, seeking whom he may devour.
—1 Peter 5:8

One hunting tactic of the lion is to isolate its prey. Without the support of a group, the lone creature becomes a likely victim of the lion's terrible strength. The lion might not make a kill immediately after he separates his prey from the group, but isolation is the first step in his overall plan.

Likewise, the devil also looks for those whom he can isolate. Since his work is dangerously sly, his victim may not always be visibly isolated. But Satan may have succeeded in planting the thought, *Nobody understands me.* The victim may think she is the only one undergoing certain trials, which can result in self-pity, discouragement, and bitterness. If this path of negative thinking is not repented of, loss of spiritual life occurs, which means isolation from God.

A lion chooses a hiding spot and watches for an animal to stray away from the safety of the group. The victim, not realizing where the lion resides, may come dangerously near the lion's well-concealed hiding place.

A spiritual victim may allow a tiny thought of self-pity to cause her mind to stray from God and supportive friends. Without the secure boundaries of God's Word and Christian friends, a small thought can end in spiritual tragedy.

Sharing trials and temptations with others is a powerful weapon against such a tragedy. Part of group safety lies in the awareness that you are not alone in any trial. The devil will have a hard time finding a victim where such safety exists.

And though the Lord give you the bread of adversity, and the
water of affliction, yet shall not thy teachers be removed into a
corner any more, but thine eyes shall see thy teachers.
—Isaiah 30:20

You may begin to wonder what is going on when your daily diet becomes the bread of adversity and the water of affliction. Although you may never know why, you do have power over one thing—your response. You can believe that God is using your trial to make you a better person, or you can allow doubts to cloud your vision of God's love, causing discouragement.

"Thine eyes shall see thy teachers." Do you see your circumstances as teachers that God brings into your life? When you have made a wrong decision, a friend has betrayed your trust, or you have been misunderstood, choose to look at these experiences as teachers and see what you can learn from them.

As an act of your will, keep your eyes on what God is teaching you today. Believe that God is giving you the right lesson, the correct page numbers, and the right amount of work at just the exact time you need it. You may not understand the lesson fully yet, and perhaps you never will, but trust Him and try to understand what He is saying. It is up to you what kind of person you will become when you face adversity. Remember that God has your future in His view. ✸

....

....

....

....

....

December 3

My beloved is . . . the chiefest among ten thousand.
—Song of Solomon 5:10

What Jesus Is for Me

Companion: "Behold, I stand at the door and knock: if any [one] hear my voice, and open the door, I will come in to [her], and will sup with [her], and [she] with me" (Revelation 3:20).

Leader: "He leadeth me in the paths of righteousness for his name's sake" (Psalm 23:3).

Provider: "But my God shall supply all your need according to his riches in glory by Christ Jesus" (Philippians 4:19).

Protector: "Yea, though I walk through the valley of the shadow of death, I will fear no evil: for thou art with me; thy rod and thy staff they comfort me" (Psalm 23:4).

Counselor: "Thou shalt guide me with thy counsel, and afterward receive me to glory" (Psalm 73:24).

Helper: "The Lord is my helper, and I will not fear what man shall do unto me" (Hebrews 13:6).

Husband: "For thy Maker is thine husband" (Isaiah 54:5).

All in All: "Where there is neither Greek nor Jew . . . but Christ is all, and in all" (Colossians 3:11).

Look not every man on his own things, but every man also on the things of others.

—Philippians 2:4

"Miriam," said Betty, "tell me something. You and Joyce are the same age. Joyce is beautiful, with petite features and wavy, golden hair. She has an amazing alto voice. Her income lets her buy anything she wants. Now take no offense at this, but your looks are . . . average." At this, Miriam smiled and nodded in understanding. "Your job pays enough for only a few extras," Betty went on. "But I notice that you have many more friends than Joyce. No matter where you go, people are glad to see you come. When you go to town, visit another community, or just stay at home with your family—young and old alike enjoy your company. Joyce seems lonely at times, almost sad, and yet she has what every young woman could wish for. What is the difference? What is your secret?"

After a pause, she received an answer. "Betty, I try to take an interest in other people. I know people are lonely and sometimes afraid to express their thoughts, so I ask questions to get them to talk about themselves. It works almost every time! You show an interest in another person's life, and you have gained another friend. But it takes special effort. If I get too busy for others, I can soon tell that they do not need me either. Old people love to be remembered. Young people respond favorably when you listen to their interests. My secret, friend, is this: love others and you will be loved in return!"

December 5

And the barbarous people shewed us no little kindness: for they kindled a fire, and received us every one, because of the present rain, and because of the cold.

—Acts 28:2

The primitive people witnessed quite a sight as these wet swimmers come in from the sea. It was cold and raining, and the survivors of the shipwreck must have been chilled to the bone. The hosts of the island kindled a fire for the refugees to warm themselves. But they didn't stop there—they kindly provided lodging for three months. Without hesitation, they showed true hospitality to these strangers.

We need to be willing to show hospitality too. Sometimes it hardly seems worth all the bother to invite others into our homes. Our orderly homes may become disorganized. If someone stays for the night, our schedules are disrupted. These are selfish reasons for not inviting others to our home; our excuses do not please God.

Take the challenge: invite others to your home for a meal. If you find it awkward to invite a married couple because you have no husband to visit with your friend's husband, invite a second couple so the men can keep each other company.

If young girls or other women visit your community, invite them to stop in or stay for the night. Your home may be the one in which they can best relax.

God will bless your efforts as you open your doors and share your home with others. He desires that we show hospitality.

Thy words were found, and I did eat them; and thy word was unto me the joy and rejoicing of mine heart: for I am called by thy name, O Lord God of hosts.

—Jeremiah 15:16

"Please land on the bird feeder," I encouraged the little bird outside the window. "Don't you see the perches there for you? And there is plenty of food inside the feeder, so stay and eat."

But in spite of all the food in the bird feeder outside my window, the bird did not stay. I would have been delighted to see him enjoy a meal. But he only hovered near, beating his wings wildly, and then flew away. Maybe he saw me inside the window and, regarding me as an enemy, did not dare settle down. Maybe he had just come from another feeding station and was not hungry enough to stay. Maybe this particular kind of bird was a picky eater and preferred different food from what was available in the feeder. For whatever reason, it did not stay, leaving me disappointed after putting forth efforts to help the feathered creature survive.

Sometimes I am like that bird. The Word of God is open before me, but I do not partake of it. It could direct me, calm my fears, and brighten my day, but I do not benefit from any of these blessings. Perhaps it will convict me in areas that I fail, so I regard it as an intrusion that will force me to make a decision. My mind can be so occupied with duties and activities that I spend only the time it takes to hover near, glance rapidly, and fly away. Sometimes I spend too much time reading other books, taking away my yearning for God's Word. Whatever the reason, God is disappointed when I do not partake of His provision for my spiritual survival. He has plenty of resources to fill me.

December 7

Cast away from you all your transgressions, whereby ye have transgressed; and make you a new heart and a new spirit.
—Ezekiel 18:31

If I am interrupted during my sewing, I tend to almost automatically remove the thimble from my finger and misplace it. When I return to my sewing project, that previous thoughtless act wastes precious time. I look on, under, and into almost everything before I finally find it—exactly where I left it. If only I would learn to remember where I put it!

The lost thimble reminds me of times when I feel my peace with God slipping away. If I lose that peace, I cannot expect to regain it by attending another church or just trying to be more loving and kind. Talking with other people about it usually doesn't help; I tend to keep talking until someone gives me an answer that my flesh enjoys. I will not regain that peace until I find out what I did to lose it, and then repent of that thing.

God will aid me in my search for His peace if I ask Him, and He will let me know where the problem lies. Sometimes He shows me that I have been carrying a burden instead of allowing Him to carry it. Sometimes there is doubt and worry in my heart. Sometimes I have fallen into the habit of being unthankful or too hasty with my devotions. Other times God shows me that I have been discontented, wishing I could be someone or somewhere else. Whatever the problem, it becomes a handicap, hindering my relationship with God.

Careless thinking, like careless placement of the thimble, brings difficulties. Just as the thimble turns up in unexpected places, so my soul-searching turns up some surprises. My thoughts had fallen into questionable areas and then slipped into a state I had not intended. Yet God's grace was always there, waiting to reveal my problem and offering His love and forgiveness. Accepting His love restores my peace.

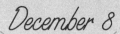

Also I heard the voice of the Lord, saying, Whom shall I send,
and who will go for us? Then said I, Here am I; send me.

—Isaiah 6:8

What Christian youth does not aspire to serve the Lord? A young Christian desires to share the love he has found in the Lord. Sometimes teenagers even envision serving God in difficult situations and faraway lands.

But as you get older, you may feel God calling you to serve in a completely different way than you had anticipated. The place might be at home, and the task much more menial than you dreamed about in your youth. Your life may seem unnoticed and unremarkable, but God clearly shows you what He wants done.

You had no idea what price you would need to pay when you sincerely responded as Isaiah did. Now God may be asking you to sacrifice something precious, and you find that it is even more difficult than going across the ocean.

Remember that God utilizes every willing heart. He may not make an Isaiah out of you, but He will use you in the place you are most suited for. And it is only in that place that you will be free and at rest in your spirit. ❊

By faith Noah, being warned of God of things not seen as yet, moved with fear, prepared an ark to the saving of his house; by the which he condemned the world, and became heir of the righteousness which is by faith.

—Hebrews 11:7

Has the Lord asked you to do something that has left you with questions and doubts? Perhaps He has given you few details, and you do not understand how it can possibly work out. The way ahead seems almost too dark to take the first step.

Have you considered Noah and his faith as he undertook the task God had assigned him?

Noah probably never saw rain before. Yet God said He would destroy the earth with a flood. Consider the faith it took to present this message to the people. If Noah had relatives other than his immediate family, they would be destroyed. What would *they* think of his preaching? If he spent many years building the ark, how would his own needs be met? How could he round up so many wild animals, let alone birds and insects?

After he had done everything God commanded and was safely inside the ark with his family, he again had a waiting period that tested his faith. Would the flood really come? When the torrents of rain beat on the ark, it again took faith to believe that the ark built according to God's plan would not leak. When their dwelling place rose and floated on the water, it took faith to believe that God was in control and would keep them safe. When the rain continued to pour from heaven, it took faith to believe that it would stop sometime. Perhaps Noah knew that God had commanded Adam and Eve to fill the earth, and now the earth was empty except for Noah and his small family. Would the earth be filled again?

By faith Noah took the first step, and then God revealed the second one. God kept His promises. You will observe the same provisions in your life when you take the first God-given step.

December 10

Shall the axe boast itself against him that heweth therewith? or shall the saw magnify itself against him that shaketh it? as if the rod should shake itself against them that lift it up, or as if the staff should lift up itself as if it were no wood.

—Isaiah 10:15

We would never expect an axe to rebel against the hand of the woodsman. It only does the task its master puts it to.

We are like axes in God's hand. God is the hewer, and He has a job for us to do. Are we allowing Him to use us according to His plan?

The saw does not tell the woodsman which tree to cut down. Do we tell God how to order our lives? Do we tell Him what we will or will not do? Do we demand that God answer our prayers the way we pray them?

A rod and staff are tools used by a shepherd. Neither one does more or less than the shepherd intends it to do. Do you wait on God to put you to use, or do you push yourself out into the frontlines, hoping God and people will notice how well you accomplish things? ✳

371

December 11

To the intent that now unto the principalities and powers in heavenly places might be known by the church the manifold wisdom of God.
—Ephesians 3:10

As a child I was enthralled with a clock's mechanism. All the gears, from the tiniest to the largest, whirling swiftly or turning slowly, fascinated me. Then there was the little hammer that slowly raised itself, without any human aid, and beat down on a shiny dome to pound out the hour. The professional clockmakers of Switzerland come to mind as I think about the intricate workings of clocks. They have honed their talents to an impressive degree.

Now if I would find one of these gears or any other clock part lying somewhere by itself, it would not thrill me. I might not even know what it is or where it comes from, and I would throw it away. By itself it does not fulfill any purpose.

Principalities and powers in heavenly places look with awe upon the church and its function. They acknowledge that no mind except a Mastermind could establish such a perfectly planned organism. As each member bows to Christ and abides under His lordship, everything functions harmoniously. With the aid of the Holy Spirit, the glory of the Gospel will sound forth.

I am not the entire church, and I am unable to demonstrate God's wisdom by myself. The smooth functioning of many parts together is what shows wisdom. A faulty part does not show wisdom; withdrawal and resistance do not result in unified worship and service. The principalities in heavenly places will not see God's glory when disunity occurs, but they cannot help but acknowledge a divine power when they see individual members in the church crowning Jesus as Lord and giving their service to Him.

....

....

For as many as are led by the Spirit of God, they are the sons of God.

—Romans 8:14

An evangelist was trying to explain the first part of 1 Corinthians 11 to a woman one day. When he finished, he asked her if she understood the chapter.

"No," the lady replied. "I do not understand what you are saying."

The evangelist tried again with what he thought was a simpler explanation. "Ma'am, do you understand now what I mean?"

"No, I do not," she replied again.

"Well, ma'am, if you understood this Scripture, would you be willing to wear a veiling?"

Without hesitation, she answered, "No, sir, I would not."

Sometimes we may say we do not understand God's will for us. But do we really *want to know* His will? Are we open to more than what we already are doing?

Maybe God cannot lead us to the mission field because we would not want to go if we were asked. He might not give us ideas for a scrapbook we're preparing for an ill person if we have not cultivated a caring heart for that person. God will not likely inspire us to write a story for children if we have no interest in young lives.

On the other hand, there are no limits to where God might lead us if we are open to His will. It might be a different place than we had thought or hoped for, but it will be the best place for us. If we are led by God's Spirit, we will be called daughters of God. No position could be more honorable! ✳

....

....

....

....

December 13

Remember the days of old, consider the years of many generations: ask thy father, and he will shew thee; thy elders, and they will tell thee.
—Deuteronomy 32:7

If you are single, you will probably need to make some important decisions by yourself. Since these decisions could change the course of your life, the responsibility may lie heavily on your heart. But God does not intend for you to feel all of that weight.

Asking counsel is of utmost importance. You need another person's view of your situation. Carefully consider who to ask for advice—ask someone who will support you even if the decision you make results in many trials for you. The friendships of women are strengthening and helpful, but you should also have the support of your father, minister, or another trusted Christian man when facing a major decision. He can be the hands and feet of Christ to you.

When you ask advice, you must be willing to share the details of what you are considering. Be open; trust your advisor with the whole scenario. He cannot give clear direction if the facts are vague. It may feel risky to share openly, but God will care for your heart as you take the risk and earnestly seek godly counsel. ✹

> Be still, and know that I am God: I will be exalted
> among the heathen, I will be exalted in the earth.
>
> —Psalm 46:10

Our bodies become stressed when we maintain a hectic pace of doing many good things. Sometimes we get so caught up in *doing* that we forget about the importance of simply *being*. We do not sit still often enough and long enough to get a true vision of God, His desires, and His thoughts.

Isaiah, not mincing words, called God's chosen people wicked and unrighteous because their thoughts were not God's thoughts. Their errant thoughts did not come about through lack of activity, because he tells them that although they labor, it is spent for that which does not satisfy (Isaiah 55:2). That makes me uncomfortable because it comes dangerously close to home.

I know there is no lasting satisfaction in always having the floors swept, the windows clean, and the sink free of dishes—they will be dirty again tomorrow. And sometimes, even after a day of helping someone else, I can come home and still not feel satisfied. This unsettled feeling is the result of a restless heart.

The antidote for a restless heart is found in the text verse: "Be still." Instead of always doing things for myself or others, I need to be still and do things for Him. I need to meditate on Him, delighting in His presence. I need to think of His purposes and His will. I need to think of my redemption and position in Christ. I need to listen to His voice, even in nature—the rustle of the wind, the raindrops pattering on the roof. They can remind me that God is saying, "This is me. I am here." I need to look deeply into the starry heavens until I get such a glimpse of His glory that I bow my head in reverence. I need to think about His coming and my heavenly home. I need to think about His all-sufficient companionship and His ability to supply all my needs. I need to search and see if I have other gods besides Him.

Only when I am still do I hear what God would have me to do. If I take time to keep my body, soul, and spirit still before Him, that state of rest will bring satisfaction in all my duties. And when I am still, God can take His exalted position within my being. 🕊

December 15

And we know that all things work together for good to them that love God, to them who are the called according to his purpose.
—Romans 8:28

"H-m-m, now I see. This puzzle piece I was trying to place for such a long time belongs where the water goes back under the trees. And this one fills in the center of that big rock." I had been so absorbed with putting pieces into place that I did not notice how each piece blended into the scene. But when I sat back and studied the picture, I could see how each piece fit into the whole.

The different "pieces" of my life complete a scene. I may not always understand what the Lord is doing when He fills in the pieces, but when I sit back and reflect on past experiences, I see where each one filled a vital place. One puzzle piece has to be laid down before the next one can fit into it. Some pieces are brightly colored and some are dark or drab. Placed where they belong, together they make a beautiful scene.

The picture on the puzzle box helped me know where to put pieces because it showed the complete scene. In the same way, God has a vision for my life, and He sees the whole picture. By adding each "piece" where and when He does, He is fulfilling that vision. I may not always understand, but someday I will see His wisdom in it all.

I enjoy putting a puzzle together more if, after I place each piece, I think about how that piece helps the overall picture. In the same way, I receive a greater blessing from my varied life experiences if I pause to consider how each one helped me in my walk with the Lord. Even if I do not understand how it blends into the whole plan, I can still benefit from what it adds to the immediate scene of my life.

God is a master at putting together the puzzle pieces of each person's life. Unless we meddle with His plan and mar the picture, He will create a beautiful, complete masterpiece in each of our lives.

Ye have compassed this mountain long enough: turn you northward.

—Deuteronomy 2:3

God speaks to you today and says, "You have worked on this problem long enough. It is time to move on." Get into the Word of God and find comfort even in the trials and struggles you face. "For whatsoever things were written aforetime were written for our learning, that we through patience and comfort of the scriptures might have hope" (Romans 15:4). God wants you to know where you are going. He wants you to spend time with Him. If you want to live a life of victory, you need to move on in faith, keeping your eyes on the Lord.

God has a purpose in the trials He sends your way. There is a daily cross to bear. That is where God's will and your will meet and become one. Great blessings come in quietly submitting to the will of God. May you look past the circumstances in life and simply believe God. He will bring you through everything you face and take you beyond each mountain until you reach your glorious goal of heaven. Keep moving on with courage.

....

....

....

....

....

....

....

December 17

Behold, what manner of love the Father hath bestowed upon
us, that we should be called the sons of God.
—1 John 3:1

We become very impressed with the words *service* and *commitment*. When one "goes into service," he is "doing great things for the Lord," having "made a commitment" for several months or years. As good as this type of work is, we can become so enthralled with the idea that we forget that our most important commitment is daily surrender to God and His will for us, and our most important service is worship and obedience.

When we serve the Lord in daily obedience, we can rest, knowing we are in His will. We do not have to feel less "committed" when others "go into service" and we "just stay at home." We should continually rejoice that the greatest privilege is being children of God. Without a clear understanding of this concept, all our efforts in serving will fail.

Jesus was unimpressed with Martha's frantic hustle and bustle because she had a wrong concept of service. His approval rested on Mary, who sat in quiet reverence and devotion.

As children of the King, we may be called to certain fields, but our primary purpose is still to be His children and wait upon Him continually. Genesis 15:6 says that Abram simply believed God, and it was counted to him for righteousness. All those who choose to believe while leaving the details of their lives to God can have the same legacy.

Charity . . . doth not behave itself unseemly.

—1 Corinthians 13:4-5

"I do not even want to see her right now. I am so mad at her. In fact, if I'd meet her on the street, I would like to kill her—but I wouldn't. I would just beat her up and tell her this was for all the tales she started about me." The man sharing his thoughts with me was too infuriated to listen when I tried to point out what Jesus could do for him.

I was appalled to think of anger so strong that it would make someone want to kill another person for spreading a rumor. But then I had to think of how I react when someone hurts me. I usually stuff it inside, but my thoughts are not pretty.

First John 3:15 tells us, "Whosoever hateth his brother is a murderer." We might not think of physically hurting someone or showing our hatred, but we often retaliate in our thoughts and with our words. We might not say much to the person who hurt us, but it is so easy to tell others of the great hurt the person has done. We can soon kill someone's reputation among all our willing listeners and sympathizers. This is not an attitude of love; and if we do not love, we hate. I remember well what a minister once said: "When we have been accused of something we have not done, there is no need to tell everyone how we have been hurt. The truth will speak for itself."

Extend forgiveness to someone today. It goes against human nature, but it shows the heart of God—and it will free your spirit.

If any man among you seem to be religious, and bridleth not his tongue, but deceiveth his own heart, this man's religion is vain. Pure religion and undefiled before God and the Father is this, to visit the fatherless and widows in their affliction, and to keep himself unspotted from the world.
—James 1:26-27

Three conditions for a worthwhile religion are stated in the above verses: a controlled tongue, a caring heart, and a pure life.

A woman unable to bridle her tongue has a useless religion to offer another. A virtuous woman allows only kind words to come from her lips. Yet even if a woman is able to control her tongue, she does not have a valuable religion if she does not care about needy people. The woman whose religion is untainted by selfishness will show genuine concern for the widows and the fatherless. She will not limit her love to her family and members of her church, although they should be her first concern. Her love will also reach out to the neighbors, the blind, and the lonely. It will even reach to those who do not seem lovable.

The third condition for a pure religion, though a broad statement, is nevertheless the personal responsibility of every Christian woman. She will keep herself unspotted from the world. She will not allow Satan to get a grip on her thought life. The spots begin in her mind, and if she allows them to grow, they can contaminate her whole life.

A religion worth following will be found in the woman who builds up people with her words, looks after the needs of others, and carries a heart unspotted by the sin that surrounds her. ❋

> Now no chastening for the present seemeth to be joyous, but
> grievous: nevertheless afterward it yieldeth the peaceable fruit
> of righteousness unto them which are exercised thereby.
>
> —Hebrews 12:11

Wringer washers usually do an admirable job of wringing out clothes, applying just the right amount of pressure in the rollers to squeeze out the most water. That's why I was dismayed one day to see my laundry after it passed through the wringers. Sopping heaps fell limply into the laundry basket. Instead of staying together and squeezing out the excess water, the rollers had parted to let a whole lump of clothes pass through. I had to subject the clothes to some severe hand-wringing, knowing that clothes hung inside the house will smell sour if they do not dry fast enough.

This helped me see why I should be thankful when I feel pressure in my life. Sometimes I would rather slip through the pressure in a big, ugly lump than to be conformed and changed to what I should be. It would be easier. Or would it? For clothes to pass through the wringer, they must be reasonably flattened out. But to be wrung out by hand is worse yet; the clothes get twisted in all sorts of ways. Spiritually, if I refuse to conform to God's will the first time I feel pressure, it could be much more severe the second time.

If I want to be useful and not smell sour, I can expect pressure. It may come by conviction as I listen to a message or as I read the Word. It may come through someone's admonition or through a lack of peace with God. It is the love of God that puts pressure on me to help me get rid of excesses. I want to recognize and appreciate these pressures so that I will be beautiful and useful to Him.

But the word of God is not bound.

—2 Timothy 2:9

Paul, in a prison cell in Rome, was writing a letter of encouragement to Timothy. Looking down at the cold, restraining chains around his hands and feet, he penned the words, "But the word of God is not bound." Even though Paul could no longer go on missionary journeys to tell others of the glorious salvation in Jesus, the Word of God would go far beyond the chains of iron that restrained him. He continued writing, "Therefore I endure all things for the elect's sakes, that they may also obtain the salvation which is in Christ Jesus with eternal glory" (2:10). His only desire was that others would know his Lord, even if he could no longer go tell them.

Is your tongue bound with the chains of fear so that you cannot speak for your Lord? Are your hands bound with doing your own wishes, making God's work wait? Remember that the Word of God is not bound. Even if we do not always do or say things just right while witnessing for Him, His Word will go forth. Your walk of life speaks loudly as well; remember that you represent Christ even when you are not speaking about Him.

"For God hath not given us the spirit of fear; but of power, and of love, and a sound mind. Be not thou therefore ashamed of the testimony of our Lord" (2 Timothy 1:7-8).

An hypocrite with his mouth destroyeth his neighbour:
but through knowledge shall the just be delivered.

—Proverbs 11:9

In Ezekiel 9, the man with the inkhorn was asked to put a mark on all the righteous people so that they would not be killed. Sometimes we do the opposite. We tend to put marks on people whom we do not especially appreciate.

When we talk about others in a degrading way, we put a mark on their character that may ruin their reputation. Often we do not know the reason for someone's decisions; we really do not understand the situation. If we put a mark on their good intentions, we may reveal a need in our own lives. Perhaps they are accomplishing more for the Lord than we are.

One young man began to forget things repeatedly. People began to disrespect him for his seeming irresponsibility and criticized him behind his back. Months later a tumor was discovered in this man's brain, revealing the cause of the young man's mental blocks. But it was too late for the critics to recall their words. The damage had been done.

"Speak not evil one of another, brethren" (James 4:11).

"Judge not, that ye be not judged" (Matthew 7:1).

When King Nahash of the children of Ammon died, David wanted to show sympathy to the king's son, Hanun. He sent his servants to comfort King Hanun, but the princes of Ammon sowed seeds of doubt in Hanun's mind concerning David's sincerity. This made the king respond negatively to David's sympathy. In the end, war resulted because of what the princes of Ammon had said—a negative mark had been placed on David's intentions (2 Samuel 10).

Today, ask God to give you a sympathetic heart for those around you so that you will put only good marks on others. ✳

If the foot shall say, Because I am not the hand, I am not of
the body; is it therefore not of the body?

—1 Corinthians 12:15

Because my leg was damaged by a childhood disease, it is especially dependent on my hand to lift it into certain positions. But just because the leg needs the hand does not mean that the hand should be where the leg is. Imagine how handicapped I would be if such were the case! As it is, my appendages cooperate beautifully with each other, and I get along fine.

Now the hand, even though it is often called upon to help, is not constantly getting in the way trying to help when there is no need. Neither does it lie idle until the leg needs help; it is busy performing usefully in other areas.

The leg, though dependent on other members, does what it can. It helps to carry my body to places where the hand can reach out and get what is needed. It does not try to perform the hand's duties, and it does not try to overachieve to cover up its own deficiency. If it did, it would bring harm to itself as well as to the rest of the body. It waits quietly until there is reason to move. The body does not require more of the leg than what it is able to do.

It is not happenstance that body parts work together harmoniously, with some doing much more than others. Their movements are dependent on the messages they receive from the head. If all the members would move because they saw another member move, chaos would result. I am thankful they do not look at each other for direction, but that they wait for a command from the brain.

The connection between how our physical bodies work and how the church body should work is obvious. When Christians listen to their head, Jesus Christ, there will be cooperation and coordination in the church body unlike anything else on the earth.

And while they looked stedfastly toward heaven as he went
up, behold, two men stood by them in white apparel.

—Acts 1:10

The disciples gazed into the sky after they had seen Jesus disappear into the cloud. They must have had a helpless feeling of loss when they realized that Jesus was gone and they would not see Him again. We can imagine that in the following days they longed to see their leader again.

I have said goodbye to my family. I am in a new community among strangers. Today at work I struggled with my new responsibilities. I have received no letters from home. On days like this when everything seemed to go wrong, I long to go home to my family. I am homesick!

I have discovered the same feeling in my Christian life. The devil seems so real today. He tries to get me to yield to temptation, and when I do, he discourages me and tells me I can never do anything right. I feel overwhelmed by the trials in life. Because of these hardships, I pray more and think more about Jesus. Suddenly I am homesick for heaven!

I am homesick for the place where there is no sadness. Homesick for relief from temptations, for a place where perfection can be attained. I am homesick to see my loved ones who are in heaven. I long to live in a place where handicapped, disease-ridden, and brain-damaged people will be made well again.

But most of all, I am homesick to be in the presence of Jesus, the one with whom I have been nurturing a relationship but have been unable to see. What joy it will be to spend time with the One I love!

But I am still on earth, and I have a purpose here. So I thank God for the hard times, because I realize that sitting at Jesus' feet is the highest joy possible for the Christian. ✽

December 25

For God so loved the world, that he gave his only begotten Son, that whosoever believeth in him should not perish, but have everlasting life.
—John 3:16

The wonderful salvation story never grows old,
We read it in the Bible and often hear it told.
It tells of God the Father, and His love for fallen man,
In meditating on it, we see His perfect plan.
The welfare of lost sinners is what He had in mind
When we rebelled against Him; how could He be so kind?
Born in a lowly stable was the Son of God who gave
His life in willing service, from the manger to the grave.
When on the cross He gave Himself to die for you and me,
He was setting an example of the way to victory;
For in becoming like Him in death from day to day,
We shall all share the likeness of His resurrection day.
Then guided by His Spirit and surrounded by His love,
We can in part experience what is planned for us above.

December 26

> Oh that men would praise the Lord for his goodness, and for his wonderful works to the children of men! For he satisfieth the longing soul, and filleth the hungry soul with goodness.
>
> —Psalm 107:8-9

My elderly friend wrote me an inspirational letter, and I want to pass on her words of wisdom:

I find that praising the Lord enriches my life. It is a testimony to others to think more on the Word of God. Hopefully they will desire to live for my Lord too.

But it was not always this way. There was a time when I missed the blessings of praising the Lord because I was not humble enough to give Him due honor and glory. Maybe it was because of the way I was brought up. We were thankful, yes, but we had a certain fear of praising God's name aloud. So today I am thrilled to see young people living a Christian life and expressing praise through song.

I experienced the above verses long before I knew they were in the Bible. The Lord has satisfied my longing soul with peace, though I do not have the joy of having my own family. I have received many blessings by taking care of my mother and sharing in the trials that she faced. When my brother and his wife went through struggles to remain true to the faith, I was happy to walk with them and fight for them in prayer.

Singing praise to the Lord gives my heart strength. It causes me to rejoice, and then I find no dull moments, though I live alone.

"It is a good thing to give thanks unto the Lord, and to sing praises unto thy name, O most High: to shew forth thy lovingkindness in the morning, and thy faithfulness every night" (Psalm 92:1-2).

I marvel at my friend's enthusiasm. I determine to praise God more!

December 27

I live by the faith of the Son of God, who loved me, and gave himself for me.
—Galatians 2:20

I gained a new appreciation for this verse some time ago while I was working for a family with small children. Numerous times the preschoolers would sit together and sing. One of their favorite songs was the chorus, "He loves me, He loves me, He loves me this I know." This little phrase, sung over and over in succession, became their song.

One day when their song was over, I asked them, "Who loves you? Who does the song mean when it says 'He loves me'?" They looked at each other blankly, so I simply told them, "It means Jesus. Jesus loves you!"

That seemed to be a precious concept to them. Later I heard them mention that it was Jesus who loved them. Their little chorus held personal meaning to them now; it was more than mere words.

Sometime later I walked through the room where they were once again singing their song. One of the little girls looked up at me and with sweet innocence said, "Jesus loves you too!"

Her words sent a thrill of joy through me. I had known it before, of course, but coming so simply from those childish lips blessed me in a new and personal way.

Why do we ever need to feel sad, distressed, or restless if we live in the realization that Jesus loves us? Really, what else matters except that we love Him in return? Herein lies our joy, hope, fulfillment, and peace—for time and eternity.

> And the peace of God, which passeth all understanding,
> shall keep your hearts and minds through Christ Jesus.
> —Philippians 4:7

We tend to think, *If I could have this or that, then I could be at rest.* If you are single, you may desire a husband and children. You may wish to stay at home instead of working away from home to support yourself. If you are married, you may wish for more quiet time away from your responsibilities, or you may long for a meaningful job instead of endless household tasks. The truth, however, is that things and circumstances will not bring peace, but submission to God will bring a peace that we cannot fully explain or understand. That peace is what will keep our hearts and minds fit for God's use. Praise be to Jesus Christ through whom this is possible!

Real Peace

Like the restless tossing sea
Churning up the dirt and mire,
Fearful what may come to light,
So the troubled wicked are—
They cannot have real peace.

Pleasure-seeking though men be,
Always out some fun to hunt,
Trying still to fill that void,
Laughing, putting on a front—
They cannot have real peace.

Man needs peace that God can give;
Peace that comes from sins forgiven,
Knowing that the Spirit's there,
Sure they're on their way to heaven—
That is peace . . . real peace!

December 29

Brethren, let every man, wherein he is called, therein abide with God.
—1 Corinthians 7:24

In the summertime I often gaze at the woods as I eat lunch. At noon the sun shines with full splendor on the trees, dazzling me with their brilliant hues of green. But right now it is winter and the brilliance is only a memory tucked away in the recesses of my mind. The lush green has been replaced by the drab grays and blacks of this season. Here and there a pale birch adds its gauntness to the bleak scene. I search for a ray of cheer, but find none in my woods.

In the distance I see another woods. At first it looks like a cheerless, gray mass. But then I see the sun shining on it, and a transformation takes place. Dainty bits of color, invisible before, turn the fuzzy grayness into soft beauty.

I sigh wistfully. Why is the distant scene more beautiful than the one near at hand? Why does the light of the sun not fall onto *my* woods? Why must I face such a depressing situation while those farther away are privileged to experience light and glory?

Then I stop to think. If I see beauty in that distant place, is it possible that I am not looking hard enough for the beauty nearby? Maybe I simply need to see it from a different vantage point. The people who live far away from my woods might even be looking in my direction wistfully, seeing beauty where I haven't found it. Maybe each of us should stay where we are and count the blessings that are near at hand.

> But when he saw the wind boisterous, he was afraid; and
> beginning to sink, he cried, saying, Lord, save me.
>
> —Matthew 14:30

As long as Peter kept his eyes on Jesus, he stayed on top of the water. The going was smooth. But when he took his eyes off Jesus and saw the storm and the waves around him, he began to sink.

On a ship out in the middle of the ocean, the sailors noticed dark clouds in the western sky. A young sailor was sent to the top of the rigging to trim the sails in preparation for the storm. As the young man was climbing the main mast, he looked out at the storm and became dizzy. The old captain watching below shouted, "Young man, look up!" The sailor looked up, regained his balance, and continued his labors.

At times we find ourselves like Peter and the young sailor. We see the obstacles and begin to sink in despair.

Jesus said to Peter, "O thou of little faith, wherefore didst thou doubt?"

Instead of looking at the waves around us, we need to look up to God in faith. God never sends a storm too hard for us. He would not have told Peter to come if He had not been able to keep Peter from sinking.

When we find ourselves sinking, we need to cry out to Jesus as Peter did, "Lord, save me!" Jesus is ready today to lift us above the waves. He is ready to give us strength to rise above the trials and obstacles. Let us keep our eyes on Jesus, look past the waves, and see God!

....

....

....

....

December 31

That our daughters may be as corner stones, polished after the similitude of a palace.
—Psalm 144:12

As a daughter of the King, you can be a cornerstone—a supporting pillar in your home, church, and community. A building rests upon the inconspicuous but solid cornerstones.

Think of yourself as a cornerstone in a beautiful and costly building. The cornerstone must be polished and refined in order to reflect the grandeur of the building. Is your life beautifully adorned with godly graces and virtues? Is your life polished to a shine, cleansed of defiling influences? Being willing to fill your place and take more than your share of responsibility will make you a more refined cornerstone. When you are pleasant and cheerful, kind toward everyone, and robed in purity, your steady presence will immeasurably bless the building of which you are a part.

When your life has been polished, the reflection of your Master is clearly seen. You came into the world sadly tarnished, but you are sanctified as you yield yourself to God. He will purify and polish you until you shine in His image. Do not become weary and settle for a mediocre dusting.

"Whose adorning . . . let it be the hidden man of the heart, in that which is not corruptible, even the ornament of a meek and quiet spirit, which is in the sight of God of great price" (1 Peter 3:3-4).

....

....

....

....

....

Verna Mast

Verna Mast was stricken with polio at three years old. After numerous surgeries, she could walk again, but not without the aid of a support to lift her drop foot. Though often confined physically, her mind remained active and contemplated deep truths. She always felt her handicap was a blessing in disguise.

After working briefly at Pathway Publishers, she turned to teaching. This, along with writing, became her lifelong interest. She had already taught three terms when we met and began teaching together. We spent seven happy years at Nebo Valley School, a one-room Amish school in Wayne County, Ohio.

A year after I married and moved to Mt. Perry, Ohio, Verna also moved into the community and stayed in a trailer on our property. Our community became her home. She learned to enjoy the church and became a member. She taught school here and in several other states for a total of seventeen years. Her summers were mostly devoted to writing. She edited textbooks and Sunday school books for Rod & Staff Publishers and wrote articles for various publishers.

In the spring of 1991 while teaching school in Kentucky, Verna called with the sad news that she was diagnosed with breast cancer. She terminated her teaching and came home for surgery and medical treatment. She felt the Lord had called her aside to allow her to accomplish her dream of writing a devotional book for singles. After counseling with others, she began writing the book. In 1992 she laid the book aside to prepare for another term of teaching, this time in Pennsylvania. However, after only one week in school, she fell ill and returned home. Her cancer had spread to her brain. Her mind became confused, and she suffered much mental agony. However, she often felt calmer when someone read Scripture to her.

On November 7, 1992, God called her home. We found the following words copied in the back of her Bible.

—*Edna Miller*

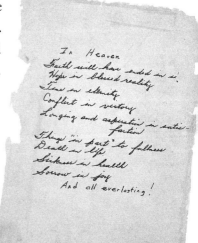

In Heaven
Faith will have ended in si...
Hope in blessed reality
Time in eternity
Conflict in victory
Longing and aspiration in satisfaction
Things in part to fullness
Death in life
Sickness in health
Sorrow in joy
And all everlasting!

Susan Schwartz

I was born in Lancaster, Pennsylvania, and grew up on a farm in upstate New York. I began teaching school when I was twenty years old, and I taught for the next eight years. I learned a lot from the children and greatly enjoyed those years. At twenty-three, I stepped into unknown waters when I left home to teach in Mt. Perry, Ohio. Five years later Moses and I were married.

The first time I met Verna Mast, she shared a devotional article that had blessed her life. Several years later, she told me that this same article blessed her with the assurance that she was going where the Lord wanted her to go the day she moved to Mt. Perry—a move that was difficult for her. When she testified about this blessing, I could not have dreamt that one day I would be placing articles into a devotional book.

Writing has been one of my hobbies since I was young. My parents and my eighth-grade teacher did much to encourage me to continue. Writing and compiling the remainder of this book has been the greatest challenge I have undertaken in the writing field. My sincere thanks to my husband, whose careful thought and final word in everything has greatly improved the manuscript.

We wish to give the Lord the glory, and we hope your Christian life will be blessed and strengthened as you read this book.

Acknowledging Our Other Contributors

We express a special thanks to the following women for the articles they contributed to this book. May God bless each one.

Lois Kuepfer

Donna Miller

Ruth Brubaker

Aletha Petre

Helena Buhler

Anna Ruth Witmer

Rebecca Kauffman

Martha Miller

Merna Shank

Evelyn Kropf

Rachel Mae Stutzman

Rachel Kuepfer

Sovilla Yoder

Martha Esh

Karen Rissler

Iva Miller

Sarah Bender

Edna Miller

Grace Putt

Amy Herr

Helena Schrock

Crystal Shank

Lizzie Ann Schwartz

Luci Zimmerman

Susie Bender

Leona Coblentz

Mary Hursh

Marjorie Otto

Lorraine Yoder

Catharine Amstutz

Susan Schlabach

Mary Mast

Lydia Ann Miller

Eva Witmer

Juanita Christner

Ida Mae Miller

Joan Martin

Nancy Zook

Esther Beechy